Yale Football
Through the Years

ALSO BY RICH MARAZZI
AND LEN FIORITO

*Baseball Players of the 1950s: A Biographical
Dictionary of All 1,560 Major Leaguers*
(McFarland, 2004; paperback 2010)

Yale Football Through the Years

Rich Marazzi

McFarland & Company, Inc., Publishers
Jefferson, North Carolina

Photographs are courtesy Yale Athletics unless otherwise indicated.

Library of Congress Cataloguing-in-Publication Data

Names: Marazzi, Richard, author.
Title: Yale football through the years / Rich Marazzi.
Description: Jefferson, North Carolina : McFarland & Company, Inc., Publishers, 2020. | Includes bibliographical references and index.
Identifiers: LCCN 2019049988 | ISBN 9781476680361 (paperback) ∞
  ISBN 9781476638553 (ebook)
Subjects: LCSH: Yale University—Football—History.
Classification: LCC GV958.Y3 M373 2020 | DDC 796.332/63097468— dc23

British Library cataloguing data are available

ISBN (print) 978-1-4766-8036-1
ISBN (ebook) 978-1-4766-3855-3

© 2020 Rich Marazzi. All rights reserved

No part of this book may be reproduced or transmitted in any form or by any means, electronic or mechanical, including photocopying or recording, or by any information storage and retrieval system, without permission in writing from the publisher.

Front cover image design and photograph by Gary Marcinick from items courtesy of Yale Athletics; back cover photograph of the championship 2017 Yale football team with the Ivy League trophy (Bill O'Brien)

Printed in the United States of America

McFarland & Company, Inc., Publishers
 Box 611, Jefferson, North Carolina 28640
 www.mcfarlandpub.com

To the late Bob Barton (Yale '57), the ultimate Yale
football historian who was a friend and mentor to so many.
Some material contained in this book
is the result of Bob's impeccable research.

Acknowledgments

To Gary Marcinik, a former Ohio State football player, who designed the Yale football history montage for the front cover of the book. Marcinik's son, Kyle, lettered in football four years at Yale from 2015 to 2018.

To Mike Gambardella, the Yale University Associate Athletic Director, Strategic Communications for his statistical and photo assistance.

To Steve Conn, the Yale University Senior Assistant Director, Strategic Communications for his statistical and photo assistance.

To Sam Rubin, the Yale University Assistant Director, Strategic Communications for his statistical assistance.

To John Napolitano, for assistance in the gathering of photos for this book.

To freelance photographer Bill O'Brien for providing many images in this book.

To the late Greg Hall, the former Yale football player whose networking of former Yale players and promotion of Yale football history has not been forgotten.

To Bill Santillo, the president of the New Haven Gridiron Club, for his support and promotion.

To Ray Peach, a veteran Yale football fan for his support and promotion.

To Bob Lewis, a veteran Yale football fan and professional Yale Bowl tailgater for his support and promotion.

To executive editor Lisa Camp and assistant editor Dré Person for their assistance and interest in this project.

To my wonderful wife, Lois, sons Rich and his wife, Trisha, Brian and his wife, Rachel, and my awesome grandchildren—Caitlin, Richie and Landon—for their utmost support and interest.

Table of Contents

Acknowledgments vi

Introduction 1

THE HIGHLIGHTS 3

Appendix 187

Bibliography 197

Index 199

Introduction

Yale football is arguably the fountainhead of college football. In 2020, the Bulldogs will field its 148th team and the venerated Yale Bowl celebrates its 106th anniversary. The first football team on any level to reach 800 wins, Yale has won recognition as national champion or co-champion in 27 seasons from one or more of the selection systems listed by the NCAA Record Book.

From 1872 until 1909 Yale was the scourge of college football. The Elis sat atop Mount Olympus as a national football power with a mind-numbing 324 wins against 17 losses and 18 ties. The impregnable Yale dynasty piled up wins like cordwood.

Walter Camp, who played and coached at Yale, is the high priest of Yale football. And many consider him the father of college football. John Heisman said, "What Washington was to his country, Camp was to American football: the friend, the founder and father."

College football began as an upper-class Ivy League endeavor. The sons of the rich and famous experimented with this new game which was an amalgam of rugby and soccer. It was Camp's rule revisions that helped modernize a game that was viewed as crude and barbaric.

Yale has had a cascade of talented players. More than 100 All-Americans, including two Heisman Trophy winners, Larry Kelley (1936) and Clint Frank (1937), have worn the Blue uniform. And a total of 26 players and four coaches are enshrined in the College Football Hall of Fame. Yale has launched 34 players to the NFL including such stars as Calvin Hill (Cowboys), the NFL Rookie of the Year in 1969, Mike Pyle, who captained the Chicago Bears and others like Gary Fencik (Bears), Dick Jauron (Lions), Eric Johnson (49ers) and more recently, Tyler Varga (Colts), Foyesade Oluokun (Falcons), and Jaeden Graham (Falcons).

Introduction

The Yale football program has won or shared 16 Ivy League titles since the Ancient Eight began formal play in 1956. Entering the 2020 season, the Bulldogs have a lifetime 915–380–55 record. Yale ranks nationally in the top ten in lifetime wins. A forfeit win against Penn in 1997 is not recognized by the NCAA.

In addition to their traditional Ivy League opponents, Yale has played and defeated Notre Dame, Michigan, Wisconsin, Maryland, Georgia, Virginia, Virginia Tech, North Carolina, Villanova, Rutgers, Boston College, Penn State, Army, Navy, Air Force, Hawaii and others. The Bulldogs are the only team that has played and defeated all of the United States military academies.

The Yale Bowl, constructed in 1914, defines tradition. It was declared a National Historic Landmark and was chosen by the *Sporting News* as one of the 40 best college football stadiums in its 2005 book, *Saturday Shrines*. The Bulldogs have played 631 games in the historic Bowl where their mark stands at 397–213–21 entering the 2019 season.

George "Papa Bear" Halas, the legendary Chicago Bears coach was honored at the Walter Camp annual dinner in 1981 at the Yale Commons. While in New Haven, he said, "Do you know what the greatest football program in America was? It wasn't the Chicago Bears; it wasn't the New York Giants; it was Yale!"

Knute Rockne, the iconic Notre Dame football coach, had deep respect for Yale football as well. When asked where he got the idea for the famed Notre Dame shift, he is said to have replied, "Where everything else in football came from—Yale!"

The Highlights

1872 (1–0) **Captain: David S. Schaff**
From 1872 to 1887 the team captain assumed coaching duties and was empowered to appoint field coaches.

Oct. 31: David Schley Schaff, Elliot S. Miller, Samuel Elder, and other members of the class of 1873 called a meeting of the Yale student body. From it emerged the Yale Football Association, the first formal entity to govern the game at Yale. Schaff, who attended the Rugby School in England where he played football, was elected president and team captain.

Nov. 16: With faculty approval, Yale met Columbia and won, 3 goals to 0, in the first (so-called) football game ever played by a Yale team. According to *The New York Times*, "some of Columbia's team arrived on the morning's boat and some of them on the eleven o'clock train."

The contest, that started at 2:45 p.m. at Hamilton Park in New Haven, drew 400 to 500 fans, mostly Yale students who paid a 25-cent admission fee. It was a time when patrons rode in their carriages from Whalley Avenue to Hamilton Park, a fairgrounds with a trotting track on the edge of town.

Schaff did not play because of an injury incurred the day before in practice.

Tommy Sherman booted the first Yale goal and Lew Irwin the other two. The team that scored five goals first was to be the winner, or if darkness prevented the game from going further, which it did, the team with the most goals would be the winner.

The New York Times referred to the contest as "the match game of foot-ball." Although it has been recorded as a football game, it was not the football we know today. Instead, it was a soccer match with 20 players on a side played on a field 400 by 250 feet. The game was played with a rubber ball. Players were allowed to be more physical than in today's typical soccer style. Batting the ball with the hands and arms and pushing other players with the body were permitted. Goals as they still are scored were executed by kicking the ball between two posts. A crossbar was added to the goal 15-feet off the ground.

After the game both teams enjoyed dinner together at Lockwood's Restaurant.

According to the *New Haven Register,* "The contest excited considerable applause," and what's more, "Yale discipline prevailed over Columbia muscle."

1873 (2–1) Captain: William Halstead

Yale was led by captain William Halstead, who became one of the most prominent surgeons in the history of the United States. Dr. Halstead was a pioneer in various surgical techniques and is credited for introducing surgical rubber gloves in the United States.

Nov. 15: Led by captain Cyrus Dershimer, the Princeton Tigers beat Yale, 3 goals to 0, at Hamilton Park to inaugurate Yale's oldest rivalry. A Yale player, George M. Gunn, and a Princeton player both kicked the ball at the same time and the ball rose into the air about 20-feet and fell with the stuffing kicked out of it. A half-hour delay was necessary until another ball could be obtained. In 1926 Gunn turned the ball over to Princeton University. On May 23, 1944, fire destroyed the University Gymnasium at Princeton. Reportedly lost in the fire were many athletic trophies including the relic ball from the 1873 Yale-Princeton game.

1874 (3–0) Captain: Hugh J. McBirney

Yale played a three-game schedule at Hamilton Park, defeating Stevens Institute and Columbia twice. There were 20 players to a side.

1875 (2–2) Captain: William Arnold

Arnold was photographed in front of the original Yale Fence which has since become a landmark for every Yale captain in each sport. The Yale Fence used today and located in the Ray Tompkins House is not the original that inexplicably escaped the university after 1952 and at this writing is in the hands of a Connecticut resident.

From 1872 to 1875 goals were earned by kicking the ball "into the net" as we know in soccer with the exception of the 1875 Yale-Harvard game when a goal was earned only after a successful kick "over the crossbar" following a touchdown. Field goals were given equal weight (one goal). This was the method of scoring from 1876 to 1882.

A goal was kicked over the crossbar from a point in front of where the touchdown had gone over the line.

Yale played a four-game schedule from November 6 to December 4 that included Rutgers, Harvard, Wesleyan and Columbia, finishing 2–2. The wins came against Rutgers and Wesleyan.

Oct. 20: Yale defeated Wesleyan, 6 goals to 0, launching a series in which the Blue piled up 46 wins without a loss in a 38-year span. The overmatched Cardinals scored just 12 points in the series: two field goals and one touchdown.

Nov. 13: The dawning of the storied Yale-Harvard rivalry began when the two schools played at Hamilton Park in New Haven on a slightly overcast day with no wind. The game was triggered by Harvard captain Nathaniel Curtis who challenged Yale captain William Arnold. It was advertised as a "Foot Ball Match" with the starting time at 2:30 p.m. In the morning the Yale men gave the Harvard team a tour of New Haven. The Harvard players wore crimson shirts, stockings and knee britches setting them off in vivid contrast to the dark trousers, blue shirts and yellow caps of the Yalies. The elegantly designed four-page game day program measured 5.5 × 4 inches in size. Yale reportedly promised Harvard $75 for its visit.

A total of 15 men comprised a side and it was agreed that the game would be divided into three 30-minute periods. Because each team had its own notion of football, it was known as a "concessionary game," a hybrid form of today's game with the teams using a combination of soccer and rugby rules.

It was agreed that the players would be allowed to use their hands to carry the ball as Harvard preferred. Yale football resembled the sport of soccer whereas Harvard played a more physical rugby style. Tutored by McGill in Canada from its two games played the year before, Harvard played Canadian rugby that some called "Boston Football." A player was allowed to run with the ball, pass it and dribble it. Also, the man with the ball could be tackled. It was reportedly the second "ball carrying" contest of football ever waged. Touchdowns only counted if they were followed by goals that were kicked over a crossbar. The field measured 140 by 70 yards.

The Crimson won the inaugural, 4 goals to 0, in front of an estimated 1,500 to 2,000 fans who paid a 50-cent admission price, twice the normal charge of a Yale game. Walter Camp, who would enroll at Yale the following year, attended the contest. H.C. Leeds, W.S. Seamans, A.C. Tower, B.S. Blanchard and H.W. Cushing figured in the Harvard scoring. Harvard scored four touchdowns but was not credited with a score because the kick after was not made.

The Elis had to familiarize themselves with the oval rugby ball that was a bit rounder than the one in use today, still a contrast to the round soccer ball. During the course of the contest the ball collapsed and had to be re-inflated on the field.

Although the fledgling, rugged Elis lost in battle, they learned their lesson well and reportedly enjoyed the Harvard rugby style better than their soccer style. "In the evening the teams were entertained at supper and representatives of the two colleges sang in the college yard," wrote Thomas Bergin in *The Game: The Harvard-Yale Football Rivalry, 1875–1983.*

1876   (3–0) Captain: Eugene V. Baker

For the first time Yale played rugby football with 11 players on a side. Only goals counted in scoring. A goal was earned if the kick was made after a touchdown. Field goals were given equal weight to a goal that was scored by a TD and followed by a successful kick.

Nov. 18: For the only time in Yale football history, Yale opened the season against Harvard, a 1 goal to 0 victory at Hamilton Park. There were 11 players on a side, a rule that Yale firmly requested. Only goals counted in scoring.

Harvard scored four touchdowns, but no goal followed. Thus, it did not register any goals (points). Yale won on a 35-yard field goal kick over the crossbar by Oliver Thompson. This ignited the Yale following to enter the playing field and carry the Yale combatants on their shoulders, delaying action for 20 minutes.

Nov. 30: Yale edged Princeton, 2 goals to 0, in Hoboken, New Jersey, the first time a Yale football team played on the road. The Tigers wore their colors for the first time showing up with black shirts and an orange

P on the chest. Walter Camp threw a forward pass to teammate Oliver Thompson. The referee, apparently perplexed by this unorthodox tactic, tossed a coin to make his decision and permitted it to stand. Camp, however, could not be credited with throwing the first forward pass because it was illegal until 1906.

Dec. 9: Yale beat Columbia, 2 goals to 0, in a rugby-style game with 11 players on each side. It was the latest date in the season that the Yale football team ever played.

1877 (3–0–1) Captain: Eugene V. Baker

Baker captained the Yale team for the second straight year. Yale beat Tufts, Trinity and Stevens Institute in games with 11 players on a side. Harvard and Yale did not meet because Harvard opposed Yale's insistence on playing with an 11-man team. The debate over 11 players or 15 players on the field was the source of controversy for the first several years of Yale football.

Dec. 8: Yale and Princeton played a scoreless tie in Hoboken, New Jersey. Yale acquiesced to playing with 15 players to a side in that contest.

1878 (4–1–1) Captain: Walter Camp

Walter Camp captained the 1878 and 1879 Yale teams. An 1880 graduate, he also played in '81 and '82 since postgraduates were allowed to participate at the time. Camp was elected captain again in 1881 but had to stop playing because of his medical school studies. All games in 1878 were played with 15 players on a side. Touchdowns were used as tiebreakers.

Nov. 23: Yale beat Harvard, 1 goal to 0, at the Boston National League Baseball Grounds, home of the Boston Red Stockings baseball team. Again, it was Oliver Thompson's field goal that proved the difference. During the game the ball rolled off the field into a pool of water in which players from both sides flung themselves. "After some competitive wallowing Camp emerged with the ball, soaked but triumphant," wrote Parke H. Davis in *Football, The American Intercollegiate Game*.

Nov. 28: Yale's only loss of the season came at the hands of Princeton, 1–0.

1879 (3–0–2) Captain: Walter Camp

From 1879 to 1884 Yale went 36–0–5.

Nov. 8: Yale and Harvard played to a scoreless tie. There were 15 players on a side and only goals were counted in scoring: Touchdowns were used as a tiebreaker. Camp, the Yale captain, kicked the only field goal of the game but it was nullified because the ball was touched by a Harvard player. The game day program from that game sold for nearly $1,500 in 2010.

The week after the Yale-Harvard game, Camp refereed the Harvard-Princeton game in Hoboken.

Nov. 27: Yale and Princeton also played to a scoreless tie.

1880 (4–0–1) Captain: Robert W. Watson

Walter Camp successfully advised a rules committee in Springfield, Massachusetts, that teams should consist of 11 men on the field, rather than 15. Camp, who was a guiding spirit of Yale football through most of its first 50 years, is credited for the 11-man team and the line of scrimmage instead of the rugby scrum. The line of scrimmage allowed both teams to deploy their forces in contrast to the continuous style of rugby. The purpose was to increase scoring. The quarterback position was now able to use spoken signals and numerical scoring was introduced. The field was reduced to 110 by 53 yards.

The snap from center to quarterback was also instituted. Originally, the snap was executed with the foot of the center. Later changes made it possible to snap the ball with the hands, either through the air or by a direct hand-to-hand pass. From this season on, teams were composed of 11 players.

Walter Camp is considered by many to be the father of college football because of his many rule innovations.

Nov. 20: After shutting out Columbia, Brown and Penn, Yale beat Harvard, one goal to zero, at the Boston National League Baseball

Grounds. Camp scored the only goal of the game, a 35-yard drop-kick penalty goal. The game was played under the rules that Camp had argued for: 11 men to a side and the replacement of the scrum by the scrimmage.

Yale captain Robert Watson returned a kickoff 100 yards but because the kick following the TD failed, Watson's record run was nullified. Touchdowns were used as tiebreakers.

1881 (5–0–1) Captain: Franklin M. Eaton

Camp was central to several more significant rule changes that came to define American football. The ridiculous rule that allowed a team to control the ball an entire half remained because there was no provision for making the possessing team give up the ball. There was no "downs" system as we know today. Blocking the opposing team from gaining possession of the ball allowed a team to control the ball for long periods of time.

Nov. 12: The oddity of winning a tie game occurred as Yale and Harvard played to a scoreless finish but Yale was declared the winner on "fewest safety touchdowns," a quirky rule that was used that season. Yale attempted the first onside kick ever in front of an estimated 1,500 at Hamilton Park in New Haven on a rainy day.

Nov. 24: Five days after Princeton and Harvard played to a scoreless tie, Yale and Princeton played to a scoreless stalemate in a game that extended into two overtimes. This was known as the "block" game. Princeton held the ball the entire first half and Yale did likewise in the second half. The Tigers used stalling tactics which led Camp to create a downs system in the rules for 1882. Camp recommended that a team must gain five yards in three downs, retreat 10 yards, or give up the ball.

1882 (8–0) Captain: Ray Tompkins

The "down" system was introduced by Camp. If on three successive downs a team did not advance the ball five yards or lost ten, it was required to give up the ball to the opposing team at the spot of the fourth down. This became the heart of the modern game and necessitated the linear markings (grids) on the field parallel to the goal lines for the measuring of the distance advanced with the ball. The term *gridiron* was born from the grid markings. This was also the last year that a touchdown counted only if the kick following the TD was good.

Yale began using voice signals before the ball was snapped.

The Ray Tompkins House, next to the Payne Whitney Gymnasium is the headquarters for Yale's athletic offices. The facility is named in honor of Tompkins, who captained the 1882 and 1883 national championship Yale football teams. Funds for the facility were provided by the bequest of Sarah Wey Tompkins, wife of the former Yale captain. Also in his memory, Mrs. Tompkins gave the Athletic Association more than 750 acres west of the Yale Bowl on which was built the Yale Golf Course.

Oct. 28: Yale blanked Rutgers in New Jersey, 5–0. This was the last game Camp ever played before he suffered a knee injury in practice a few days later.

Nov. 25: Yale edged Harvard, 1–0, at Holmes Field in Cambridge before an estimated 3,000. The Blue made three touchdowns but converted only one goal kick after the TD, thus the 1–0 score. Touchdowns by Yale's Louis Hall, Charles Beck and Arthur Farwell were erased because the goal kick failed following the TDs. Yale's only score was registered in the second half by Beck, who recovered a fumble and ran it for a TD which was validated by Eugene Richards's kick.

A scathing report from the *Hartford Herald* read, "Harvard cannot defeat Yale at football unless she consents to place on her team men who would substitute toughness for skill and professional enmity for amateur courtesy. But such a team will never represent Harvard and may never bear its honored name." [Yale won the next six games that the two teams played.]

Nov. 30: Led by Tompkins, Yale finished 8–0, beating Princeton, 2–1, in the Polo Grounds, then located at Fifth Avenue and 110th Street in New York City. The Tigers' James Haxall provided the highlight of the game when he drop-kicked a jaw-dropping 65-yard field goal.

1883 (8–0) Captain: Ray Tompkins

Thanks to the innovation of Camp, a touchdown was now valued at two points, the goal after the touchdown four points, a field goal five points and one point for a safety. No longer was a goal validated by the kick following the TD. Proper blue uniforms were worn by the Yale team.

Nov. 6: Yale waxed Rutgers, 98–0, in Brooklyn. Wyllis Terry kicked five field goals.

Nov. 17: Yale demolished Columbia, 93–0, its largest margin of victory ever against the Lions.

THE HIGHLIGHTS   1884

Nov. 29: Yale downed Harvard, 23–2, on Thanksgiving Day at the Polo Grounds in New York before an estimated 10,000 fans. The two points were the only points the Elis gave up the entire season

1884 (8–0–1) Captain: Eugene L. Richards

A touchdown now counted for four points until 1898. A goal after the touchdown was worth two points and a safety was valued at 2 points while the field goal stayed at five points. The two points after touchdown goal was kicked from a spot in front of where the touchdown had gone over the line. It wasn't until 1922 that the ball was spotted directly in front of the goalposts for the try for point following the touchdown.

Because Yale wanted a field of its own, two members of the class of 1881—Adrian S. Van de Graaff and Henry S. White—spearheaded the purchase of land on the south side of Derby Avenue which became the new site of Yale Field, the current site of the baseball field. The football team played on that field starting this year. The field ran from center field to right field on the baseball field. The author has designated this as Yale Field I.

Oct. 1: The Elis defeated Wesleyan, 31–0, to inaugurate Yale Field I on Derby Avenue. That season the Elis shutout the Middletown, Connecticut, liberal arts college three times (31–0, 63–0 and 46–0). The two teams played three games in a season seven different years.

Oct. 25: Yale met a neophyte Dartmouth team for the first time in a game that was played at Hanover, New Hampshire. Halfback Wyllys Terry and Alex Coxe, a 290-pound guard, each scored four touchdowns as Yale rolled, 113–0. It was the first time that Yale scored 100 points in a game. Despite the lopsided score, *The Dartmouth* headlined, "Dartmouth Eleven Acquit Themselves Very Creditably." The news story began, "The money which was spent to bring the Yale Rugby team up here seems to have been well invested. Our men have gained much practice, which it would be impossible for them to obtain from any picked eleven."

Nov. 5: Wyllys Terry set a record that still stands by running the length of the field—110 yards—in Yale's 46–0 win over Wesleyan. It wasn't until 1912 that the field was shortened to 100 yards.

Nov. 22: Yale scorched Harvard, 52–0, in New Haven. Many years later, Red Smith wrote, "it tied the track record for cruel and unusual punishment." Henry Flanders's 100-yard run was the highlight play of the game. Sophomore QB Nervy Bayne scored three TDs for Yale. Bayne's extracurricular activities outside the playing field eventually resulted in his leaving Yale. In 1893, he organized LSU's first football team made up of former college men from Tulane and the Southern Athletic Club.

1885 (7–1) Captain: Frank G. Peters

Per Camp's recommendation, the offside penalty was determined to be five yards. Harvard did not compete in football that season, a decision by the Harvard faculty, who viewed the game of football as dangerous and degrading. "At the time a player could hack throttle, butt, trip, tackle below the hips, or strike an opponent with closed fist three times before he was sent from the field," wrote Thomas Bergin in *The Game: The Harvard-Yale Football Rivalry, 1875–1983*.

Nov. 21: Princeton's Henry "Tillie" Lamar picked up a teammate's fumble of a punt and ran 95 yards for a touchdown and a 6–5 victory over Yale in New Haven. Lamar's feat broke a 47-game (42–0–5) Yale unbeaten streak. Yale would not lose again until the final game of the 1889 season. And again, it was Princeton who rained on Yale's parade.

1886 (9–0–1) Captain: Robert N. Corwin

Oct. 6: Yale whipped Wesleyan, 75–0, and three days later slammed the Cardinals again, 62–0. Yale counts 46 games vs. Wesleyan, but Wesleyan only 40.

Oct. 30: Yale won by its highest score ever, embarrassing Wesleyan, 136–0, as QB Henry "Harry" Beecher, grandson of the famous preacher and abolitionist of the same name, scored 11 touchdowns. During his three-year career he scored a record 66 touchdowns. The modern record for most touchdowns is held by Mike McLeod, who reached the end zone 55 times from 2005 to 2008 (54 were rushing TDs).

Nov. 20: Yale and Harvard renewed their annual joust at Jarvis Field in Cambridge with Yale prevailing, 29–4, over a Harvard team that registered 765 points that season. Yale entered the game undefeated, untied and unscored upon. Beecher, the athletic Yale QB, scored on the fifth play of the bone crushing game. Harvard's A.F. Holden scored the only TD against Yale that season.

Nov. 25: Yale was leading Princeton 4–0 when the game was stopped

THE HIGHLIGHTS   1887–1888

by darkness, resulting in a scoreless tie. Yale suffered a similar fate in the 1884 Princeton game.

1887 (9–0) Captain: Henry W. Beecher

Game length was set at two halves of 45 minutes each. Two paid officials, a referee and an umpire were mandated for each game. Yale's hegemony over its opponents continued. The Bulldogs were undefeated and unscored upon the first six games of the season.

Nov. 5: Billy Bull, Yale's left-footed kicker, booted 12 conversions without a miss in Yale's lopsided 74–0 romp over Rutgers.

Nov. 19: Yale beat Princeton in New York, 12–0.

Nov. 24: Yale defeated Harvard, 17–8, on Thanksgiving Day at the Polo Grounds in New York in front of an estimated 15,000. Pa Corbin scored with a recovered kick and Billy Bull, who booted a 25-yard FG, followed with a successful kick. Billy Wurtenberg's 35-yard TD run followed by a Bull kick completed the scoring.

1888 (13–0) Coach: Walter Camp; Captain: William H. Corbin

Walter Camp became Yale's first head football coach. In Camp's first season, Yale went 13–0, outscoring their opponents, 698–0. Camp coached the team from 1888 to 1892, compiling an unmatched record of 67–2–0. Three of his five teams did not give up a point the entire season. Camp also coached at Stanford in December 1892 and from 1894 to '95, compiling a record of 12–3–3.

Tackling was now allowed below the waist. This led to mass formations with linemen and backs grouped closely together to power their way at the point of attack. The violent wedge formation resulting is serious injuries evolved from the rule.

Yale won the Harvard game by a forfeit because Harvard refused to play the game in New York, which had been mutually agreed on by both schools. It was probably unfortunate for the Cantabs that the game was never played because Harvard finished 12–1 that year. However, Yale does not include the forfeit as one of the all-time wins in their record book.

Sept. 29: Camp coached his first game and led the Elis to a 76–0 win against weak sister Wesleyan. Yale's 24-year-old captain, William "Pa" Corbin, who sported a handlebar mustache, unofficially named Mrs. Walter Camp co-coach of the team. "Sir Walter" was chairman of the Board of Directors of the New Haven Clock Company and his time was occupied by business. Because his boss would not allow him to leave to attend practices, Camp's wife, Alice, volunteered to go to the field every afternoon, bringing her husband's instructions. Mrs. Camp, who paced the sidelines during practices, jotted down notes for her husband and became an expert in her analysis. She even monitored the diets of the players.

Oct. 16: Unheard of by today's standards, Yale played the first of three road games over a period of five days facing Wesleyan, Amherst and Williams. The Amherst and Williams games were played on back-to-back days (October 19 and 20). Yale outscored those opponents, 115–0.

Nov. 17: Yale beat its ever-obliging sparring partner, Wesleyan, 105–0. It was the fourth time that the Elis scored over 100 points in a game. Three of the four times the opponent was Wesleyan.

Nov. 24: Yale upended Princeton, 10–0, in a game played at the Polo Grounds in New York. Billy Bull kicked two field goals, each worth five points. The 698 points scored during the season did not include the six points gained by Yale in the Harvard forfeit.

1889 (15–1) Coach: Walter Camp; Captain: Charles O. Gill

Yale twice played a 16-game schedule. The first time was this season. The Elis were led by Captain Charley Gill, who played five varsity seasons and never missed a game or called for a substitute. His iron man streak is unmatched in Eli annals.

Officials were given whistles and stop watches to use on the field. The center rolled the ball back, and it had to be touched by two of the players before it was in play.

Handsome Dan, the Yale bulldog mascot, arrived. The dog was owned by Yale student Andrew B. Graves. The dog followed his master to classes and to games and tradition says it barked whenever Yale scored. Handsome Dan was befriended by the players and students and is believed to have been the first live college mascot. It was at this time that Yale became known as the Bulldogs.

Graves returned to his native England but Dan stayed on the Yale campus with Graves's brother, who, prior to baseball and football games, would lead the Yale mascot across the field, drawing applause from the crowd. A fine specimen, the popular Yale bulldog won many awards at dog shows including a first prize at the Westminster Kennel Club show.

In 1897, Handsome Dan I was reunited with his master in England and died the following year. Graves had him stuffed by a taxidermist and returned him to Yale where he remains in a sealed glass case on display in the lobby of the Payne Whitney Gymnasium.

Nov. 23: Yale beat Harvard at Hampden Park in Springfield, 6–0. Thomas Lee "Bum" McClung scored on a 1-yard run when he reportedly was pushed and pulled over the goal line by the whole Yale team. McClung then kicked the goal.

Nov. 28: Yale entered the game 15–0 before losing to Princeton, 10–0, at the Polo Grounds, ending their 48-game (47–0–1) unbeaten streak. This was the first game Camp lost as Yale's head coach.

At the conclusion of the season, Walter Camp picked an All-America team for the first time. It is speculated that it was a collaborative effort between Camp and Caspar Whitney, the manager of *The Week's Sport*. Camp picked or collaborated on an All-America team every year through 1924.

1890 (13–1) Coach: Walter Camp; Captain: William C. Rhodes

The Yale football machine rolled on in the 1890s going 116–7–5. Of Yale's seven losses, four came at the hands of Princeton.

Yale reportedly introduced cheerleaders for the first time. While records from this era are unofficial, it is believed that Hall of Fame back Lee "Bum" McClung scored 510 points from 1888 to 1891. He scored 63 touchdowns when a touchdown's value was four points. "Bum" also kicked 129 goals after a touchdown (two points each). In 1909 McClung was appointed the 22nd Treasurer of the United States by President Howard Taft, a Yale alum.

Nov. 22: Harvard's undefeated, untied team ruined Yale's perfect season by defeating the Bulldogs, 12–6, in Springfield, Massachusetts, before an estimated 15,000. Jimmy Lee (40-yard sweep) and D.S. Dean (70-yard run with a recovered fumble) were the TD heroes for the Cantabs. McClung scored Yale's only TD on a 6-yard run. This was the only other loss Camp suffered as head coach. Some consider the victory the greatest in the history of Harvard Crimson football and Arthur Cumnock, team captain, Harvard's greatest football player.

Nov. 27: Yale beat Princeton, 32–0, at Eastern Park in Brooklyn, New York, to finish the season 13–1. McClung scored four touchdowns in the rout. Yale's share of the gate was $11,185. This brought the football revenue for the year to $18,392 (value about $474,000 today), enough to pay for the entire athletic program. Before the start of the game, tragedy struck when 2,000 spectators were thrown to the ground because a movable grandstand that stood 20 feet high and 150 feet long collapsed. An estimated 50 fans were injured, two reportedly were likely to die.

The game was immortalized in art by former Yale player Frederic Remington whose classic work, *Foot-Ball—A Collision at the Ropes*, appeared in *Harper's Weekly*.

1891 (13–0) Coach: Walter Camp; Captain: Thomas L. McClung

The 1891 team went 13–0 and was unscored upon. Frank Hinkey, an exciting 5-foot-9, 20-year-old freshman end, surfaced that year. Hinkey, who captained the 1893 and 1894 squads, saw his Yale teams suffer defeat only once in his career, a 6–0 setback to Princeton in 1893. He played the game with reckless abandon, hurling his body at opponents with disregard for its consequences. Pop Warner called him "the greatest player of all-time." Hinkey stayed up late, smoked cigars despite having a lung condition and drank the worst brands of whiskey. Walter Camp referred to him as the "disembodied spirit." Yale's head football coach in 1914 and 1915, he was elected to the College Football Hall of Fame in 1951.

Nov. 21: Yale beat Harvard, 10–0, at Hampden Park in Springfield, Massachusetts, before an estimated 25,000 fans. Stan Morrison (1-yard run) scored in the first half for four points but the kick failed. In the second half Laurie Bliss ran to paydirt on a 25-yard run with a recovered fumble for four points and McClung made the kick for two more points. Players on both teams played the entire game as substituting was rare at the time.

An official Yale-Harvard scorecard was issued as well as a game day program. The trend for cigarette advertising in college football programs began with this program with the advertising of such cigarette brands as Egyptian Deities and Pall Mall. For many years Chesterfield sponsored color centerfolds in college football programs.

Nov. 26: Yale ended its perfect season with a 19–0 win over Princeton in a game that was played at Manhattan Field in New York in front of 40,000. Manhattan Field, the first sports stadium with all-iron grandstands, was the second Polo Grounds, home of the New York Giants National League baseball team. It was located just south of the Polo Grounds III that was built in 1890 and renovated after a fire in 1911. Then it became known as

Polo Grounds IV, the one generally indicated when the Polo Grounds is referenced. Manhattan Field was known as Columbia Field in 1899 and 1900.

1892 (13–0) Coach: Walter Camp; Captain: Vance McCormick

Research indicates that Yale Field II was first used for football. It is the current site of the Dewitt Cuyler Athletic Complex that includes Clint Frank Field and is a practice field for the Yale football team. The field ran perpendicular to Yale Field I and route 34 (New Haven Avenue). This was also Walter Camp's final season as Yale's head coach. The undefeated Bulldogs were not scored upon for the second straight season. (From here on, the author will refer to Yale Field II as Yale Field.)

Nov. 19: Frank Hinkey, a ferocious tackler, is said to have neutralized Harvard's flying wedge first used in Yale's 6–0 win in Springfield. The invention of Harvard assistant coach Lorin Deland, the Crimson first used the brutal mass formation in the second half. A total of 10 players would lock themselves together in a V formation to protect the ball carrier using their hands and arms and rush forward. Pop Bliss scored Yale's TD on a 1-yard blast and fullback Frank Butterworth, a two-time All-American, made the kick.

Nov. 24: Walter Camp coached his final game at Yale, a 12–0 win over Princeton at the Polo Grounds.

1893 (10–1) Coach: William C. Rhodes; Captain: Frank A. Hinkey

Bill Rhodes, the captain of the 1890 Yale team took over the head coaching duties. As the story goes, his motivation to become the Yale head football coach resulted from officiating the 1891 Yale-Amherst game, a contest he believed Yale played substandard football. He reportedly took over the team the remainder of that season but is not credited for any Yale wins.

Nov. 11: Yale beat Penn in New Haven, 14–6. It was the first time a team had scored against Yale in 35 consecutive games dating back to the 1890 Harvard game.

Nov. 25: Yale won their 37th straight game, beating Harvard, 6–0, at Springfield in front of a crowd of 25,000. Yale's six points came on a touchdown by Frank Butterworth, followed by a "Wild Bill" Hickok kick.

Betting appeared heavy, ranging from $10 to $1,000 at places like the Massasoit House, Cooley's Hotel, Shean's Exchange and other places. Harvard appeared on the field in knickerbockers and vests made of leather.

The failed idea was that the leather breeches would hinder Yale's tackling. But the Elis blanked the Crimson for the third straight year.

Handsome Dan, the Yale mascot, was on the field. One of the Harvards made a big dog out of red cloth, stuffed with rags. He was displayed with the placard, "Where's Dan?" After the game, Handsome Dan tore the dummy to pieces.

Nov. 30: Undefeated Princeton was poison to Yale. Led by three-time All-American Phil King, the Tigers spoiled Yale's perfect undefeated, untied season and Yale's 37-game winning streak with a 6–0 win at the Polo Grounds before 50,000.

1894 (16–0) Coach: William C. Rhodes; Captain: Frank A. Hinkey

For the second and last time, Yale played a 16-game schedule. Two-time All-American guard and Hall of Famer William Orville Hickok, known as "Wild Bill," and All-Americans Frank Hinkey (end), George Adee (QB), Frank Butterworth (FB), and Philip Stillman led the team to an undefeated 16–0 season, the most wins in a season by any team in college football history. Under coach Bill Rhodes, the Elis outscored their opponents, 485–13. Yale's record 16-win season was noted during the 2019 College Football Playoff National Championship game played between Clemson and Alabama, the finalists in the Division I Football Bowl Subdivision for the 2018 season.

In this era, it was not uncommon for teams to play lengthy schedules. The University of Chicago under coach Amos Alonzo Stagg played 22 games (14–7–1) in 1894.

Nov. 24: In what has become known as the "Springfield Massacre" and the "Bloodbath in Hampden Park," Yale beat Harvard, 12–4, led by Hinkey and Hickok. The Yale scores came in the first half when Phil Stillman ran across the goal line on a blocked punt followed by a Hickok kick. Sam "Brinck" Thorne scored on a 5-yard run supported by a Hickok kick.

The game that was played in Springfield, Massachusetts, was so violent, the series was suspended for two years. Hinkey had allegedly broken the collarbone of a Harvard player following a fair catch. Yale tackle Fred Murphy broke the nose of Harvard's Bob Hallowell during an officials' conference; in turn, Murphy absorbed a hard hit later in the contest that hospitalized him. False rumors circulated postgame that he died in a local hospital. Violence ensued among fans in the streets of Springfield.

THE HIGHLIGHTS   1895–1896

Many years later Red Smith wrote in the *New York Post*, "No father or mother worthy of the name would permit a son to associate with the set of Yale brutes on Hinkey's football team."

Dec. 1: Yale completed a 16–0 season by defeating Princeton in New York, 24–0.

1895 (13-0-2) Coach: John Hartwell; Captain: Sam Thorne

Nov. 23: Yale finished its undefeated season with a 20–10 win over Princeton. Hall of Famer and All-American halfback Samuel Brinckerhoff Thorne proved to be a one-man wrecking crew as he scored two touchdowns, set up a touchdown with a 45-yard punt return, kicked two conversions and blocked a punt. The two ties came against Boston A.C. and Brown.

1896 (13-1) Coach: Sam Thorne; Captain: Fred T. Murphy

Frank Merriwell, Yale's fictional hero, who excelled in multiple sports, made his debut in *Street and Smith's Tip-Top Weekly*. Brought to life by Gilbert Patten, who wrote under the pseudonym, Burt L. Standish, the Merriwell stories sold at a rate of 200,000 copies per week. The character appeared in more than 200 dime novels between 1896 and 1930. Subsequently, there were numerous radio dramas and a book that centered on the alpha male.

Oct. 24: Yale beat the Carlisle Indians, 12–6, in East Orange, New Jersey, in a game that was marred by a quick whistle from former Yale All-American "Wild Bill" Hickok, one of the officials on the game. The incident occurred in the second half, robbing a touchdown run by Carlisle's Isaac Seneca, Jr. Seneca, the first American Indian to be selected as an All-American in 1899, busted through the center of the line. He squirmed and shook off the Yale tacklers, dodged a man or two, and, made an apparent spectacular TD run down the field. But Hickok prematurely blew the whistle, calling the play dead before Seneca broke loose.

When Seneca broke away, Hickok realized that he had made a mistake and wanted to change his decision and allow the touchdown. Fred Murphy, the Yale captain, objected, claiming that the whistle had been blown and the ball was down. The Indians, of course, objected, and a wordy war followed.

Hickok told Murphy that if the touchdown was not allowed the Indians would leave the field. Murphy was obstinate and would not give in. With the influence of Josh Hartwell, the umpire, Hickok concluded that he ought not to change his ruling and ordered the ball down on the 35-yard line. He then had a long talk with the Indians, and finally persuaded them to continue the game, which they did.

Nov. 21: The men from Old Nassau did it again. This time Princeton stopped a 44-game (42–0–2) unbeaten Yale streak and a perfect season with a 24–6 victory at the Polo Grounds.

1897 (9–0–2) Coach: Frank Butterworth; Captain: James O. Rodgers

Grandstands were put up at Yale Field, increasing the seating capacity to 15,000 fans.

Oct. 23: Yale beat the Carlisle Indians at the Polo Grounds in New York, 24–9. *The New York Times* wrote, "There were 22-men in perfect condition ... meeting in equal numbers, man against man, on equal terms."

Nov. 13: After a two-year armistice, thanks to the efforts of Walter Camp and W.A. Brooks (Harvard), Yale and Harvard resumed their rivalry and played a scoreless tie at Soldiers Field in Boston. The stalemate that was played in two 35-minute halves was witnessed by approximately 24,000. Yale used the same 11 players the entire game.

Soldiers Field, which subsequently became Harvard Stadium, was donated by philanthropist Henry Lee Higginson, an officer in the Union Army during the Civil War. Higginson, who was also the founder of the Boston Symphony orchestra, donated the 33 acres of land as a memorial to his friends who died in the Civil War.

Nov. 20: Yale beat Princeton in New Haven, 6–0. The highlight play of the game was executed by Yale QB Charles de Saulles's zig-zag 55-yard run.

1898 (9–2) Coach: Frank Butterworth; Captain: Burr Chamberlain

Yale won its first nine games by a combined 146–11 score then was shut out by rivals Princeton and Harvard the final two games. Touchdowns and field goals both counted five points and a goal after touchdown was valued at one point. A safety was two points.

Nov. 12: In front of ex–President Grover Cleveland and his wife, Frances, Princeton continued to haunt Yale, again ruining an undefeated season with a 6–0 win at Brokaw Field in New Jersey. The Tigers' consensus All-American end Arthur Poe's electrifying 95-yard game-winning touchdown was the highlight of the game. Poe picked up the ball on the Princeton 5-yard line after Yale back Alfred Durston failed to catch the snap from center. He fumbled and thought the ball was "down," according to *The New York Times*, who also reported that Poe's race to the goal line was "one of the most sensational ever witnessed on a football field." The *Times* added, "Pandemonium broke loose on the Princeton side. Flags were waved, women took off their bouquets of chrysanthemums and waved them in the air." Benjamin Ayres kicked the extra point.

It should be noted that Poe was the second cousin twice removed of the American author Edgar Allan Poe.

A 100-page game day program was produced with player photos, ornate Victorian ads and much more. The cover of the program pictured three-time Yale All-American Burr Chamberlain and Arthur Hillebrand, a Princeton player who was later inducted into the College Football Hall of Fame.

Nov. 19: Harvard beat Yale, 17–0, at Yale Field in heavy rain before 17,500. Crimson sophomore fullback Bill Reid, known as "William the Conqueror," charged into the end zone twice on runs of 5 and 12 yards. He became the first Harvard player ever to score two touchdowns against Yale in one game. Because of a leg injury, Reid did not play his senior year. Instead, he became the team's head cheerleader.

1899 (7–2–1) **Coach: J.O. Rodgers; Captain: Malcolm L. McBride**

Oct. 21: Yale remained undefeated, untied, and unscored upon after the first five games, blanking the Wisconsin Badgers in New Haven, 6–0. The two teams would not play again until 1947.

Nov. 18: Yale and Harvard played to a scoreless tie at Harvard. The game was witnessed by 36,000 spectators, including Governor (and future U.S. President) Theodore Roosevelt of New York and Governor Roger Wolcott of Massachusetts, both Harvard graduates. Yale stopped Harvard on the goal line when Harvard fullback S.G. Ellis ran straight into the arms of Malcolm McBride, who was braced against the goal post which was on the goal line at the time.

Nov. 25: Despite Albert Sharpe's 50-yard drop-kick field goal, Yale lost to Princeton, 11–10, in New Haven to close out the 19th century in which the storied Yale football program produced an astonishing record of 223-13-13.

1900 (12–0) Coach: Malcolm L. McBride; Captain: F. Gordon Brown Jr.

The era of four-time All-American and Hall of Fame guard Francis Gordon Brown ended with the Bulldogs going 37–5–3. The national champion 1900 team, called the "Team of the Century," included seven first-team All-Americans. Yale outscored their opponents, 336–10 with the 10 points divided between Columbia and Princeton.

Nov. 17: Yale waltzed by Princeton, 29–5, at University Field in New Jersey.

Nov. 24: Yale and Harvard both entered the contest undefeated. The Bulldogs won the game, 28–0, in New Haven to finish a perfect season. Harvard would win their next 23 games. The big play of the game came in the second half when Sherman Coy recovered a fumbled pass in the Crimson backfield and ran 75 yards. Yale played the entire game using 12 players. All Yale starters except for All-American center Herman Olcott played the full game.

"Boola-Boola" was sung for the first time. It appears that three Yale students, Allan M. Hirsch, F.M. Van Wincklen and A.H. Marckwald, wrote the words to fit the tune of "La Hoola Boola"—a song African American entertainers Bob Cole and Billy Johnson performed in New Haven in the 1890s.

1901 (11–1–1) Coach: George S. Stillman; Captain: Charles Gould

Two-time All-American tackle (1899–1900) George Schley Stillman was handed the coaching baton for the 1901 season. Stillman subsequently entered the banking business and died at age 27 after contracting typhoid fever.

Jan. 1: Century Milstead, an All-American tackle at Yale in 1923 who also played in the NFL with the New York Giants, is born on this date. He got his unusual name for being born on the first day of the twentieth century. Of course, the debate as to the first year of a century rages on.

Nov. 16: The Bulldogs tripped Princeton, 12–0, before 19,000 at Yale Field.

Nov. 23: Yale entered the Harvard game 11–0–1 but the Crimson spoiled the Elis' undefeated season winning, 22–0. It was the worst shellacking a Yale team had ever received. All three Crimson TDs were scored on 1-yard runs by Crawford Blagden, Albert Ristine and Thomas Graydon.

THE HIGHLIGHTS   1902–1903

Midway through the season, Harvard officials raised the issue that Yale All-American guard Edgar "Ned" Glass had played at Syracuse prior to coming to Yale and because Yale transfers were required to sit out one year, he should be ineligible. Yale sat him for the Princeton and Harvard games, beating the Tigers but losing to the Crimson.

The Yale and Harvard Glee clubs had a joint concert as part of the Yale-Harvard weekend, a tradition that has endured.

1902 (11–0–1) Coach: Joseph R. Swan; Captain: George B. Chadwick

Nov. 1: Yale battled Army to a 6–6 tie before a then-record crowd of 8,000 at West Point.

Time ran out on a Yale drive that had gone from the Blue's 10-yard line to the Army 20.

Nov. 22: Ned Glass returned and helped Yale break Harvard's 23-game winning streak with a 23–0 victory at Yale Field. It was Harvard's first loss since Yale beat the Cantabs, 28–0, in 1900. In this game a Yale player faked an injury so a teammate could get a letter. In an article by 1902 Yale captain George Brewster Chadwick for the November 15, 1958, Yale-Princeton game day program, Chadwick wrote,

> In my time, men could not get a "Y" unless they played in the Princeton game or the Harvard game.... A few days before the Harvard game, George Goss one of our guards, came up to me and said, 'If all is going well toward the end of the game, I'll pretend I'm hurt, so that Chan Hamlin can take my place. No one needs to know about it except you and me.
>
> Toward the end of the game all indeed was going well; we led Harvard 23–0. After a certain play, I saw Goss lying on his back. I ran over to him, and knelt beside him, fearful that he had been really hurt. But he winked at me and then I remembered. Thus, Hamlin got into the game not knowing the why of it. I kept that incident a secret until a 25th anniversary dinner of the team. Hamlin appreciated the gesture.

1903 (11–1) Coach: G.B. Chadwick; Captain: C.D. Rafferty

Stands were increased at Yale Field to hold 29,000. A rule change allowed a running back to run with the ball between the 25 yard lines as long as he was five yards on either side of the center when he crossed the line of scrimmage. The next season the rule was extended for the entire field. The field was thus marked with longitudinal lines.

Nov. 14: The Yale-Princeton game in New Haven, won by Princeton,

11–6, was filmed by Thomas Edison Films using a Kinetograph motion picture camera. The big play in the game occurred when Yale's Ledyard Mitchell was attempting to drop kick a 41-yard FG when he was hit by two Tigers. After he was hit, Princeton's Ridge Hart gave the ball impetus toward the Yale goal. Tigers All-American John DeWitt picked up the ball, which was technically a fumble, and ran for a 26-yard touchdown. DeWitt also kicked a 53-yard field goal following a fair catch. The length of the FG remains open to question. There is no evidence that Edison attended the game. The field was marked in a checkered gridiron.

Harvard Stadium opened on the same day, but Dartmouth spoiled the party defeating the Crimson, 11–0. Its U-shaped architecture resembles Panathenaic Stadium in Athens, Greece.

Nov. 21: Yale won the inaugural Y-H appearance in the new stadium, 16–0. The game was played in two halves, a practice that continued until 1909. The Elis scored in the first half on a 3-yard run by Ralph Kinney that was set up by a long Harold Metcalf run. In the second half, two blocked kicks were downed by Jim Hogan behind the Crimson goal line. Harvard Stadium was the nation's first sports venue to use the term *Stadium*. The next oldest was the original Yankee Stadium that opened in 1923.

1904 (10–1) Coach: C.D. Rafferty; Captain: James J. Hogan

The team was noted for Yale's "Irish Line" that was led by three-time All American tackle James Hogan. A native of Glenbane, Tipperary, Hogan was elected to the College Hall of Fame in 1954. He was joined on the line by tackle Ralph Kinney, guard Ned Glass, center Henry Holt, guard George Goss, and end Tom Shevlin. This was the last year that Yale played more than 10 games in a season. Two-time All-American quarterback Foster Rockwell helped the Bulldogs go 32–2–1 between 1902 and 1904.

Oct. 22: Army edged Yale, 11–6, at West Point to give Yale their only loss of the season. Army and Syracuse were the only teams to score against the Elis during the season.

Nov. 12: Yale beat Princeton at Princeton University Field, 12–0. "Down the Field" was sung for the first time. The song was composed by Stanleigh Friedman ('05) and written by C.W. O'Connor.

Nov. 19: Yale shut out Harvard for the third straight year, this time,

12–0. Sammy Morse (from 2 yards) and Rex Flinn (1 yard) crossed the goal line for the Bulldogs. Flinn's score came on a blocked Harvard kick by Roswell Tripp that was carried over the goal line by Flinn. One of Harvard's reserves was William Clarence Matthews, the first black to play in the Y-H series.

1905 (10–0) Coach: J.E. Owsley; Captain: Thomas L. Shevlin

Nov. 25: Harvard lost to undefeated Yale, 6–0, before an estimated 43,000 in Boston, finishing 8–2–1. Yale scored in the second 30-minute half after Bob Forbes recovered a fumble on the Harvard 30-yard line before crossing the goal line on a 4-yard run several plays later.

The game had a violent tone to it. Yale's Tom Shevlin, the alpha male All-American end, ignored Harvard's Francis Burr's fair catch signal and tackled him low. The Elis' Jim Quill then broke Burr's nose. Quill claimed it was retaliation because Burr had bitten him earlier in the game. When referee Paul Dashiell failed to penalize Shevlin, the Harvard crowd became boisterous. Before the Burr incident, Yale's Sammy Morse was banished for punching Jack Wendell, who he claimed had been repeatedly holding him without being penalized by Dashiell.

Harvard coach Bill Reid saw to it that Dashiell would never officiate another Harvard game. The violent play prompted the delivery of a note from Henry Lee Higginson, a Civil War veteran, who was wounded at the First Battle of Bull Run. Higginson, a benefactor who donated to Soldiers Field, sent the note to Reid, requesting the withdrawal of the Crimson team from the playing field. Reid ignored the request.

1906 (9–0–1) Coach: Foster Rockwell; Captain: Samuel F.B. Morse

In this era of mass formations such as the flying wedge, the casualty football list for 1905 was fearful. There was a total of 18 to 26 gridiron fatalities reported by various sources, including 11 in high schools and three in colleges. There were 149 serious injuries, 47 on the college level. Columbia, Northwestern and Union gave up the game. Stanford and Columbia replaced it with rugby.

Jan. 27: President Theodore Roosevelt had called upon representatives of college football to make the game safer. The football rules committee comprised of 14 members including three Yale men, Walter Camp,

Amos Alonso Stagg (coach at the University of Chicago) and Dr. Henry Williams (coach at Minnesota) agreed to legalize the forward pass. A rule was also established requiring teams to gain 10 yards in three downs. There were several restrictions, however, regarding the forward pass. One rule read, "If a pass hit the ground before it was touched by a player of either side, the ball automatically went to the opponent on the spot where the pass was thrown." Also, passes over 20 yards were illegal. Camp, who reportedly was initially against the forward pass, devised the "Statue of Liberty" play, according to writer Tim Cohane.

Oct. 3: Yale defeated Wesleyan, 21–0. One source credits the birth of the forward pass to this game when Sam Moore of Wesleyan threw a pass to Irwin Van Tassel that gained 18 yards for the Methodists. According to writer Dan Parker, "this marked the dawn of the aerial era." However, most sources credit the birth of the forward pass to Saint Louis University's Bradbury Robinson when he tossed a 20-yard pass to Jack Schneider on September 5, 1906, 28 days earlier when SLU, coached by Eddie Cochems, defeated Carroll College, 22–0.

Oct. 20: Yale clipped Penn State in New Haven, 10–0. From 1899 to 1906 the two schools played seven times with Yale winning every game. The Elis outscored the Nittany Lions, 148–0, in the series.

Nov. 3: In a game in which Yale failed to record a first down and both teams each used only one sub, Yale pulled out an unlikely 10–6 victory over Army at West Point. The Cadets became the first (and only) team to score against Yale all season. Trailing, 6–0, at the half, Clarence Alcott recovered a blocked punt for Yale's touchdown worth five points. Alcott was reportedly all over the field and recovered several fumbles. Paul Veeder made the extra point to tie the score. Lucius Horatio "Ray" Biglow (often spelled Bigelow) made the deciding field goal (worth four points then) in the last two minutes on a free kick after a fair catch by William Knox.

The *New York Times* bannered, "Yale Field Goal Earns Luckiest of Victories." The NCAA eliminated the free-kick FG following a fair catch in 1950 but it is still legal under high school and NFL rules. There have been six such documented free-kick field goals in NFL history, the last being in 1976 when Ray Wersching of the San Diego Chargers booted a 45-yarder against the Buffalo Bills following a fair catch.

Nov. 17: For the seventh time, Yale and Princeton played to a scoreless tie. The stalemate nets undefeated seasons for both programs and a co-national championship.

Nov. 24: Yale blanked Harvard, 6–0, to spoil Harvard's 10–0 season. A fumbled punt set up Yale's only TD scored by Howard Roome on a 3-yard run. This was the first Y-H game that was impacted by the forward pass when Paul Veeder connected on a 30-yard toss to Clarence Alcott, a substitute end who brought the ball to the Harvard 4 yard line to set up Roome's TD.

1907 (9–0–1) **Coach: William Knox; Captain: L.H. Biglow**

Yale's only loss from 1907 to 1909 came against Harvard in 1908. Ted Coy, an All-America fullback in each of those years, was elected to the College Football Hall of Fame.

Nov. 16: Led by Coy, the indomitable sophomore fullback, Yale edged Princeton, 12–10, in New Haven. With the Tigers leading, 10–0, Coy ran roughshod over the Tigers, scoring two touchdowns and kicking both extra points.

Nov. 23: Yale beat Harvard, 12–0, in a dogged battle at Harvard Stadium. It was the Bulldogs' sixth consecutive shutout win over the Crimson. Coy scored Yale's two touchdowns on runs of 4 yards and 1 yard. Hamilton Fish III, captain of the 1909 Harvard team (and acting captain in 1908 when that year's captain was injured) was a mainstay at tackle from 1907 to 1909.

1908 (7–1–1) **Coach: L.H. Biglow; Captain: Robert B. Burch**

In its final addition, stands at Yale Field were constructed to hold 35,000.

Oct. 17: Thanks to Coy's punting and plunging, Yale defeated Army, 6–0, at West Point before 10,000. Coy scored the only TD late in the game.

Nov. 14: In one of the most amazing finishes in Yale football history, the Elis trailed Princeton, 6–0, in the final minutes on a blustery, snowy day in New Jersey. The Tigers' diminutive captain Eddie Dillon delivered an onside kick. The idea was to let Yale kill the remaining time with an ineffectual offense. But Coy, also known as "Terrible Ted," shot through the snow and brought the ball down to the Princeton 10. Triggered by the crowd who were chanting, "Coy, Coy, Coy," the Yale QB trotted over and pulled Coy from his end position into the backfield where he crashed through for a touchdown. Because of the rule at the time that allowed the team that scored to receive the kickoff, Coy received the ball and ran to the Princeton 30. On the next play he tore across the goal line, leading Yale to an unlikely 11–6 win.

Nov. 21: Yale's six-year hex over Harvard ended when left-footed drop kicker Vic Kennard booted a 25-yard field goal in the first half to give Harvard a 4–0 lead which proved to be the final score. The Harvard win also ended Yale's 42-game (39–0–3) unbeaten streak. Percy Haughton, Harvard's first year coach, gambled by putting Kennard in the game in the first half. The rules at the time stipulated that once a player was removed from the game, he could not re-enter. Kennard remained in the game for a time until he was injured after tackling Coy, Yale's All-American fullback. Despite fears that his leg was broken, Kennard's mother, who was in the stands dismissed the injury. "I don't care," she said. "He stopped Ted Coy."

According to legend, Haughton strangled a bulldog during a fiery pregame speech. Contemporary research concludes that at worst Haughton "strangled" a papier mâché bulldog and tied another such creation to the back fender of his automobile.

When told the score, President Theodore Roosevelt, a Harvard alumnus, interrupted a doubles tennis match at the White House with the French ambassador to dance an impromptu jig.

At the end of the season it was discovered that Ham Andrus, Yale's All-American guard, had played the game with a broken arm.

1909 (10–0) Coach: Howard H. Jones; Captain: Edward H. "Ted" Coy

Former Yale player Howard Jones, who gained fame as the longtime head coach at Southern California, coached his alma mater to an undefeated, untied and unscored-upon 10–0 season. Yale outscored its opponents, 209–0. It would be the Elis' fifth such trifecta season. Periods were changed from two halves of 35 minutes to four quarters of 15 minutes. Field goals now counted three points instead of four.

Five Yale Glee Club undergraduates decided to spend Monday evenings at Mory's on Temple Street in New Haven and assumed the name "Whiffenpoof." The origin of the name is generally traced back to a Broadway actor named Joseph Cawthorn who, during a sequence of dialogue in a musical entitled *Little Nemo*, claimed to have caught a Whiffenpoof fish.

THE HIGHLIGHTS   1910

The typically 14-member senior-only gentlemen rankers group was pictured in formal attire in the October 25, 1969, Yale-Cornell game day program standing on the crossbar of the south end goal post in the Yale Bowl.

Oct. 2: Yale beat Syracuse, coached by Howard Jones's brother and former Yale player T.A.D. (Thomas Albert Dwight) Jones, 15–0. It marked the first time that two brothers coached against each other at the major college level. (They would again coach against each other in 1922 when Howard's national champion Iowa Hawkeyes beat Yale.)

Nov. 20: In a "Battle of the Giants," Yale defeated Harvard, 8–0, for the national championship. Entering the game, Yale had not allowed a point the entire season while Harvard, on an 18-game undefeated streak, had outscored their opponents, 103–9. Coy kicked two field goals and Yale scored a safety when Wayland Minot recovered a punt blocked by Carroll Cooney. Coy was the team's leading scorer despite missing four games because of an appendectomy.

Yale coach Howard Jones would coach at Ohio State in 1910, leading the Buckeyes to a 6–1–3 record. He then spent the next several years in private business before returning to Yale in 1913. Jones subsequently coached at the University of Iowa, Duke University and the University of Southern California. At USC, Howard's teams went 121–36–13 and won five Rose Bowls. His overall coaching record is 194–64–21 and includes five national championships, one at Yale and four at USC.

All-American fullback Ted Coy led Yale to an undefeated, untied and unscored on 10–0 team in 1909. Notice the players are participating without helmets and numbers on their jerseys.

1910 (6–2–2) Coach: Edward H. "Ted" Coy; Captain: Fred J. Daley

Yale lost its role as lords of the college football oligarchy. In the 10 previous seasons the Elis went 80–4–5. In the next decade the Bulldogs recorded 59 wins against 20 defeats with five ties—impressive by today's standards but perhaps, not dynastic.

Passes over 20 yards were illegal and the rules stipulated that the offense had to have seven men on the line of scrimmage. Backs were allowed to cross the line of scrimmage at any point.

Ted Coy replaced Howard Jones as head coach but did not enjoy the success he had as a player. The Yale Corporation appointed and incorporated the Committee of Twenty-One to study ways of improving the athletic facilities. It was this committee that spearheaded the Yale Bowl project.

Nov. 5: Brown beat Yale, 21–0, for the first time in the history of their series that began in 1880. After this game, Henry Holt took over the Yale coaching duties for the final two games of the season.

Nov. 12: Yale beat Princeton, 5–3, in New Jersey. Junior quarterback Art Howe's touchdown pass to John Reed Kilpatrick accounted for the decisive score.

The Bulldogs employed the "Minnesota shift," designed by Dr. Henry L. Williams at the University of Minnesota and brought to Yale by former Yale great Tom Shevlin, who served as an assistant under Williams and was a coaching advisor at Yale late in the 1910 season. Shevlin taught it to the Yale team in one week.

Nov. 19: Despite Shevlin's teachings, Yale and Harvard played to a scoreless tie in New Haven. Several fires broke out under the wooden stands at Yale Field.

1911 (7–2–1) Coach: John Field; Captain: Arthur Howe

Cole Porter, a junior at Yale, wrote Yale's fight song, "Bulldog." The song continues to be played when the team enters the playing field and after every Yale score. Yale's two losses came at the hands of Army and Princeton.

Nov. 18: Yale and Princeton set a record that may stand forever, punting 64 times (36 by Princeton) as the Tigers defeated the Bulldogs, 6–3, in a downpour at Yale Field. Art Howe, Yale's quarterback and future Hall of Famer, returned a collegiate record 17 punts (some accounts say 18) for 130 yards. The Tigers featured Hobey Baker, "the blond Adonis of the gridiron." Because of the fires the previous year during the Harvard game, smoking was prohibited. In this era, cigar ashes were the cause of many fires.

Nov. 25: For the second straight year, the Yale-Harvard game ended in a scoreless tie. The stalemate was highlighted by a kicking duel between Walter Camp Jr., and Harvard's Sam Felton. John Field coached his last game for Yale.

1912 (7-1-1) Coach: Arthur Howe; Captain: Jesse Spalding

The value of a touchdown was stabilized at the current six points, a conversion one point, a field goal three points and a safety two points. The field was reduced from 110 to 100 yards and downs increased from three to four to make 10 yards.

Oct. 19: Yale beat Army, 6-0, at West Point. Yale sophomore guard Theodore York broke two ribs that would lead to his death.

Nov. 2: The Yale-Colgate game was cancelled when York died in New Haven Hospital. He developed blood poisoning and pneumonia set in. This was one of four games cancelled in Yale football history. The October 1, 1949, contest against Fordham was never played because Yale officials feared a polio epidemic on campus. Dale Liechty, an end on Herman Hickman's team, was diagnosed with polio along with two other cases on campus. The 1985 Yale–UConn contest scheduled for September 28, was cancelled because of Hurricane Gloria and the September 15, 2001, Yale-Towson game was cancelled because of the events of 9/11.

Nov. 16: Yale and Princeton played to a 6-6 tie in New Jersey. With Yale trailing, 6-3, with one minute remaining in the game, Yale's Harold Pumpelly, a substitute player, drop-kicked a 49-yard field goal to tie the game. "Pump" always claimed that the ball traveled 52 yards and three inches.

Nov. 23: In keeping with tradition, it was common for Yale and Harvard to have special songs for The Game. One of the classics was a Yale song that appeared in the 1912 program called "The Undertaker Song." The lyrics read:

> Oh! More work for the undertaker
> Another little job for the casket maker
> In the local cemetery they are very,
> very busy on a brand-new grave.
> No hope for Harvard.

But it was the Crimson who buried the Elis, 20–0. For the third straight year, Yale failed to score against the sons of John.

1913 (5–2–3) Coach: Howard H. Jones; Captain: Henry H. Ketcham

Howard Jones returned to Yale to coach the Bulldogs for one season. He was paid $2,500, making him the first salaried Yale coach. Two-time Pulitzer Prize poet Archibald MacLeish was a center on this team.

June 23: At 5:00 p.m., Yale University President Arthur Twining Hadley led the groundbreaking ceremonies for the Yale Bowl. The name "Bowl" was first suggested by Noah H. Swayne Jr. (class of 1893), a member of the Committee of Twenty-One, a group appointed by the Yale Corporation in 1910 to study ways of improving Yale's athletic facilities.

Aug. 1: Construction of the Yale Bowl began with a crew of 145 men hired by the Sperry Engineering Company of New Haven. The Bowl was designed by architect Charles Ferry, an 1871 Yale alum. The architectural features of the Bowl were worked out by Donn Barber (Yale 1893). Yale grad Everard Thompson directed the construction details.

The construction process was called "cut and fill." The plan was to dig a giant hole or crater, then use the 320,000 cubic yards of soil to build the surrounding walls or berm. From ground level an excavation was made about 27½ feet to the floor (playing field) which was the "cut" process. The earth that was dug-up was used for building the surrounding berm to a height of 26 feet. This was the "fill." Therefore, the top of the Bowl to the bottom measures 53½ feet. When a spectator walks into the Bowl, they are 27½ feet from the playing field and 26 feet from the top. The Rose Bowl that opened in 1922 was patterned after the Yale Bowl.

Nov. 22: Harvard's Charley Brickley, known as the "da Vinci of the drop kick," kicked five field goals for all of Harvard's points in the Crimson's 15–5 win in Boston to cap off an undefeated season.

1914 (7–2) Coach: Frank A. Hinkey; Captain: Nelson S. Talbott

The opening of the Yale Bowl on November 21 ushered in a new era.

Oct. 17: Notre Dame, with their great fullback Ray Eichenlaub, carried a 27-game winning streak and were favorites to defeat Yale in New Haven following a 103–0 win over Rose Polytechnic the week before. But the undaunted Elis staged an upset by defeating the Irish, 28–0. That game was targeted to open the Yale Bowl but it was not yet completed so it was played at Yale Field.

Knute Rockne was an assistant coach for the "Irish" under head coach Jesse Harper. He later would call the defeat "the most valuable lesson Notre Dame ever had in football. It taught us never to be cocksure."

Rockne later wrote in his autobiography, "I sat on the sideline at New Haven that Saturday and saw a good Yale team captained by Bud Talbott with a crack halfback named Harry LeGore leading the attack. They made Notre Dame look like a high school squad." It is believed that this game launched Notre Dame into the era of modern football.

Nov. 14: In a numerological oddity, the 1914 Yale-Princeton game is won by the Elis, 19–14 at the new Palmer Stadium. For a time, Palmer Stadium was the largest college stadium in the country behind the Yale Bowl.

Nov. 17: The Bowl was reported as completed. Oddly, however, there were no rest rooms in the Bowl, an apparent oversight. In 1916, Ferry wrote a report to the American Society of Civil Engineers that stated, "The cost of permanent toilets was not included in the original estimate of the Bowl." Portable toilets were used until the current eight exterior rest rooms that surround the Bowl were added in 1931.

Nov. 21: The Yale Bowl, the largest stadium yet built in America, opened with an estimated crowd of 70,000 as Harvard beat Yale, 36–0. It was the worst defeat in the history of Yale's 42-year-old football program. A writer quipped, "Yale had the Bowl but Harvard had the punch." In attendance was eight-year-old Al Ostermann, a New Haven resident, who would attend 499 of the first 500 games played in the Bowl. The only game he missed was on November 8, 1930, when Yale beat an inferior Alfred team, 66–0, the same day Army had a date with Illinois at Yankee Stadium. Ostermann chose to attend the big intersectional contest in the Bronx.

Harvard's Tack Hardwick scored the first touchdown ever in the Bowl on a 5-yard pass from Packy Mahan. The highlight play of the game occurred in the second quarter when Harvard's Thomas Jefferson "Jeff" Coolidge picked up a Carroll Knowles fumble on the Harvard 5-yard line and raced 95 yards for a touchdown. When the game ended, the Harvard crowd lit firecrackers on the goal posts and did a snake dance around the field.

During the game the Yale undergraduate Red Cross relief committee collected $7,463.91, the equivalent of $187,000 today. Following the game that ended at 4:17 p.m., seven Harvard students were fined $5.29 apiece for disturbing the peace in the streets of New Haven.

The Harvard team dined at the Hotel Taft in New Haven before most departed for New York City where they were the guests of the Harvard Club for the evening.

Ironically, football was not the first athletic event ever staged in the Bowl. On the day the Bowl opened, a cross-country meet, won by Cornell, started and ended in the Bowl long before the start of the game.

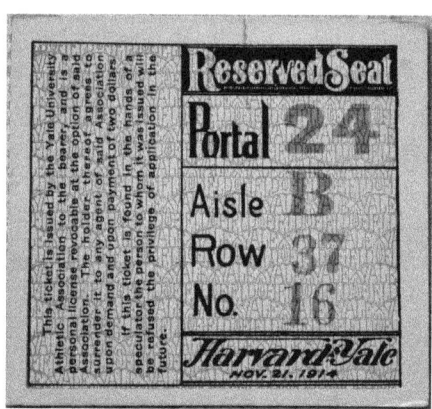

This ticket is for the first game ever played in the Yale Bowl (courtesy John Hayden).

1915 (4–5) Coach: Frank A. Hinkey; Captain: Alex D. Wilson

Yale suffered the first losing season in the 44-year history of the their football program. The new Bowl was open weekdays for public inspection.

Sept. 25: Yale opened the season with a 37–0 victory over Maine in a game played before only 7,000 fans in the Bowl. It was still the largest number ever present at a Yale opening match. Yale scored 21 points in the first quarter, all within a minute, helped by the former rule that the team scoring would get the ball back by receiving the ensuing kickoff. Beverly V. Thompson, the QB in the single wing, scored the first Yale touchdown ever in the Bowl on a 10-yard run in the opening quarter and added another.

Because of excessive heat, the game began at 4:00 p.m., one hour after the scheduled start. A popular feature of the contest was the public address announcer who was positioned on the field with a megaphone. He announced the names of players who scored touchdowns. At the time, players were not numbered.

Nov. 6: Brown's Fritz Pollard became the first African American to play in the Yale Bowl. Pollard led the Bears with long runs and exciting punt returns in defeating the Bulldogs, 3–0. Pollard was received with racial animosity from the Yale side. For security reasons, he was instructed to enter the field through a separate gate.

THE HIGHLIGHTS   1916

Nov. 13: Otis Guernsey drop-kicked a 54-yard field goal to help the Elis beat heavily favored Princeton, 13–7, in front of 50,000 at the Bowl. The *New York Times* reported, "Princeton came here today to take part in the obsequies of Yale's misfortune, but the flowers and condolences were wasted, for there was no Yale funeral."

The 54-yard field goal is still an Ivy League record for Yale, duplicated by Tom Mante in 2009.

Nov. 20: Harvard's captain, Eddie Mahan, crossed the goal line four times as the Crimson whitewashed the Elis for the second straight year, this time, 41–0. Mahan, a three-time first team All-American, also kicked five conversions accounting for 29 of Harvard's 41 points.

1916 (8–1) Coach: T.A.D. Jones; Captain: C.R. Black Jr.

Yale players wore numbered jerseys for the first time in the Princeton and Harvard games.

Oct. 13: Former United States President and Yale alum William Howard Taft attended Yale's football practice. Taft's son, Charley, a junior center, was scheduled to start his first varsity game at Yale the following day against Lehigh. Charley captained the Yale basketball team the previous year.

Oct. 14: Because the Yale Bowl was being used as a rehearsal for an elaborate pageant involving a cast of 8,000 to celebrate the 200th anniversary of Yale's move from Saybrook, Connecticut, to New Haven in 1716, Yale played a home game outside the Bowl at Yale Field across the street and beat Lehigh, 12–0.

Oct. 20: Yale beat Virginia Polytechnic Institute, 19–0, in the only Friday game ever played by the Yale varsity in the Bowl. The Friday game was scheduled because of the 200th anniversary pageant the following day in the Bowl.

Nov. 18: The sons of two former United States presidents were in opposing uniforms—Charley Taft (Yale), son of William Howard Taft and Richard Cleveland (Princeton), son of Grover Cleveland. A green and crippled Yale team emerged victorious in the Elis' 10–0 win over the Tigers at Palmer Stadium in front of 42,000, the largest crowd ever to see a game at Princeton. The scoring came from halfback Harry LeGore's touchdown and Jim Braden's 25-yard field goal.

Prior to the game, former Princeton great Hobey Baker, in a Curtiss

"Jenny" flown by Cord Meyer (a Yalie), joined a squadron of New York National Guard Jennies led by Captain Raynal Bolling, the most to have ever flown in military formation, and flew to Palmer Stadium. The planes performed several maneuvers to the delight of the crowd, and Baker landed on the field, becoming the first person to reach a football game by air.

Nov. 25: Yale bounced back from the previous year's humiliating 41–0 defeat to edge Harvard, 6–3, in the second matchup ever of the ancient rivals in the Bowl. Following the game, a large number of Yalies went by train to Grand Central Station in New York City where the contingent made its way to the Yale Club on Vanderbilt Avenue. It was the first Yale victory celebration over Harvard commemorated at the 22-story clubhouse. The euphoric Blues, numbering 1,200, partied into the morning. "A brass band of six sturdy performers was worn to a frazzle before midnight because it tried to play *Boola Boola* every time a grad called for it," wrote Fred Lieb in the *New York Sun.* At 9:00 p.m. the band led a procession of 600 club members through Vanderbilt Avenue to West 44th Street. When they reached the Harvard club, they serenaded the crestfallen men of John Harvard.

1917 (3–0) Coach: T.A.D. Jones; Captain: Artemus L. Gates

Because so many athletes were in the military in World War I, Yale played a three-game schedule with an informal assemblage of ROTC students. They defeated Loomis Institute, New Haven Naval Base and Trinity.

America mobilized its National Guard forces after the United States declared war against Germany on April 6. The 1st Connecticut from the Hartford area and the 2nd Connecticut from the New Haven area were sent to Camp Yale in the vicinity of the Yale Bowl for encampment and training. The 1st and 2nd combined to become the 102nd Infantry and was made part of the 26th "Yankee" Division of Massachusetts. The reason why they were called the "102nd" is because of the numbers 1 and 2 and nothing (zero) in between.

Military tents spread out over the current site of the Coxe Cage, Lots B, C and D where the Armory and lacrosse fields are located. The officers were quartered in tents across the street at the now Dewitt Cuyler Field, adjacent to the Yale baseball field. In the beginning of the war, Yale trained

American artillery officers. France sent four 75mm howitzers, one of which is on display at the West Haven Veterans Museum and Learning Center.

Although there was no Handsome Dan during this time, a mongrel named Stubby wandered into the encampment and befriended the soldiers. In October 1917, the unit shipped out for France and Stubby was smuggled aboard the troop ship S.S. *Minnesota* by private J. Robert Conroy and became the official mascot of the 102nd Division. Stubby, who served in 17 battles, provided morale lifting visits up and down the line and occasionally early warning about gas attacks by waking a sleeping sentry to alert them. His sensitivity to poisonous gas resulted from his exposure in France. Later in the war he was injured in a grenade attack, receiving large amounts of shrapnel in his chest and leg.

The war dog also saved lives by leading paramedics to wounded soldiers when he heard the sound of the English language. Stubby was honored by three United States presidents and was the first dog to be promoted officially on orders to the rank of sergeant. Conroy returned to the United States with Stubby and when Conroy studied law at Georgetown University, Stubby became the mascot of the Hoyas. At halftime of football games, he would nudge a football around the field to the amusement of fans. He died in Conroy's arms in 1926.

In 2018 a movie titled *Sgt. Stubby: An American Hero*, was released.

1918 (no games—war year)

Because of the Great War, this would be the only year that Yale did not field a team from 1872 to the present. Yale's 1915 football captain, Alex Wilson, who was an infantry captain, died in combat on September 29 in the Battle of Argonne Forest in France. Other players never to return included Joseph Stillman, James E. Miller and Andrew Ortmayer.

Nov. 14: A trio of ex–Harvard and Yale players participated in a unique fundraising drive on New York's Wall Street for the United War Fund. In front of thousands of spectators, Charley Brickley, Harvard's great drop kicker, was successful in booting a football from the steps of the Sub-Treasury building across Wall and Broad Streets and into the hands of Yale man Jack Gates. Brickley kicked while standing on one of the balconies in front of the Stock Exchange.

1919 (5–3) Coach: Albert H. Sharpe; Captain: J. Timothy Callahan

Former Eli great running back Albert Sharpe, a medical doctor, returned to Yale as athletic director and football coach. Following the 1919 season, he was replaced by T.A.D. Jones, who had coached the team before entering government service during World War I. Sharpe remained to coach the basketball team for two more years.

June 1: Three military planes were flying over the area of the Yale Bowl when two collided 1,000 feet in the air. Lieutenant Melvin B. Kelcher and Corporal Joseph Katzman were instantly killed when their plane crashed in a sandy terrace in front of the property of C.E. Libbey on Westwood Avenue near Yale Avenue.

Oct. 11: Yale defeated North Carolina, 34–7. This would be the first of six consecutive years that the teams would play. In this game, Fred "Chuck" Pharr, a 5-foot-6, 150-pound running back, scored the only touchdown for the Tar Heels. It would be the only TD that North Carolina would score in the six-year series dominated by Yale.

Nov. 15: Princeton got by Yale, 13–6, in the Bowl in front of more than 60,000. Perhaps the most interesting spectator was Mrs. Mary Callahan, the mother of the rival centers, Tim and Mike. She reportedly sat on the Yale side. Tim captained the Yale team in both 1919 and 1920. Mike captained the Tigers in 1920. Tim is one of five players who captained the Yale football teams for two years. The others were Eugene Baker (1876–77), Walter Camp (1878–79), Ray Tompkins (1882–83) and Frank Hinkey (1893–94).

Nov.22: Coach Bob Fisher's Harvard football team concluded an undefeated regular season with a 10–3 victory at Harvard Stadium before an estimated crowd of 50,000. Arnold Horween, who would later coach the Crimson, kicked a field goal and Eddie Casey scored on a reception in the first half. Only one touchdown was scored against Harvard during the season. Yale's Jim Braden drop-kicked a series record 53-yard FG.

1920 (5–3) Coach: T.A.D. Jones; Captain: J. Timothy Callahan

Yale went 58–20–5 in the "Roaring Twenties" and enjoyed its winningest decade in the Yale Bowl, going 54–13–5. Opponents who walked into the gauntlet of the Bowl felt like Christians on their way to the Roman

Colosseum. Because of the size of the Bowl and economic advantage for Yale and its opponents, the Elis only played 11 away games in the entire decade. Attendance soared in this era when the average attendance at Yale games was 37,405.

It was a time when radio broadcasts reached coast-to-coast and newspapers created sports legends. Many of the gilded writers covered games in the Bowl.

Yale alum Rudy Vallee, a saxophonist and arguably the first crooner and first mass media pop star, would play a solo with the Yale band on occasion and sit with the Yale cheerleaders on the bench.

It was decided in November that the Yale players would wear numbered jerseys for the Princeton and Harvard games. Captain Tim Callahan was given uniform No. 1. In general, the rest of the Yale team was numbered in alphabetical order from John Acosta to Leon Walker.

Nov. 13: Princeton spanked Yale in New Jersey, 20–0. In what may have been a first in major college football history, brothers Tim (Yale) and Mike (Princeton) Callahan served as opposing captains. This time Mrs. Callahan sat on the Princeton side with her daughter, Eunice. Before the game she said that she might sit on the Yale side for a time.

Nov. 20: The largest crowd (reportedly 76,000 to 80,000) in the history of sports in the United States jammed the Bowl and saw Harvard edge Yale, 9–0. To accommodate the large throng, temporary wooden seats were erected on the lower rim of the Bowl and a tier of temporary seats was completed around the top of the enclosure.

All the scoring occurred by virtue of three Harvard field goals, two by Charley Buell (32 and 15 yards) and the other came from captain Arnold Horween (38).

Fido Kempton, Yale's tawny-haired QB, and Harvard end John Gaston were banished for fighting. Unlike the Yale eleven, the Harvards remained unnumbered. Crimson coach Bob Fisher was quoted as saying, "football is a team game and not a game of eleven individuals." Harvard would go on to beat the Oregon Webfoots, now known as the Ducks, 7–6, in the East–West Tournament Bowl, now known as the Rose Bowl.

1921 (8–1) Coach: T.A.D. Jones; Captain: Malcolm P. Aldrich

This was the first year the Yale team wore numbered jerseys for every game.

Oct. 22: Yale beat Army, 14–7. The entire Army Cadet Corps traveled by train to New Haven where they were met by the Yale Reserve Officers Training Corps and escorted to the Yale Commons. Following lunch, the Cadets marched to the Bowl and gave a dress parade at 1:45.

Nov. 12: Thanks to two fourth quarter field goals by Yale All-American halfback Mac Aldrich, Yale downed Princeton, 13–7. Among those in attendance was Marshal Ferdinand Foch, the Commander of the Allied forces in World War I. Foch, dressed in his gray-blue uniform, received a "soul-stirring" ovation from the 75,000 fans. Before the game the Eli band played the famous French marching song, "La Madelon" before marching to a point in front of Foch's box on the Yale side where the band broke into "La Marseillaise," France's national anthem. At the end of the first quarter, Foch crossed the field to the Princeton side accompanied by Yale President James Rowland Angell and Connecticut Governor Everett J. Lake. Princeton President John Grier Hibben greeted Foch on the visitors' side. Speculators (scalpers) in an apparent attempt to beat the law, sold tickets at face value if fans purchased "a very fine fountain pen" for $25.

Nov. 19: The Bulldogs again walked away licking its wounds after suffering a 10–3 defeat at the hands of Harvard in front of 55,000 in Boston. Yale drew first blood in the opening frame when captain Mac Aldrich booted a 12-yard FG. The Crimson were held scoreless until the fourth quarter when they scored 10 points. The damaging play was Charley Buell's punt return from midfield to the Yale 12-yard line before George Owen crossed the goal line two bucks later. Owen subsequently added a 30-yard FG to complete the scoring.

1922   (6–3–1) Coach: T.A.D. Jones; Captain: Ralph E. Jordan

Starting this season, the "try for point" rule (run, pass or kick) following a touchdown was made from the 5-yard line. A team could either kick an extra point after a touchdown as usual, or place the ball anywhere beyond the 5-yard line and try to score either by touchdown or by a kick and receive the one point if successful. On the try for a point, any foul by the defense awarded the offense the point, and any foul by the offense made the try no good. This was the last time that Yale played a 10-game season until 1980.

Sept. 30, 1922: Charles O'Hearn booted a 52-yard field goal as the Elis beat Carnegie Tech, 13–0.

Oct. 14: The Jones brothers, Howard and Tad, renewed their coaching rivalry that dated back to 1909 when Howard's Yale eleven blanked Tad's Syracuse team. Again, Howard came out on top when his undefeated national champion Iowa Hawkeyes edged Yale in the Bowl, 6–0. Iowa's lone touchdown came on a 9-yard run by quarterback Leland Parkin in the second quarter, capping a 59-yard drive. "He was too fast for his interference," wrote the *New York Times*. "Seeing an opening directly ahead, Parkin cut for it like a frightened rabbit making for his hole." It was the Hawkeyes' 12th straight victory in a streak that reached 20 games.

The game was carried on WOR Radio (Newark, New Jersey), marking the first professional broadcast of a Yale football game.

Nov. 18: Coach Bill Roper's Princeton Tigers, labeled the "Team of Destiny" by writer Grantland Rice, finished a perfect season with a 3–0 win over Yale at Palmer Stadium. The *Official NCAA Division I Records Book* listed Princeton, along with California, Cornell, Iowa and Vanderbilt as national champions. The Tigers were led by captain Mel Dickenson, consensus All-America Herb Treat, and the legendary Pink Baker.

Nov. 25: Harvard defeated Yale, 10–3. The Harvard scores came on a 1-yard plunge by George Owen and a 34-yard field goal by Karl Pfaffman. The Elis' only tally was a 20-yard field goal by Charles O'Hearn. Harvard dominated the series from 1909 to 1922, earning an 8–2–2 record.

For the first time in the history of the Harvard football program, the Crimson wore numbers on the backs of their jerseys. Among the 78,000 in the Bowl was French premier Georges Clemencau, the prime minister of France in World War I. Like Foch the year before, he diplomatically switched sides at halftime while both bands played the Marseillaise. Clemencau's presence did not impress Damon Runyon, the celebrated short story fictional writer, who covered the game for the *Washington Times*. He wrote, "The possibility of a break in the football relations between Harvard and Princeton recently attracted more serious attention and discussion than the purpose of Clemencau's visit."

In finishing the season with losses to Princeton and Harvard, some of the old Blues were getting restive with Yale coach T.A.D. Jones. Undaunted, he said grimly, "I will not be driven out by a crowd of tailor-shop gamblers. Nor will they dictate Yale's athletic policy."

1923 (8–0) Coach: T.A.D. Jones; Captain: William M. Mallory

The 1923 Yale team, augmented by talented transfers, finished 8–0, and is considered one of the greatest in the modern era. They outscored opponents, 230–38. Since 1920, only the 1923 and 1960 teams have enjoyed undefeated and untied seasons. Captain Bill Mallory (fullback) and Century Milstead (tackle) earned All-America honors.

"Memphis Bill" Mallory, an All-American fullback, led the 1923 Yale team to an undefeated season.

March 1: Thanks to the generous $350,000 donation of Henry G. Lapham, a wealthy Boston investment banker and president of the Boston Garden–Arena Corporation, ground was broken for the Lapham Field House on Derby Avenue. The field house has been used by athletes since that time.

Oct. 13: In the first meeting ever between the two schools, Yale blanked the University of Georgia in the Bowl, 40–0. In the battle of the "Bulldogs," Georgia won six of the eleven contests that were played between 1923 and 1934.

Nov. 3: Yale overwhelmed Army, 31–10, in front of an estimated 80,000 fans in the Bowl, the largest crowd to ever attend a game in the historic saucer. Of the 10 largest crowds to see a game at the Yale Bowl, five have come against Army. The Cadets led at the intermission, 10–7, thanks to the dazzling 80-yard run by QB George Smythe in the second quarter. But the Elis turned it around in the second half. Lyle Richeson twice picked off Smythe and Mal Stevens added another interception. Ted Blair, Richard Luman, and Newell Neidlinger crossed the goal line for the Elis. The win gave Yale a 15–3–5 mark in the 23 games played since their first meeting in 1893.

Nov. 24: Yale completed a perfect undefeated and untied season, beating Harvard, 13–0, in Boston under a pelting rain on a muddy field. Legendary writer Grantland Rice wrote, "The game was played on a gridiron of seventeen lakes, five quagmires and a water hazard." Raymond

THE HIGHLIGHTS 1924

"Ducky" Pond, future Yale head coach and All American for the season, returned a fumble 67 yards for a touchdown, Yale's first touchdown versus Harvard since World War I.

Fittingly, Ducky scored the only touchdown. It's a myth, however, that Pond earned his nickname because of his sure-footed running in the Harvard Stadium goo. He carried that moniker with him when he entered Yale from his native Torrington, Connecticut.

It was reported that Babe Ruth provided broadcast commentary during the contest.

1924 (6–0–2) Coach: T.A.D. Jones; Captain: Winslow M. Lovejoy

Starting this season, the try for point (run, pass or kick) following a touchdown was made from the 3-yard line. Christy Walsh, Babe Ruth's agent, established the All-American Board of Football. The plan was most likely intended to replace Walter Camp's annual All-America teams. Such football luminaries as Knute Rockne, Howard Jones, Glenn "Pop" Warner and Yale coach T.A.D. Jones were recruited to offer their opinions in ghostwritten columns by Walsh.

Oct. 4: North Carolina's abject failure against Yale continued as the Bulldogs defeated the Tar Heels, 27–0, in the Bowl.

Oct. 18: Yale and Dartmouth played to a 14–14 tie. Yale was on an unbeaten streak that would reach 18 games and Dartmouth was embarked on a 22-game run.

Oct. 31: The Yale and Army elevens both practiced in the Bowl. Because the Army squad did not arrive on time, Yale under the direction of coach T.A.D. Jones, took the field first. Army then drilled until after dark before returning to their headquarters at the Hotel Clark in Derby.

Nov. 1: A sold out crowd that paid three dollars each stood as an Army bugler played, "Last Call" and the Yale band played "Fair Harvard" in memory of Percy Haughton, the famed ex–Harvard coach who had died on October 27. Then Yale and Army engaged in a 7–7 tie in front of 78,000 including Secretary of War John W. Weeks. Yale's only score came in the first quarter on Ducky Pond's dazzling 47-yard run into the south end zone. Harry Wilson's last-quarter TD pulled the Cadets even.

The *New York Times* wrote, "For in addition of seeing a football game that was as hard fought as Chateau-Thierry and as thrilling as a boy's first long trousers, the great crowd witnessed a demonstration of rhythmic grace and military precision such as only West Point cadets can give."

Good tickets were scalped for $50.

Nov. 22: Yale completed an undefeated season (6–0–2) by downing Harvard, 19–6, in a chilly, persistent downpour in the Bowl. Bill Kline scored two of Yale's TDs on 1-yard plunges. Pond scored on another 1-yard run. Harvard's points were scored by Erwin Gehrke's two FGs. Both captains, Win Lovejoy (Yale) and Malcolm Greenough (Harvard), both played center and faced each other head-to-head.

1925 (5–2–1) Coach: T. A.D. Jones; Captain: John H. Joss

March 14: Walter Camp, the "Father of American Football," was found dead in his room at the Hotel Belmont in New York City between sessions of a football rules committee meeting. Accounts in the *New York Times* indicated that Camp was not visibly ill when he turned in for the night. Because Camp never showed for a morning meeting, Princeton coach Bill Roper and committee member W. S. Langford were dispatched to the hotel but got no response after calling his room. The manager of the hotel then supplied a carpenter to go to Camp's room. A panel was removed from the door and Camp was found dead.

Scores of Yale students and New Haven residents paid their respects at Camp's home on 460 Humphrey Street in New Haven. He is buried at the Grove Street Cemetery in New Haven alongside his wife, Alice, and son Walter Jr., who lettered in football at Yale in 1911 and 1912.

Oct. 10: Yale routed Georgia, 35–7, in the Bowl, extending its unbeaten streak under coach T. A. D. Jones to 18 games (16–0–2). Dan Allen had a touchdown and four conversions for Yale, which intercepted four passes.

Oct. 17: Yale's undefeated string of 18 games was snapped by Penn, 16–13.

Oct. 24: Yale opened Brown's new stadium by beating the Bears, 20–7, before 25,000 in Providence. Bill Kline, Dan Allen and Larry Noble scored for the Elis. On the same day, the Yale freshmen crushed the Culver Military Academy in the Bowl, 29–0, in front of 5,000.

Nov. 14: Princeton upset heavily favored Yale, 25–12, in the Bowl before 78,000. The Elis pulled a rock when after a Yale punt, numerous players gathered around the tumbling ball and waited for it to come to rest. A Yale player stopped the ball from rolling and turned away to line up. Thereupon a wise Tiger named Gilligan snatched up the ball and ran it far into Yale territory setting up a Princeton TD a couple of plays later. In attendance was actress Gloria Swanson with her titled husband, Henri, Marquis de la Falaise de la Coudraye. The celebrity couple sat in the last row on the Yale side of the field directly below the press box.

Nov. 21: Yale and Harvard played to another scoreless tie in front of 51,000 in Boston. Apparent poor clock management on the part of the Elis, prove disastrous. When the game ended, Yale had the ball on the 1-foot line. Instead of calling a timeout, time expired as the Bulldogs reportedly engaged in earnest discussion about the next play.

According to the claims of broadcasters, the game attracted the largest radio audience ever for a football game covering territory as far west as St. Louis.

1926 (4–4) Coach: T. A. D. Jones; Captain: Philip W. Bunnell

Actor John Wayne made his first appearance on the silver screen in the movie *Brown of Harvard* in which he played the part of a Yale football player. His lone scene took place in Harvard Stadium.

Oct. 9: Yale beat Georgia in the Bowl, 19–0. The Elis' star halfback, Bruce Caldwell, ran wild, collecting a large chunk of the 290 rushing yards Yale gained for the day, including two touchdowns.

Oct. 16: Yale ended Dartmouth's 22-game undefeated streak, winning, 14–7, in the Bowl without the services of Caldwell, who broke his ankle during a practice scrimmage three days before the Dartmouth game and was lost for the season.

Oct. 23: Led by first-year coach Tuss McLaughry, Brown beat Yale, 7–0, using the same 11 players the entire game. The following week the "Iron Men" Bears defeated Dartmouth, 10–0,, without making a substitution. Brown finished the season 9–0–1, the only undefeated season to date for the Bears.

Oct. 30: Army crushed Yale, 33–0. The following week Maryland blanked the Elis, 15–0. It is the only time Yale has suffered three consecutive shutouts.

Nov. 13: Yale fell to Princeton, 10–7, in New Jersey. It was Yale's fourth consecutive loss, the first time a Yale team had ever dropped four straight games.

Nov. 20: Yale squeezed by Harvard, 12–7, in New Haven. The Crimson were now coached by former Harvard stalwart Arnold Horween. Harvard's only touchdown resulted from a 35-yard pass from Henry Chauncey to Bill Saltonstall. Chauncey drop-kicked the extra point. His son, Henry "Sam" Chauncey Jr., served as Yale's Vice President and Secretary from 1971 to 1981. The Elis took a 6–0 lead in the second quarter when Cobbles Sturhahn recovered a blocked punt in the end zone. Two second-half field goals Jerry Wadsworth (23 yards) and Tibby Bunnell (38 yards) completed the Yale scoring.

1927 (7–1) Coach: T.A.D. Jones; Captain: William A. Webster

In T.A.D. Jones's final season, Yale allowed its opponents a stingy 32 points. All-American Bruce Caldwell emerged as one of Yale's great running backs, supported by All-American linemen John Charlesworth (center), Sidney Quarrier (tackle), Bill Webster (guard) and Dwight Fishwick (end).

The goal posts were moved 10 yards behind the goal line.

Oct. 8: Yale missed a chance at the national championship by a step when it lost, 14–10, to Georgia in New Haven. Stew Scott, who scored Yale's touchdown on a pass, caught what looked like a game-winning throw in the final minute, but his foot came down just beyond the end zone. Yale finished 7–1, Georgia went 9–1. The consensus pick as best in the land was Illinois. Some selectors chose Yale and Georgia as co-national champions.

Oct. 22: Caldwell passed, ran and kicked the Elis to a 10–6 victory over Army before 77,000. His 96 yards rushing and 46-yard field goal paved the way. Caldwell's 34-yard touchdown toss to Quarrier on a tackle-eligible play accounted for Yale's lone TD.

According to Jane Leavy in her book, *The Big Fella*, Fox Movietone News premiered its first biweekly talking newsreels in New York and around the rest of the country in December with highlights of the Army-Yale game and a New York City rodeo.

Nov. 11: The *Providence Bulletin* reported that Caldwell played as a freshman at Brown in 1923 before transferring to Yale. The writer cited a Yale-Harvard-Princeton agreement not to use any player who had competed for another college football team. The idea was to prevent "tramp athletes" from hopping from school to school, a widespread problem after

World War I. It was learned that Caldwell played in three freshmen games gaining only obscure time.

The Yale University Association, headed by Professor George H. Nettleton, established a committee that voted unanimously to declare Caldwell ineligible. Included in the committee was Yale captain William A. Webster.

Outraged Yale students staged demonstrations and rallies. Harvard and Princeton heads encouraged Yale to ignore the agreement and allow Caldwell to play against them. But Nettleton's committee did not bend. Despite his banishment, Caldwell was awarded a letter.

Caldwell was also an outstanding baseball player who had a brief career in the major leagues for the Cleveland Indians and Brooklyn Dodgers. He also played for the New York football Giants, giving him the distinction as the only Yale football player to play in the major leagues and pro football. Following his athletic career, Caldwell wore the robe of a municipal court judge in West Haven, Connecticut. He died in 1959 and is buried a drop kick away from the venues of his college sports achievements—Yale Bowl and Yale Field. John Kieran of the *New York Times* wrote, "The enemy rush line couldn't halt Bruce Caldwell, but he was stopped by a printed paragraph."

Nov. 12: Singer, comedian, actor Al Jolson, an old friend of coach T.A.D. Jones, sang "California Here I Come" for the Yale team before their 14–6 win over undefeated Princeton at the Yale Bowl.

Nov. 19: On a clear, chilly day in Boston, Yale coach T.A.D. Jones ended his coaching career with a 14–0 victory over Harvard. The Yale TDs were scored on runs by Johnny Garvey (52 yards) and Bill Hammersley (42 yards). Duncan Cox kicked the two extra points. For the first time, Harvard's massive Big Bass Drum made its appearance in the band.

Jones was the head Yale football coach in 1916 and '17 and from 1920 to 1927. His record at Yale was a sterling 60–15–4. He was 5–3–1 against Harvard. Among Yale coaches who led the team for more than two seasons, only Walter Camp, who went 67–2 between 1888 and 1892, had a better winning percentage.

1928 (4–4) Coach: Marvin A. Stevens; Captain: Maxon H. Eddy

Mal Stevens, a halfback on Yale's 1923 undefeated and untied team, replaced Jones as Yale's football coach. His tenure lasted from 1928 until 1932 in which time he compiled a 21–11–8 record.

Nov. 3: Designed by 1900 Yale grad John W. Cross, the $300,000 Walter Camp Memorial Gateway, a series of lofty stone pillars, was dedicated in the morning before the Yale-Dartmouth game. Tablets set into the walls on each side of the gateway bear the names of the 224 colleges and the numerous prep and high schools all over the nation that joined with Yale in honor of the memory of Camp by helping to finance the structure located on Derby Avenue. Professor George H. Nettleton (class of 1896) presided at the dedicatory services held at Walter Camp Field of which Yale Bowl is one unit. The Yale freshmen, captained by Albie Booth, played that day, possibly at the same time the dedication services were being held. Little did Booth know that he would one day be nearly as famous as the man who was being memorialized in stone.

The Yale varsity celebrated the event by beating Dartmouth, 18–0, in a game played through a misty haze. Captain Maxon Eddy, George Loud and John McEwen scored the three Yale TDs.

Nov. 24: Yale ended the season by suffering its third straight loss, this time at the hands of Harvard, 17–0. The Crimson were led by captain Art French and running back Dave Guarnaccia, who scored twice on runs of 11 yards and 1 yard. Not once did the Elis get beyond the Harvard 38 yard line. For the first time fans paid five dollars for a ticket.

The day ended tragically when John Winters, a preparatory student, was killed when he was run down by a car driven by Yale student Peter McAndrews, who took the car without permission from a fellow Yale student. McAndrews was subsequently sentenced to six months in the county jail and fined $500 by Judge Isaac Wolfe.

Dec. 30: Yale guard Norman Hall died of shock and exposure during the Christmas recess of his junior year after rescuing his friend's sister on Nomahegan Pond in Cranford, New Jersey. The two had gone ice skating when the ice gave way, and both fell into the frigid water. Yale doesn't retire numbers, but the only one not reissued for a time was 45, the number worn by Hall in 1927 and 1928.

1929 (5–2–1) Coach: Marvin A. Stevens; Captain: Waldo W. Greene

Albie Booth, "Little Boy Blue," emerged to become one of Yale's all-time heralded icons in this golden age of the newspaper industry with an upward tick in sports coverage. Yale traveled to Athens, Georgia, to help the University of Georgia open their new football stadium.

THE HIGHLIGHTS 1929

Oct. 5: Booth, a 5-foot, 6-inch dynamo, made his spectacular Yale football debut in Yale's opening season 89–0 win over outmanned Vermont. "Little Boy Blue" scored two touchdowns, one a 57-yard run, and kicked five extra points. The 89 points registered by the Elis were the most ever scored by a team in the Bowl and the largest margin of victory by any team that ever played in the Bowl. Tommy Taylor's 80-yard kickoff return electrified the 17,500 fans on this steamy day. The Blue amassed 632 yards rushing and 109 passing while holding the Catamounts to a total offense of minus 6 yards.

Oct. 11: The day before Yale played the University of Georgia, the 50-piece Yale band, the golf team and 40 undergraduates made the train trip where they were met by Georgia Governor Lamartine Hardman and his staff. It was the first time the team had crossed the Mason-Dixon line. The Yale band marched through the streets of Athens. Coach Mal Stevens, his 38 players, coaches and officials were guests at a dinner that evening at the Athens Country Club.

Oct. 12: Yale played its first football game in the deep South, losing to Georgia, 15–0. The game that opened Sanford Stadium in front of 35,000 on an unusually warm southern day pitted two universities separated by geography and culture. The southern boys were said to be more acclimated to the heat and humidity than the visitors from New Haven who reportedly wilted in their woolen uniforms.

The Georgia Bulldogs were led by the flamboyant left end Vernon "Catfish" Smith, who scored two touchdowns and drop-kicked an extra point. Georgia opened the scoring in the second quarter when Bobby Rose blocked a Yale punt that was recovered by Catfish in the end zone for a touchdown. A mixed Yale signal in the third period led to a safety and a 9–0 score before Smith crossed the goal line again in the fourth quarter on a long, twisting pass play from Spurgeon "Spud" Chandler, who was a two-time 20-game winner pitching for the New York Yankees in the '40s.

Oct. 14: Vance McCormick, captain of the 1892 Yale football team, and a member of the Yale University Corporation said in the *Yale Daily News* that coaches should remain in the grandstand and that the captain of a team should run the game. McCormick's suggestion was ignored.

Oct. 19: Sophomore tailback Albie Booth, inserted at the start of the second quarter, scored Yale's touchdowns on a plunge and a 12-yard run and kicked both extra points in a 14–6 comeback victory over Brown. This was a harbinger of things to come.

Oct. 26: Yale trailed Army, 13–0, in the second quarter when Booth, wearing No. 48, came off the bench again and riddled Army, scoring three touchdowns. He also drop-kicked three extra points to lead the Elis to a 21–13 comeback win before 80,000. "Little Boy Blue" scored two touchdowns, the second on a 74-yard punt return and drop-kicked both extra points to give Yale a 14–13 lead at the intermission.

Three-time All-American Army running back Christian "Red" Cagle scored first for the Cadets in the first quarter on a 45-yard run after intercepting a pass. In the second period, the Black Knights of the Hudson scored on Hertz Murrell's 35-yard run but they missed the conversion.

Early in the third quarter, Booth, as Tommy Holmes wrote in the *Brooklyn Daily Eagle*, "became an elusive blob of mercury in the backfield." When the day ended, the sophomore phenom had carried the ball 32 times for 141 yards and for the day he had 223 all-purpose yards.

Newsreels of the game made Booth a household name across the country when they captioned "Booth 21, Army 13."

Among the spectators was his mother, attending her first football game. Because of the intense interest in the game, the first of the six-passenger Fairfield monoplanes planes took off from Roosevelt Field in New York City around 10:30 a.m. and landed at the H and H Airport in West Haven.

Albie Booth's legend was carved when he came off the bench and scored three touchdowns in the 1929 Yale-Army game as a sophomore.

Nov. 16: Yale's winningest decade in the Bowl ended with a 13–0 win over Princeton. Yale's jubilation was a bit tempered because the venerated

Yale Fence, where captains of Yale athletic teams were photographed at the Pach Brothers Studio on Chapel Street since 1875, was stolen by a group of Harvard students from the *Harvard Lampoon*, the longest-running undergraduate humor publication.

Nov. 23: Yale's euphoria of beating Princeton was short-lived as Harvard broke the hearts of the Elis in Boston, 10–6, before an estimated 59,000, thanks to the addition of 20,000 seats in Harvard Stadium. This was the first matchup between Albie Booth and Barry Wood, referred to by author Thomas G. Bergin as "neophyte paladins." The game was broadcast on NBC Radio by the legendary Graham McNamee.

Nov. 24: The Yale Fence was returned to New Haven after its appearance at a banquet of the *Harvard Lampoon.* According to *Life* magazine, the *Lampoon* posed its janitor up against the fence in mockery of Yale's captains. The shipper of the three-rail fence, according to the tag attached to the bulky package described himself as Eric Gustafson. A value of $4,000 was placed on the fence by its shippers with charges totaling $8.35.

1930 (5–2–2) **Coach: Marvin A. Stevens; Captain: Francis T. Vincent**

Sept. 27: Led by captain Francis T. "Fay" Vincent, the father of future Major League Baseball commissioner Fay Vincent, Yale blitzed Maine, 38–0, in the season opener. The day before the contest, coach Mal Stevens invited Maine coach Fred Brice to attend the Yale practice, something that would be unheard of today.

Oct. 25: Yale and Army battled to a 7–7 tie. Trailing, 7–0, Army's Tom Kilday scored a controversial touchdown when he was reportedly pushed over the goal line by a teammate, a violation of Rule 10, Section 1, Article 1. The Yale Athletic Association took the high road and did not protest the game.

Nov. 15: The Elis, led by Freddie Linehan and Fred Loeser, made a famous goal-line stand to beat Princeton, 10–7, in New Jersey. Yale and Princeton began playing football against each other in 1873, but it took 57 years before the bands of the two universities combined on the field and together played Yale and Princeton songs. Another novelty was that the Yale band formed the letter "P" while the Princeton band lined up in a "Y."

Nov. 22: Harvard triumphed for the third straight year. Crimson QB Barry Wood, who played the entire game, tossed two touchdown passes to Art Huguley to beat Yale, 13–0, before 74,679. Following the game, Harvard captain Ben Ticknor traded his jersey to a young Yale fan in exchange for a piece of the goal post. Harvard coach Arnold Horween, who departed with a 21–17–3 mark, was succeeded by Eddie Casey.

Nov. 25: Albie Booth was elected captain of the 1931 Yale football team. Sportswriters compared him to Frank Merriwell, the Yale fictional sports hero.

1931 (5-1-2) Coach: Marvin A. Stevens; Captain: Albert J. Booth

Douglas MacArthur II, nephew of the famed American five-star general and commander of the Allied Forces in the Pacific Theater during World War II, was a member of the Yale varsity. Coach Mal Stevens scrapped the single wing attack for the Notre Dame box behind a balanced line. The Army game was called by Ted Husing and Graham McNamee.

Oct. 17: In a tribute to Amos Alonzo Stagg, who was then the head coach at Chicago University, Yale traveled to the Windy City and won, 27–6. Stagg, who lettered at Yale (1885–89), was one of the missionaries who helped spread the gridiron gospel from coast-to-coast.

Oct. 24: Tragedy marred the 6–6 tie between Yale and Army in the Bowl when Cadet Richard Sheridan, a 149-pound end, fractured two vertebrae attempting to tackle Bob Lassiter on a kick-off return and died two days later in a New Haven hospital. It remains the only football fatality in the history of the Bowl. Yale coach Mal Stevens and running back Albie Booth attended the funeral at West Point. Cries to eliminate the kickoff in college football have existed for decades but the idea has never fostered enough support.

Oct. 31: Despite Booth's heroics of scoring three touchdowns, Yale blew a 23-point lead, its biggest margin in the history of the storied Yale football program, as the Elis and Dartmouth played to a 33–33 tie. Booth's touchdowns came on a 94-yard kickoff return, a 22-yard pass and a 53-yard run.

Dartmouth rallied from a 33–10 deficit in the third quarter thanks to the Indians' "Wild Bill" McCall, who scored on runs of 76, 92 and 60 yards. According to the *New York Times*, Dartmouth tied the game on a third-down field goal by Bill Morton from the Yale 23. Dartmouth still had another down to try for a go-ahead touchdown but the Dartmouth quarterback (who called the plays) may have thought a field goal on third down would have given Dartmouth the lead. Although the score at the time was 33–30 in favor of Yale, the scoreboard wrongly had it as 33–31.

Yale was on the Dartmouth 18-yard line with time running out in the fourth quarter. The field judge, W.H. Friesele, of Princeton, told reporters that he warned Yale it had 15 seconds left. Some of the players apparently wanted Booth to try a drop kick for a field goal, but the field judge said he saw Albie shaking his head. While Yale was standing around unable to decide on the play, time ran out and the game ended.

Oddly, for the second year in a row, Yale played back-to-back tie games with Army and Dartmouth.

Nov. 7: Joe Crowley scored a Yale-record five touchdowns in the Bulldogs' 52–0 win over St. John's from Maryland. Mike McLeod and Tyler Varga would duplicate the effort in future years. Varga accomplished the feat twice.

Nov. 21: Booth closed out his celebrated Yale career in Boston when he drop-kicked a 26-yard field goal in the last two minutes to beat previously undefeated Harvard, 3–0, in the golden jubilee contest between the two combatants. Yale completed only one pass in nine attempts when Booth connected with Herty Barres for a 26-yard grab that set up the field goal. Barres made the play of the game when he chased down Harvard's Jack Crickard after an 80-yard return to the Yale 8-yard line.

The cover of the game day program was found to be offensive to many fans of the Blue as it showed a picture of John Harvard sitting on the famed Yale Fence where captains of all Yale sports teams have been photographed since the 19th century. One Yale official said in a light-hearted tone, "There would always be a seat for John Harvard on the Yale fence."

Booth ended his storied career rushing for 1,428 yards and returning 76 kicks for 1,138 yards. He scored 17 TDs, kicked 24 extra points and four field goals accounting for a career total 138 points. He was elected to the College Football Hall of Fame in 1966. The great running back might have been the most popular athlete in Yale sports history. He captained his freshman football, basketball and baseball teams and his varsity football and basketball teams while at Yale. The Elis went 15–5–5 during Booth's magnificent career.

On the same day, the first high school game ever played in the Yale

Bowl occurred when Booth's alma mater, Hillhouse, defeated Commercial (now Wilbur Cross), 46–0, in front of more than 16,000.

Nov. 28: Yale closed the season with a 51–14 pasting of Princeton, the most lopsided score in the history of their series dating back to 1873. Booth reportedly suffering from pleurisy didn't play in the game. Following the season, he spent several months in the Gaylord Farm Anti-Tuberculosis Sanatorium in Wallingford. He missed the team picture but thanks to some trick photography, Booth found his way into the photo.

A Yale player, who was almost the exact same size as Booth, sat in the picture in the place reserved traditionally for the captain. Later, his head was removed from the picture and a head taken from a photo of Booth was inserted. Booth returned to play baseball for a part of the '32 season. His first game, no less, came against Harvard and "Little Boy Blue" added to his legend when he walloped a full-count bases loaded home run in the first inning off his old rival, Barry Wood, to give Yale a 4–2 lead which proved to be the final score.

Dec. 5: Yale played a round robin exhibition in the Bowl with Brown, Dartmouth and Holy Cross that raised more than $45,000 for charity amid the Great Depression. Described as the "Gloomy Bowl," the event drew between 22,000 and 28,000 and raised almost $50,000. Yale beat Holy Cross, 6–0, on a Joe Crowley touchdown and had a scoreless game against Brown. A panel of judges awarded Yale the championship on the basis of a complicated scoring system. The day ended on a tragic note when James C. Kelly, age 35, fell on the pavement as he was leaving the Bowl and died three days later of a fractured skull.

1932 (2–2–3) Coach: Marvin A. Stevens; Captain: John S. Wilbur

Yale played a seven-game schedule, the fewest number of games played in any season.

On December 2, the Payne Whitney Gymnasium opened with the Yale basketball team defeating an alumni group, 38–16.

Oct. 1: Yale and Bates played to an unlikely scoreless tie at the Yale Bowl, marking the first time in their 60-year football history that Yale did not win its opening game. In seven meetings against Bates, the Elis outscored the small liberal arts college from Lewiston, Maine, 223–0. But the Bobcats can claim a moral victory from their '32 tie game.

THE HIGHLIGHTS   1933–1934

Oct. 7: Albie Booth was among the 12 players and five coaches chosen to appear in the flick *The All-American*.

Oct. 8: Yale All-American Amos Alonzo Stagg, the "Grand Old Man of the Midway," brought his University of Chicago team to the Bowl, where the Bulldogs and Stagg's Maroons played to a 7–7 draw, one of three tie games Yale would play that season.

Nov. 18: The *New Haven Register* reported that "unknown malefactors broke into the Bowl, uprooted and made off with the goal posts, and ran Y banners upside down on the flagpoles."

Nov. 19: Yale blanked Harvard, 19–0, in a game that was played in a torrential rainstorm before an estimated 35,000 fans, among them Babe Ruth, "The Sultan of Swat," and his wife, Claire, who protected themselves from the rain with a strip of linoleum. Walt Levering scored twice for Yale on short runs (1 yard and 4 yards) and Walter Marting scored on a 24-yard pass from Bob Lassiter. Marting's son, Del, scored twice against Harvard in the 1967 game, giving the Martings the distinction as the only father-son Yale duo to score a touchdown against Harvard. It was the final game for Yale coach Mal Stevens, who finished 21–11–8 during his five-year run.

1933 (4–4) Coach: Reginald D. Root; Captain: Robert Lassiter

Yale continued to hire alums for the head coaching position. Reggie Root, a tackle on Yale's vaunted 1923 and 1924 teams, succeeded Stevens. He would last just one season. Root subsequently became the longtime freshman football and varsity lacrosse coach. During the 1944 season, he found ways to coach the Hillhouse High School football team as well as the Yale freshman team. At Hillhouse he coached Levi Jackson, who would become the first black football player and first black captain at Yale.

Nov. 25: Harvard beat Yale in Boston, 19–6, highlighted by Fergie Locke's 90-yard kickoff return in the third quarter, to date The Game's longest Crimson score on a kickoff return.

Dec. 2: Princeton beat Yale in the Bowl, 27–2, on the latest date that Yale played a regular season game in the 20th century.

1934 (5–3) Coach: Raymond W. Pond; Captain: Francis C. Curtin

Raymond "Ducky" Pond, a star running back on the great '23 team, replaced Root as head coach.

Oct. 6: Al Barabas rushed for 203 yards in 28 carries and scored twice as Columbia downed Yale, 12–6, in their first meeting since 1905. A sophomore playing his first varsity game, Larry Kelley, who would win the Heisman Trophy in '36, scored Yale's touchdown on a 5-yard pass from Jerry Roscoe. The loss gave Pond the ignoble distinction of being the first Yale head football coach to lose his first game, and it was the first time Yale lost an opening game.

Nov. 10: Georgia edged Yale, 14–7, in the Bowl ending an 11-game rivalry. It marked the fifth consecutive win by the Georgia Bulldogs over Yale. No team had ever defeated Yale five straight times.

Nov. 17: In an upset for the ages, the Yale's Ironmen turned back Princeton, 7–0, in sold-out Palmer Stadium. It was the Tigers' only loss in a span of 30 games.

Yale's 11 starters played the full 60 minutes without a substitution. A scoreless stalemate continued until three minutes remained in the first quarter when Yale had a 3rd-and-13 on the Princeton 49 and pulled off a fake punt-pass play. Stan Fuller was in punt formation on third down, but center Jim DeAngelis snapped to QB Jerry Roscoe who fired a 49-yard touchdown pass to Larry Kelley. Clare Curtin then kicked the extra point and Yale led, 7–0, which proved to be the final score. It was the first time in 37 years that Yale played the same 11 players the entire game.

Yale's traveling squad numbered 28 while Princeton dressed 80 players. DeAngelis, who ran off with the game ball after the game, said, "They lined up on the sidelines, looking us over like lambs of slaughter."

The game was played in the dark ages of sports science. According to Bill Wallace in his book, *Yale's Ironmen*, at halftime the players were nourished with sugar cubes soaked in rum.

That evening the Yale team stayed overnight at the Hotel New Yorker in New York City. They went to the theater to see the musical comedy, *Life Begins at 8:40* starring Ray Bolger and Bert Lahr. According to Roscoe, it was prearranged with the thought the team would need something to cheer them up after taking a beating from a strong Princeton team, who went on to win their next 12 games.

Nov. 23: Handsome Dan II was kidnapped by Harvard operatives. They exacerbated the stunt and drew the ire of the Yalies by having the Yale mascot photographed licking the hamburger-covered boots of John Harvard. The bulldog was subsequently returned unharmed.

THE HIGHLIGHTS   1935–1936

Nov. 24: Yale beat Harvard, 14–0, before 55,000 on an overcast day in New Haven. Yale's scoring came in the first two quarters on a Strat Morton 20-yard run and a Larry Kelley 8-yard TD pass from Roscoe.

1935 (6–3) Coach: Raymond W. Pond; Captain: Mather K. Whitehead

Oct. 5: The Bulldogs spanked New Hampshire, 34–0. Clint Frank, who would win the Heisman Trophy in 1937, made his varsity debut and scored two touchdowns.

Oct. 12: Yale defeated Penn, 31–20. The Elis made their first trip ever to historic Franklin Field in Philadelphia, the oldest college football stadium in the United States, which opened in 1895. The venue stands on 33rd and Spruce Streets and was home to the Philadelphia Eagles from 1958 to 1970. A second deck was added to the stadium in 1925, making it the first double-decker football stadium.

Oct. 19: Kicking specialist Henry "Hessie" Gardner's point after Al Hessberg's 20-yard first-quarter touchdown run provided the margin of Yale's 7–6 victory over Navy before 60,000 in the Bowl.

Nov. 2: Dartmouth, in one of their signature victories, beat Yale, 14–6, for the first time in 19 tries dating back to 1884. The big play that broke the "Yale Jinx" was made by Carl Ray, who intercepted a Yale pass and ran eight yards for the clinching touchdown. With little time remaining in the game, Dartmouth students tore down both goal posts in the Bowl, creating the rare site of a football field minus goal posts.

Nov. 23: Yale edged Harvard, 14–7, on a snowy day in Boston. The Elis broke a scoreless tie in the third quarter when Roscoe fired a 35-yard touchdown pass to Kelley. Yale's final score came when Al Hessberg, "The Albany Express," crossed the goal line on a 2-yard run. Tommy Curtin kicked the extra point.

Nov. 30: Princeton got revenge after being robbed of a perfect season the year before by the Yale Ironmen when they defeated the Elis, 38–7. Jack White and Pepper Constable each scored twice for the Tigers.

1936 (7–1) Coach: Raymond W. Pond; Captain: Lawrence M. Kelley

Yale finished 12th in the Associated Press poll in 1936 (7–1) and 1937 (6–1–1).

Yale University sold to the Atlantic Refining Company the rights to broadcast six football games in the Bowl that would be broadcast over the Yankee Network of the Mutual Broadcasting Company.

Oct. 17: Controversy clouded Yale's 12–7 win over Navy in Baltimore. Trailing, 7–6, in the third quarter, Navy running back Snead Smith fumbled Tony Mott's punt on his 23-yard line, picked it up and fumbled again. Kelley rushed in and inadvertently kicked the ball down to the 2-yard line where he recovered the pigskin. The officials ruled that Kelley's kick was not intentional and allowed the play to proceed without penalty. Two plays later, Clint Frank scored the winning touchdown. The play led to a subsequent rule change which stipulated that all free balls kicked, accidentally or intentionally, would now be ruled dead at the point of contact. For the record, Kelley wore uniform No. 19 and Frank wore No. 14.

Oct. 31: Coach Earl "Red" Blaik's Dartmouth team nipped Yale, 11–7. It would prove to be Yale's only loss of the season in which the Elis finished 7–1.

Nov. 7: Kelley had another epic game in Yale's 14–6 win over Brown. He ran back an interception 54 yards, setting up a Clint Frank touchdown, then went 33 yards to score with a blocked punt. He also kicked the only extra point of his career.

Nov. 14: Yale returned to Palmer Stadium for the first time since the famous "Iron Men" game in 1934. Yale trainer major Frank Wandle posted a sign that read, IT WAS DONE IN 1934. IT CAN BE DONE IN 1936. Yale came back after trailing, 16–0 and 23–20, to win a 26–23 thriller. The passing combo of Clint Frank to Larry Kelley was too much for the Tigers.

Nov. 21: Yale's 14 first-half points stood up as the Bulldogs beat Harvard, 14–13, in the Bowl. The Bulldogs scored in the first quarter on an Al Wilson 6-yard run. In the second quarter, Frank connected with Kelley on a 42-yard TD pass. This gave Kelley the distinction of having scored a touchdown in every game he played against Princeton and Harvard dating back to 1934, the only player to do so. Bud Humphrey kicked Yale's extra points. Harvard's failed extra point in the fourth quarter allowed the Elis to walk away victorious.

Frank, who also made a bevy of tackles from his defensive halfback position, prompted Harvard coach Dick Harlow to visit the Yale locker room and congratulate Frank for his outstanding performance. "You are the greatest back I've ever seen," said Harlow.

This was Kelley's final game in a Yale uniform. In his career the 6-foot-2 All-American end had 49 receptions for 889 yards and scored 15 TDs in an era dominated by the running game. Kelley, who was also a defensive giant, was voted the Heisman Trophy winner the second year that the award was issued but the first year the trophy was issued in its present form. In December 1999, his trophy was auctioned for $328,110.

The Harvards did not rid Kelley entirely. His final game at Yale was not in a football uniform but a baseball uniform. Kelley closed his collegiate career by helping lead Yale to victory over Harvard in late June 1937. The game was played at Mercer Field in New London as part of "boat race day" when the Yale and Harvard crews met on the Thames River in the annual Yale-Harvard Regatta.

An outstanding baseball player, St. Louis Cardinals vice president Branch Rickey offered him a $5,000 contract but he refused.

Kelley's legendary accomplishments at Yale inspired Grantland Rice to pen the following:

> *If you figure they've overplayed fiction*
> *Where Merriwells rise to the fray,*
> *Without the least semblance of friction*
> *And made the star play of the day.*
> *If you figure such stuff is a breeder*
> *Of yarns that are foolish or stale*
> *Just a moment, I beg of you, reader*
> *Shake hands with L. Kelley of Yale.*

1937 (6-1-1) Coach: Ray W. Pond; Captain: Clinton E. Frank

Clint Frank won the Heisman Trophy, beating out future Supreme Court Justice Byron "Whizzer" White. For his career Frank rushed for 1,244 yards and passed for 937 yards including 9 TD tosses. The infield of the Dwyer Track at the Dewitt Cuyler Athletic Complex is named Frank Field in honor of the former Yale great. William Proxmire, a U.S. Senator from Wisconsin from 1957 to 1989, lettered for the '37 Yale team.

Oct. 16: Yale beat Army, 15–7, to begin the season 3–0. In attendance was former U.S. President Herbert Hoover, who sat in the section reserved for Yale president Charles Seymour. No sitting president has ever attended a Yale game in the Bowl.

Oct. 30: Yale, ranked No. 5 by the AP poll, hosted No. 9 Dartmouth

Two of Yale's all-time greatest players, Larry Kelley and Clint Frank, won Heisman Trophies in back-to-back years in 1936 and 1937.

and the teams played to a 9–9 draw before 71,002 fans, the largest Bowl crowd in the decade of the 1930s. It's the only time two Top 10 teams have played in the Bowl. Yale's Dave Colwell's 75-yard punt set up a safety for Yale.

Nov. 13: Yale quarterback Clint Frank played his final game in the Yale Bowl and went out in a blaze of glory when he scored four TDs on runs of 78, 4, 52 and 6 yards as Yale pummeled Princeton, 26–0, in a driving rainstorm. Frank rushed 19 times for 190 yards, at the time a single-game school record. College Football Hall of Fame member Fritz Crisler coached his final game for the Tigers. His record against Yale was 2–3–1 while at Princeton.

Nov. 20: On a cold, dark Boston day in which snow fell in the second half, Harvard stung Yale, 13–6, despite Frank's 50 tackles and 74 rushing yards that included a 1-yard TD plunge in the third quarter that tied the score, 6–6. Frank Foley scored the winning TD for the Crimson on a 10-yard dash in the fourth quarter. The Harvard win, played in front of ex–President Herbert Hoover, spoiled Yale's undefeated season. Despite the Great Depression, scalpers got $50 for a pair of tickets.

1938 (2–6) **Coach: Raymond W. Pond; Captain: William V. Platt**

The golden Kelley-Frank era (24–8–1) ended. The next four years (1938–41) were ones of famish as the undernourished Bulldog struggled, winning only seven times in 32 games.

Future United States President Gerald R. Ford began assistant football and boxing coach duties while a Yale Law School student from 1938 to 1940. The 38th U.S. president, Ford was a star center and linebacker at the University of Michigan, helping the Wolverines to national titles in 1932 and 1933.

Oct. 8: Yale lost to Penn in Philadelphia, 21–0. This was the first time in the history of the Yale football program that the Elis lost the first two games of the season, also falling to Columbia in the season opener, 27–14.

Oct: 15: Yale rebounded by upsetting an undefeated, heavily favored Navy team in the Bowl 9–7 before more than 50,000 howling fans behind the exploits of Gil Humphrey, who labored for two years in the shadow of Clint Frank. Humphrey's sons, George and Watts, followed him on the gridiron at Yale.

A contingent of 1,500 midshipmen arrived in the Elm City at 5:30 a.m. on four train cars. At the time, the Naval Academy did not allow the midshipmen to stay overnight away from the Academy. Following breakfast at the New Haven railroad station, the Middies were given the freedom of the city and the University. The Corps marched down Chapel Street and entered the Bowl at 1:15 p.m. to give a pregame marching exhibition. A detachment of 320 bluejackets from the USS *Wyoming* battleship that anchored outside the New Haven harbor in the morning supported the Middies in a losing cause.

Oct. 22: 12th-ranked University of Michigan beat Yale, 15–13, in the Bowl. Trailing, 13–8, late in the game, a roughing the kicker penalty gave the Wolverines a new life from their own 26-yard line. Tom Harmon, the 1940 Heisman winner, then led Michigan with passes and runs to spark a 74-yard scoring drive culminated by Harmon's pass to John Nicholson.

Both teams wore blue jerseys. Yale's was a notch or two lighter than the Wolverines. Michigan brought its 130-piece band to New Haven.

Nov. 19: Harvard nipped Yale, 7–0, in New Haven before 62,000 despite soggy weather and paltry records, Yale (2–5–0) and Harvard (3–4). The Crimson broke a scoreless tie in the last quarter when Torby Macdonald scored on a 10-yard pass from Frank Foley, culminating an 80-yard drive. Chief Boston kicked the extra point.

1939 (3–4–1) Coach: Raymond W. Pond; Captain: J. William Stack, Jr.

The NCAA (in 1939) and the National Football League (in 1941) made helmets mandatory. Before the invention of the football helmet, players would often grow their hair long as a protective measure to prevent a head injury.

Oct. 21: Yale beat Army, 20–15, aided by a fluke play. A Yale interior lineman blocked a punt near the 20-yard line. Yale's Hal Whiteman, who captained the 1940 team, fielded the ball in the air and scored a touchdown. Hal's son Bart also played at Yale (1967–69).

Oct. 28: Yale lost to No. 3 ranked Michigan at Ann Arbor, 27–7. Consensus All-American junior Tom Harmon, who led the nation in scoring in 1939 and 1940, scored three of the four Wolverine touchdowns, his longest a 59-yard gallop in the third quarter on a reverse around left end. The man known as "Old No. 98," added three extra points and gained a total of 203 yards in 18 carries. Harmon also tossed a 23-yard aerial TD to Forest Evashevski, a blocking back for Harmon, who subsequently coached the Iowa Hawkeyes to two Rose Bowl championships.

Nov. 25: Coming off a 13–7 loss to Princeton, the Elis entered the Harvard game at an anemic 2–4–1 against the 4–3 Crimson. Surprisingly, Yale cruised past the Redshirts, 20–7, on scores by Al Bartholemy (5-yard pass from Fred Burr), and two short Hovey Seymour TD runs.

1940 (1–7) Coach: Raymond W. Pond; Captain: Harold B. Whiteman

Oct. 12: Penn, under coach George Munger, punished Yale, 50–7 at Franklin Field in the first Yale football game ever televised. It was the worst beating the camera-shy Elis ever suffered.

Oct. 15: The *Los Angeles Times* reported, "Big-time football at Yale is dead." Ogden Miller, the director of athletics at Yale, in a speech before the Football Writers Association, including college and professional coaches, deplored the commercial aspects of college football, inferring that Yale could very well get along without Cornell, Penn and teams of similar strength on its schedule. Miller said, "We will play teams that are getting the same kind of material as we are and playing similar football." He added that the de-emphasis of football at Yale had been going on for some time. Miller saw pro football as a threat to the college game.

Oct. 19: Yale won their only game of the season, beating Dartmouth, 13–7. With the score tied, 7–7, in the final minutes, Yale had the ball on the Dartmouth 5-yard line. Yale's winning touchdown was scored by substitute end John Reid on a pass from Ted Harrison. Reid caught the ball on the 3-yard line and fought across the goal with the winning touchdown.

Nov. 2: Dick High intercepted a Yale pass late in the contest and raced 96 yards to the goal line, giving Brown a 6–2 win.

Nov. 9: Cornell, ranked No. 1 in the country by the Associated Press, beat Yale, 21–0, to win its 14th consecutive game under coach Carl Snavely. The Big Red were led by All-America tackle Nick Drahos and blocking back Walt Matuszak. It's the only time a No. 1 nationally ranked team played in the Yale Bowl.

Nov. 23: Yale continued to stumble as New Haven natives Fran Lee and Charley Spreyer led Harvard to a lopsided 28–0 win over Yale. In the last quarter Lee returned a punt 78 yards for a touchdown which remains Harvard's longest punt return for a touchdown in the Yale-Harvard series. Spreyer scored on a 2-yard blast. Ducky Pond coached his final game at Yale. From 1934 to 1940, Pond's teams went 30–25–2.

1941 (1–7) Coach: Emerson W. Nelson; Captain: Alan E. Bartholemy

Yale replaced Raymond "Ducky" Pond with 36-year-old Emerson "Spike" Nelson, who became the first non–Yale grad to head the football program since its inception in 1872. Nelson was an assistant coach at Yale under Pond for two years and a former star tackle at the University of Iowa.

The return of the old T-formation became fashionable as the old single wing gradually vanished for the most part with the exception of Princeton, who employed it until 1969. Unlimited substitution, which led to platooning, was legalized. Before the rules mandated it, Yale became one of the first colleges to number their players by position: ends (80s), tackles (70s), guards (60s), centers (50s), backs (1–20) etc.

Oct. 4: Nelson made an auspicious coaching debut as Yale made one of the school's greatest upsets, beating the University of Virginia, 21–19. The Cavaliers boasted the likes of great running backs "Bullet Bill" Dudley, who is in both the College and Pro Football Hall of Fames, and C. Edgar (Eddie) Bryant.

Trailing at the half, 19–0, the Elis staged a garrison finish by scoring 21 unanswered points before an estimated 22,000. Several thousand were Virginians, 500 of whom came to New Haven on a special train.

The Bulldogs scored in the third quarter on a 60-yard drive, as sophomore Ed Taylor scored from the 2 followed by Hovey Seymour's extra point. After an exchange of punts, Yale had a 7-yard scoring pass from Jack Ferguson to sophomore Fred (Ted) Harrison. Fred Dent, who would serve as the U.S. Secretary of Commerce under Presidents Richard M. Nixon and Gerald R. Ford, converted the extra point. Early in the fourth quarter, Townsend (Tim) Hoopes tossed a 12-yard TD pass to captain Alan Bartholemy, giving Yale the lead. Seymour converted to make it 21–19, which proved to be the final score.

As the winds of war swirled throughout the nation, the Yale band captured the patriotic spirit by reportedly playing the national anthem before the game for the first time ever at the Bowl.

Oct. 18: Coach Earl "Red" Blaik led Army to a 20–7 win over Yale. Blaik became the first coach to take a visiting team into the Yale Bowl in back-to-back years, having coached Dartmouth the year before. This was duplicated in 2015 when Columbia coach Al Bagnoli ushered his Columbia Lions into the Bowl the year after he took his Penn Quakers into the historic saucer.

Nov. 22: Harvard triumphed over Yale, 14–0, in Boston. Yale had a touchdown nullified by a penalty in the first quarter that nixed an 82-yard drive. The Cantabs scored in the first quarter on a Don McNicol 1-yard run and in the fourth quarter on a 4-yard pass from captain Fran Lee to Don Forte. McNicol accounted for 179 yards on 25 carries.

It was Nelson's last hurrah as the Elis finished 1–7 under the first-year coach.

The game marked Harvard senior Endicott Peabody's final performance versus Yale. Peabody, who later served a term as governor of Massachusetts, started three straight seasons on the offensive line for the Crimson.

Dec. 22: Spike Nelson resigned as Yale's head football coach. He was popular with students and alumni and was expected to remain on the job. But with World War II still in progress, and because of, as he put it in his letter of resignation, "uncertainty of athletics and general conditions," he accepted an offer to join the staff of the procurement department of the U.S. Engineer Corps in Philadelphia.

1942 (5–3) Coach: Howard Odell; Captain: Spencer D. Moseley

Howie Odell, a former running back and punter at the University of Pittsburgh, succeeded Nelson as Yale's head coach. He served as an assistant coach at Pittsburgh, Harvard, Penn and Wisconsin before coming to Yale. From 1938 to 1941 Yale won only 7 games against 24 losses and 1 tie, reaching its nadir in '41. Odell led the football program to its former glory. In his six-year tenure, he went 35–15–2, during which time he was 4–0 against Harvard and 4–1 against Princeton.

The NCAA permitted freshmen to play on varsity teams for the first time since 1905. Bob Pickett, a 205-pound fullback, and Stan Weiner were frosh standouts for the Bulldogs in '42. Freshmen would be allowed to compete on the varsity at Yale from 1942 until 1946. About 350 colleges, including Harvard and Princeton, dropped their varsity football programs for a season or more because of a shortage of players during the war years.

Wartime All-Americans at Yale included center and linebacker Spencer Moseley (1942) and end Paul Walker (1943–45). Walker, a consensus All-American in '44 and third team in '45, went on to play in the NFL with the New York Giants. Moseley, who captained the '42 team, was the son of George Moseley, Yale's 1916 All-American end, giving the Moseleys the distinction of being the only father-son All-Americans at Yale. Spencer, who played most of the 1941 season with a broken jaw, became a Marine pursuit pilot in World War II and flew as a Marine reservist in the Korean War.

The horrors of war claimed the lives of several Yale lettermen including 1940 captain Hovey Seymour, Frank Gallagher, Strat Morton, Quentin "Monk" Meyer, Gene Constantin, Bert Martin, Bill Knapp, Kay Todd Jr., Webster M. Bull, Kevin Rafferty, Cyrus R. Taylor and "Memphis Bill"

Mallory, the All-American fullback who captained the undefeated 1923 eleven. Mallory, who joined the U.S. Army Air Forces as an intelligence officer, did not die in combat. On his return home from discharge in 1945, he was aboard a transport plane that crashed in Italy. At age 42, he was scheduled for release from the Army because of over-age regulations. An intelligence officer of the Tactical Air Force, Memphis Bill received the Legion of Merit Medal for the famed "Operation Mallory," which resulted in the cutting of 24 bridges crossing the Po Lombardy.

George Mead, the manager of the 1940 team, also lost his life. It would be impossible to determine how many others died from various effects of the war.

During World War II, Yale Heisman winner Clint Frank served as a Lieutenant Colonel in the United States Air Force as an aide to General Jimmy Doolittle. Lieutenant Raymond "Ducky" Pond (former Yale player and coach) coached the Georgia Pre-Flight Skycrackers. John Reed Kilpatrick, Yale's 1910 All-America end who had been a colonel in World War I, served in World War II as a brigadier general.

Oct. 3: Yale ran away from Lehigh, winning, 33–6, in Odell's head coaching debut.

Nov. 14: The Bulldogs beat Princeton, 13–6. To reduce wartime travel, the game was played at Columbia's Baker Field on a frigid day. For the first time, no special trains ran.

Nov. 21: Yale edged Harvard, 7–3, in the Bowl to win its first Big Three championship in six years. The game was attended by an estimated crowd of only 23,500, affected by gas rationing and travel limitations.

All-American center Spencer Moseley made 19 tackles to lead the Elis. The Bulldogs scored in the fourth quarter on a 61-yard touchdown pass from Hugh Knowlton to Tim Hoopes. Fred Dent kicked the extra point. The Crimson score came in the second quarter on a 27-yard FG by Bob Fisher, the son of the erstwhile Harvard coach. Following the Yale score, Harvard staged a 90-yard drive to the Yale 7-yard line. The final play of the game was a dropped pass in the end zone by Harvard fullback Wayne Johnson, who was transferred to Yale the following year in the V-12 program after he enlisted in the Marine Corps.

1943 (4–5) Coach: Howard Odell; Captain: Townsend W. Hoopes

College football survived in large part because of the U.S. Navy's

V-12 program that commenced on July 1. The program was based at 131 campuses in 43 states, including Yale. The purpose of the program was to give prospective Navy, Marine and Coast Guard officers a college education in areas the Navy most required. A total of 20,000 trainees in the armed forces studied at Yale during this time. Marines could play varsity football because they were under the Department of the Navy. Army soldiers, who were placed in Yale's Berkeley College, were permitted to participate only in intramural sports. Army Air Forces personnel used Yale facilities but were not formally affiliated with Yale and thus could not engage in varsity sports.

Sept.11: Yale opened the season with a 13–6 victory over Muhlenberg, coached by Al "Doggie" Julian. Wayne Johnson, who played for Harvard the year before, broke his neck in the first quarter and was temporarily paralyzed. He never played again, but he was awarded a letter at the team's banquet in December. He remains the only athlete to win varsity football letters from both Yale and Harvard.

Oct. 23: No. 2 ranked Army ambushed Yale in the Bowl, 39–7. The game started at 3:00 p.m. because of wartime classes. Glenn Davis, the 1946 Heisman winner, only notched 22 yards rushing on 10 carries but passed for two touchdowns and made a touchdown-saving tackle of Yale's Ray "Scooter" Scussel, a 5-foot-8, 165-pound Marine transfer from UConn.

Nov. 13: The hungry Yale Bulldog fed on Princeton Tiger meat, winning, 27–6, in front of a wartime crowd numbering 17,000. Scussel scored three of Yale's four TDs. Two pairs of brothers played in the game. There was Yale's All-American end Paul Walker and his brother Blake, who quarterbacked the Elis. Walter Brown played left end for Yale and his identical twin brother Charley was at center for the Tigers. The twins had played together at Hotchkiss in 1941 but never against each other. Their father, H.G. Brown, lettered for Princeton in 1913 and sat on the Princeton side while Mrs. Brown added to the divided house by sitting on the Yale side and rooted for the Blue even though Yale wore white uniforms instead of their traditional blue.

1944 (7–0–1) Coach: Howard Odell; Captain: Macauley Whiting

Odell went from the single wing to the T-formation and led the Elis to a 7–0–1 mark, the first undefeated team in 20 years. Yale wore white jerseys for most home games. Marlin "Buzzy" Gher, a star halfback, was an Air Medal–winning aerial gunner in the South Pacific in 1942 and 1943. A fan favorite, Buzzy Gher fan clubs were formed by local youngsters. Tackle John Prchlik left for active naval duty midway through the '44 season before returning in '46. The 6-foot-4, 215-pound tackle, who played in the East-West game in 1948, played for the Detroit Lions from 1949 to 1953.

Charley Loftus, the legendary Yale sports publicity director (1943–68) was reportedly credited with coining the term "tailgating."

July 15: Albie Booth joined Yale's coaching staff as the junior varsity coach. "Little Boy Blue" assisted Mal Stevens in 1932 and when Stevens shifted to NYU, Booth assisted him there in 1934.

Oct. 31: Marine Nick Fusilli, one of Dartmouth's best linemen, was transferred to Yale. This helped to offset the loss to the military of linemen John Prchlik and Westi Hansen, plus halfback Frank Gillis.

Nov. 4: Yale edged Dartmouth, 6–0. Wearing a Yale uniform that day was Fusilli, who was a starting Dartmouth guard the week before in Dartmouth's 14–13 win over Brown. Fusilli oddly appeared in the Dartmouth team photo in the game day program but was listed on the Yale roster.

Nov. 25: Because Harvard and Princeton did not have a formal football schedule in 1944, Yale ended the season with a 6–6 tie vs. Virginia. The tie deprived the Elis of a perfect 8–0 season.

1945 (6–3) Coach: Howard Odell; Captain: Paul Walker

The pressures of playing football paled in comparison to the experiences of war. Four members of Yale's 1945 team—Martin Dwyer, Fritz Barzilauskas, Valleau Wilkie and Bill Schuler—were all lieutenants in the Army Air Corps, and all had been shot down while on aerial missions over German-held territory. All were Nazi war prisoners until freed by advancing American troops and all returned to play football at Yale. Following his Yale career in 1946, Barzilauskas, a guard, was chosen in the first round of the NFL draft by the Boston Yanks, becoming the third player taken overall. He received a record salary for a rookie lineman—$9,000. He played professional football for the Boston Yanks, New York Bulldogs and New York Giants between 1947 and 1951. His son, Tony, lettered for Yale in '69. Schuler, an outstanding tackle, began his collegiate career at Auburn and enrolled at Yale following the war. The outstanding tackle, who lettered in 1945 and 1946, played for the New York Giants in 1947 and 1948.

April 14: William "Pa" Corbin, the captain and center on the 1888 Yale team, died at age 81 in the Hartford Hospital where he had been a patient since March 18 when he was struck by an automobile.

Sept. 22: In an exhibition game tune-up for the '45 season, Yale defeated the New London Sub Base, 42–13, in the Bowl. Larry Dalley, an 18-year-old freshman, scored on a 68-yard run for the Elis, the highlight play of the day.

Sept. 29: The Elis kicked off the season with a 27–7 victory over Tufts. "Handy Vandy" Kirk, Yale's talented 18-year-old sophomore pre-divinity student, tallied all four of Yale's TDs. One came on a 57-yard sprint up the middle to the delight of the 20,000 shirt-sleeved fans.

Oct. 6: Air Forces veteran Stan Koslowski caught one touchdown pass, threw another and kicked three conversions as Holy Cross crushed Yale, 21–0, in the Bowl, ending Yale's 10-game unbeaten streak. The loss became a trifle more palatable when Holy Cross (8–2 that season) went on to play Miami (Florida) on New Year's Day in the Orange Bowl.

Nov. 17: Yale won its 500th game, defeating Coast Guard, 41–6.

Nov. 24: In one of the most unusual statistical games in Yale football history, the Elis held Princeton to one first down and minus four yards rushing compared to their 22 first downs and 357 yards in their 20–14 win over the orange and black.

Dec. 1: Yale beat Harvard, 28–0, before an estimated 35,000 at the Yale Bowl. It was the only time that The Game was played in December and the first time it was played in an odd-numbered year in New Haven. Because Harvard made a late decision to participate in football in '45, Yale agreed to add Harvard to their schedule after the Princeton game. The late date that was agreed upon in October was announced as a post-season game. It was the only time the game was played in the Bowl two consecutive times—1942 and 1945. From 1946 on Harvard has hosted the annual rivalry in the even numbered years and Yale the odd numbered years.

Yale fullback Art Fitzgerald, a third-string transfer from Notre Dame, scored three times on runs of 1, 15, and 4 yards. Vandy Kirk added the final TD on a 3-yard run in the fourth quarter. Yale captain Paul Walker tackled Harvard's Charley Roche in the end zone for a safety in the third quarter. Fitzgerald would go on to represent Yale in the East-West Shrine game and the NCAA basketball and baseball tournaments.

H.B. Bullard, a Yale cheerleader in '45, remembered Handsome Dan V (1940–47) keeling over near the end of the game. "I carried him off the field," recalled Bullard. "I think he was overwhelmed by the roar of the crowd after Yale had completed a pass play." The head Yale cheerleader in '45 was Homer Babbidge, who subsequently became president of the University of Connecticut from 1962 to 1972.

Dec. 14: Yale, shattering 73 years of football history, announced that coach Howie Odell's contract would be extended five years. Odell received offers from several colleges and professional teams including the University of Nebraska. Odell turned down the Cornhuskers offer as he prepared to board a plane to Lincoln.

1946 (7–1–1) Coach: Howard Odell; Captain: Richard M. Hollingshead III

Several war veterans returned, the campus exploded in numbers and the debut of Levi Jackson made it an exciting year for Yale and its fans.

Sept. 28: Freshman Levi Jackson, Yale's first African American football player, made a memorable debut in the Elis' 33–0 win over the Merchant Marine Academy, also known as Kings Point. Jackson scored on a 59-yard jaunt late in the first period and a 6-yard run early in the third quarter. He also intercepted a pass on the Yale 8 and ran it back to the 30 which led to Vic Tataranowicz's 8-yard run across the goal line.

Oct. 12: Jackson made an electrifying 84-yard TD kickoff run to help give the Blue a 20–6 lead, but Yale was unable to contain the passing talents of Columbia quarterback Don Kasprzak and the receiving skills of All-American Bill Swiacki and lost to the No. 11 Lions, 28–20, in the rain. It was Yale's only loss of the season. The Elis entered the game ranked 15th in the country.

Nov. 9: Yale's diminutive kicker Billy "Boola Boola" Booe made a record seven extra-point conversions in Yale's 49–0 win over Brown. Booe was successful in 23 of 25 extra-point attempts in '46.

Nov. 23: Both teams entered The Game with sterling records (Harvard 7–1 and Yale 6–1–1) as they prepared for battle on a bitterly cold day along the Charles in front of 57,000. The Elis, apparently confused at first over Harvard's triple wing "L formation" employed by coach Dick Harlow, overcame a 14–0 Crimson lead in the first quarter to win, 27–14. Accord-

Left to right: Carm Cozza, Bill O'Brien and Levi Jackson (courtesy Bill O'Brien).

ing to author Tom Bergin, this was the first Y-H game that the team that did not score first won.

Levi Jackson's 17-yard pass to halfback Art Fitzgerald put the Elis on the board in the second quarter. Ferd "The Bull" Nadherny subsequently scored on runs of 9 and 5 yards. Yale ended the season ranked 12th by the AP poll. Jackson, who ran for 806 yards, the fifth most in the nation, was cited by the Gridiron Club of Boston as the best college football player in New England, earning the Bulger Lowe Award. Yale QB Tex Furse led the nation in efficient passing at 61.4 percent.

1947 (6–3) Coach: Howard Odell; Captain: Endicott P. Davison

Yale averaged 47,560 fans per game at the Bowl, a record for a single season. This was Howie Odell's final season as Yale's head coach. Odell, who recorded a 35–15–2 mark from 1942 to 1947, departed to become head coach at the University of Washington. Yale assistant coach Reggie Root joined Odell.

Feb. 7: Odell suffered a double fracture of his right leg while playing handball at the New Haven YMCA with Ivy Williamson, the end coach and the head basketball coach. He was taken to New Haven Hospital.

Oct. 4: Yale blanked Cornell, 14–0, in the Bowl. Levi Jackson suffered a head injury that led to a four-day hospital stay.

Oct. 18: Wisconsin downed the No. 12 ranked Bulldogs, 9–0, in the first meeting between the two schools since 1899. The game was played in 79-degree heat before a crowd of 65,000 customers in the Bowl.

Nov. 1: Yale defeated Dartmouth, 23–14, in a game that was marred by a referee's mistake in not allowing a fourth down near the end of the first half. Late in the second quarter, the Indians tried a rush and two passes from Yale's 45 at which point the officials turned the ball over to Yale on its 43-yard line. With five seconds remaining in the half, Billy Booe, with Roger Barksdale holding, kicked a 35-yard field goal to give Yale a 17–0 advantage at the intermission.

Following the game, Yale coach Howie Odell checked with the chart kept by one of his aides and realized that Dartmouth only had three tries late in the first half. If the winning margin had resulted from the egregious boner the officials pulled in allowing the Green only three downs on one sequence of plays, it would have been highly embarrassing for Yale.

Nov. 8: Brown beat Yale, 20–14, in a game that was played in a 55-mph gale and a lashing rain. Writers Hank O'Donnell and Gus Langner, both 40-year veterans of the press box, called this "the most wretched day the Bowl had seen." Rain made the field a quagmire. Booe began a string of 28 consecutive extra points through November 20, 1948.

Nov. 15: Princeton beat Yale, 17–0, in the first of six successive victories by the Tigers over the Blue. In coach Howie Odell's six-year tenure, this would be his only loss to either Princeton or Harvard.

Nov. 20: Two days before the Harvard game, the legendary Amos Alonzo Stagg addressed the Yale team at practice. He told the group to strike the first blow and to keep striking without letting down. "To let down is human," said Stagg. "Don't let Yale be human on Saturday." The team responded with a roar of "yeas" and rushed to resume their workout.

Nov. 22: On a day in which the open trolley made its final trek to the Bowl for a Yale game, QB Tex Furse, directing the T-operations, scored three times and Booe kicked his third field goal of the season, a 39-yarder, to lead Yale to its fourth straight win over Harvard, 31–21, in front of 70,896 chilled fans, the largest crowd to see a Yale-Harvard game since 1930. Slowed and shackled by injuries, Levi Jackson had his best game of the season as he rushed for 76 yards, including a 15-yard TD run in the third quarter that put Yale ahead, 21–14. His 45-yard pass to Larry McQuade before the end of the first half was key.

Bobby Kennedy, a future U.S. Senator and U.S. Attorney General, was an end on the Harvard team. He got in for only one play because of a leg injury he suffered earlier in the year. RFK reportedly hobbled down the sidelines on a kickoff with his leg encased in a special brace. He earned his major football letters in '45 and '46. The Game was the swan song for both Yale coach Howie Odell and Harvard coach Dick Harlow.

Nov. 27: The final trolley ride ever to the Bowl occurred for the annual Hillhouse–West Haven high school game on Thanksgiving Day.

1948 (4–5) Coach: Herman Hickman; Captain: William E. Conway

With Odell's departure, Rip Engle, the Brown coach at the time, was prominently considered to be a candidate for the Yale job but withdrew his name from any consideration and went on to coach Penn State from 1950 until 1965. Columbia coach Lou Little (real name Luigi Piccolo) also spurned the position. It was rumored that Little was on the brink of going to Yale shortly before General Dwight D. Eisenhower took over as Columbia's president. Eisenhower reportedly said that his acceptance of the Columbia post was based on a package deal that would keep Little as the coach. Little stayed and Ike took the job. He served in that position from May 1948 until January 1953.

The colorful Herman Hickman succeeded Odell. A hefty, jocular man with scholarly wit, he was as comfortable talking Kipling and Shakespeare as he was football. Writer Hugh A. Mulligan referred to Hickman as "Yale's Falstaff with a football under his arm." An All-American guard at the University of Tennessee, he also played for the NFL's Brooklyn Dodgers (1932–34) and was a professional wrestler known as "The Tennessee Terror." Before coming to Yale, he was an assistant at West Point under Earl "Red"

Blaik. When he arrived at Yale, he was surprised to see so many small linemen as compared to the Army players he coached. He referred to his undersized linemen as "The Seven Dwarfs."

Success did not follow Hickman to the ivy walls of Yale. His teams compiled a disappointing 16–17–2 record over four years but his '48 edition did upset Wisconsin on the road.

In an effort to increase scoring possibilities, a one-inch tee was legalized whenever the ball was placekicked.

Sept. 25: Hickman launched his four-year Yale head coaching career with a 28–13 victory over Brown. Backup QB Joe Paterno, the future Penn State football coach, threw a pass from the Yale 20 in which pass interference was called, putting the ball on the 2 yard line. Brown scored and pulled to within 14–13 but that would be the Bears' last score of the day.

Oct. 2: In the first matchup ever between the state rivals, Yale and the University of Connecticut, Yale beat UConn, 7–0, as Levi Jackson scored the lone TD. Except for 1951 and 1985 (when the game was canceled because of Hurricane Gloria), the two teams played every year from 1948 until 1998.

Oct. 9: In one of the most exciting games ever staged at the Bowl, Columbia beat Yale, 34–28, before 55,000. Trailing by six points late in the fourth quarter, the Elis marched 59 yards to the Columbia 27 when the game ended.

The Lions were led by Columbia's "Gold Dust Twins," quarterback Gene Rossides and halfback Lou Kusserow, who scored three touchdowns operating out of coach Lou Little's winged-T offense. The game that was carried on NBC national/regional TV, was the first televised game ever from the Bowl. Ironically, Kusserow, the star of the game, who still holds Columbia's all-time scoring (282 points) and TDs (47) records, became a well-known producer for NBC Sports following his playing career.

The Lions attacked quickly scoring on the fourth play of the game when Rossides connected with Bill Olson. Yale answered when Charley Keller raced 76 yards on the ensuing kickoff. Later in the quarter Kusserow scored from the 11, giving Columbia a 13–7 lead that was never relinquished. QB Tex Furse (two touchdown runs) and halfback Bobby Raines also scored for the Elis.

Oct. 16: Avenging the 9–0 loss the year before, Yale defeated Wisconsin in Madison, 17–7. It was the farthest west any Yale eleven had ever traveled, a total distance of 1,019 miles by train each way. A capacity crowd of 45,000 jammed Camp Randall Stadium. The Badgers wasted no time getting on the board, scoring the first three minutes of play when Clarence Self ran for a 42-yard touchdown. Later in the quarter, Wisconsin's Bob Petruska fumbled, and Yale's Walt Clemens recovered on the Wisconsin 19. The Bulldogs' Bob Raines ran down to the Wisconsin 8-yard line before Levi Jackson punched over the goal line from the three. Billy Booe converted to tie the game, 7–7. The Elis scored early in the second half on a Ferd Nadherny touchdown set up by Raines's 48-yard run. Booe again kicked the extra point, his 17th consecutive try, giving Yale a 14–7 lead. Booe added a field goal in the third quarter from the Badgers' 6-yard line and Yale never looked back.

A group of disgruntled Wisconsin students unfurled a 10-foot banner that read, GOOD-BYE HARRY and sang "Goodnight, Harry" to the tune of "Goodnight, Ladies" in reference to Badgers coach and athletic director Harry Stuhldreher, the former QB of Notre Dame's famed Four Horsemen. The banner spearheaded a statewide assault on the beleaguered Stuhldreher, who had been the head coach since 1936. At the end of the season, Stuhldreher resigned his coaching position after finishing 2–7 but retained his role as athletic director for another year.

Oct. 17: A crowd of 1,000 students and fans, including the Yale band and New Haven mayor William Celentano greeted the Yale team and coaches at the New Haven railroad station. Several players and coach Herman Hickman rode in a motorcade back to the campus and many marched back. Hickman gave a brief speech in front of Wright Hall. "If the team keeps showing the old Yale fight, they had at Madison, we ain't gonna lose many games," said Hickman. But the Bulldogs lost four of their last five games.

Nov. 20: Harvard beat Yale, 20–7, at Harvard Stadium under first year coach Art Valpey. The Crimson's Hal Moffie ran for an 80-yard TD on the first play from scrimmage on a reverse, the highlight play of the day. At the final practice of the year, Hickman recited "Spartacus to the Gladiators" in a failed attempt to motivate his team.

It is believed by some that the title of *THE GAME*, was born with this contest. According to an article written by William Wallace of the *New York Times*, the title came into being in 1948 when both sides had losing records and the event needed a little boost in the opinion of Yale sports publicity director Charley Loftus, who boldly christened the annual joust as THE GAME.

Nov. 22: Levi Jackson was elected Yale's football captain for the '49 season. He was the first black sports captain in Yale's athletic history. In response to the honor, Jackson said modestly, "It's swell." The vote that was held on the second floor of the Ray Tompkins House was 49–1 for Levi. Yale's 70th captain refused to vote for himself. The other Yale black football captains include Rudy Green (1974), Jordan Haynes (2011) and Deon Randall (2014).

1949 (4–4) Coach: Herman Hickman; Captain: Levi Jackson

Oct. 1: The game against Fordham was canceled after Yale fullback Dale Liechty contracted polio. Because the Yale administration did not know whether this was an isolated case or an epidemic, it was decided to err on the side of caution.

Oct. 15: After opening the season with victories over UConn and Columbia, Cornell pummeled Yale, 48–14.

Nov. 5: Brown upset Yale, 14–0. Notably absent from the sidelines was Yale coach Herman Hickman, who scouted the Harvard-Princeton game.

Nov. 19: Yale tripped Harvard, 29–6, before an NBC national/regional TV audience, ending Harvard's most disastrous season in history at 1–8. The Elis, who finished 4–4, hoisted Hickman, their hefty 300-pound coach, on their shoulders.

Captain Levi Jackson, playing in his final game, scored on a 34-yard run in the first quarter and on a 7-yard pass from QB Stu Tisdale in the second frame. Jackson, who played with a calcified ankle during the season, ended his career rushing for 2,049 yards and owned 13 team records.

Ferd Nadherny and Jim Fuchs, who held the world record for the shot put, crossed the goal line on 1-yard runs. Bobby Raines had nine carries for 99 yards. Raines's roommate, Dale Liechty, who was sidelined for most of the season with a light attack of polio, was sent into the game during the failed extra-point attempt after Fuch's TD in the final frame. Liechty was stationed well out to the right where there would be no danger of any contact. Apparently, the idea was for Liechty to get a varsity letter.

This was Harvard coach Art Valpey's final season. He was replaced by Lloyd Jordan, who guided the Crimson through the '56 season.

THE HIGHLIGHTS 1950–1951

1950 (6–3) Coach: Herman Hickman; Captain: Bradford H. Quackenbush

Sept. 30: Yale foiled Brown, 36–12. Bob Spears scored Yale's first two touchdowns. Jon Bush, the brother of George H.W. Bush, the 41st president of the United States, kicked three extra points and booted a field goal from the 17-yard line.

Oct. 7: Despite being handicapped by the absence of Ed Senay, Yale's most dangerous rusher, the Bulldogs held on to defeat Fordham, 21–14. The contest was highlighted by Jim Ryan Jr.'s 95-yard kickoff return in the second quarter, giving Yale a 14–7 lead. In an apparent prank by Fordham students the week of the game, a directional sign on the Merritt Parkway read FORDHAM BOWL. The word *Yale* had been covered by paint and the word *Fordham* substituted above it.

Another sidebar to this game was Yale's regular right halfback, John E. Lohnes, being declared ineligible for the game because he married the week before without the university's permission. Regulations required an undergraduate to obtain approval of university authorities before taking a bride.

Nov. 18: Princeton, No. 7 in both the AP and UP polls, took the Elis to school, winning, 47–12. It was the most points ever registered by a visiting team in the Bowl. All-American Dick Kazmaier rushed for 147 yards and a touchdown. He also completed 8 of 10 passes for 102 yards and three touchdowns as the Tigers remained undefeated. Princeton would win the Lambert Trophy as the top team in the East and finish No. 6 in the AP poll.

Nov. 25: The Game was played in Boston in a 55-mph gale wind with the Elis prevailing, 14–6, after falling behind, 6–0, in the fourth quarter. The Cantabs struck first on an overland route from Carroll Lowenstein to David Warden, a play that covered 63 yards. Yale scored on 3- and 5-yard runs from Senay and Bob Spears.

1951 (2–5–2) Coach: Herman Hickman; Captain: Robert Spears

Sept. 22: Yale opened the season by bullying Bates, 48–0. Bates, coached by former Eli coach Ducky Pond, recorded just one first down the entire game.

Sept. 29: Yale and Navy played to a 7–7 tie before 54,000 in the Bowl. Navy's Ned Snyder missed a 42-yard field-goal attempt as the Yale denizens held their breath with time running down.

Nov. 17: Heisman winner Dick Kazmaier threw three touchdown passes and ran for another as No. 6 ranked Princeton, the winner of the Lambert Trophy for the second straight year, leveled the Elis in New Jersey, 27–0. Two days later, Kazmaier appeared on the cover of *Time* magazine.

Coach Hickman, the laureate of the locker room, was driven to beat Princeton but never did. He was absent from the '48 Kings Point game and the '49 Brown game because he was scouting the Princeton-Harvard game both years.

Nov. 24: In Herman Hickman's swan song as the Eli's head coach, Yale and Harvard scuffled to a 21–21 deadlock, the highest-scoring tie game in the history of the series that had seen five scoreless ties. The Crimson overcame a 14–0 Yale lead when John Ederer's 84-yard touchdown run set up a 14–14 tie in the third quarter. Jim Ryan scored two of the Yale TDs on runs of 47 and 2 yards. The Elis, trailing 21–14, scored with 1:01 remaining in the game when substitute quarterback Ed Molloy connected with Ray Bright on a 14-yard pass. Bob Parcells kicked all three extra points including the game-tying kick.

1952 (7–2) Coach: Jordan Olivar; Captain: Joe Mitinger

Herman Hickman, who became a TV personality, unexpectedly resigned as Yale's head coach before the start of the season. He was replaced by Jordan Olivar, who was hired as an assistant on Hickman's staff. Born Giordano Olivari, he was a master of the Belly-T offense. He served as head coach at Villanova and Loyola Marymont before coming to Yale.

Yale captain Joe Mitinger has the distinction as being the last football captain photographed on the original Yale Fence in the Pach Brothers studio on Chapel St. in New Haven.

Chin straps were now made to fit snugly across the point of the chin, rather than under it. The Ivy League presidents decreed in the interests of not overemphasizing football that postseason games and spring practice would be banned.

Aug. 15: Olivar was named Yale's head coach five weeks before the start of the season after Hickman resigned.

Sept. 20: Yale beat UConn, 34–13, in Olivar's debut as head coach.

Oct. 4: Yale end Ed Woodsum scored four TDs in the Elis' 28–0 win over Brown. Woodsum snared three TD passes and pounced on a fumble in the end zone for the other. Bob Parcells kicked the four extra points.

Nov. 15: The Tigers clawed the Bulldogs for the sixth straight year. The game was highlighted by Homer Smith's 93-yard run that gave Princeton a 20–7 lead in a game they would win, 27–21. The Tigers finished No. 6 in the country in 1950 and 1951.

Nov. 22: In a game called by legendary announcer Russ Hodges, Ed Molloy tossed a Yale-record (vs. Harvard) four touchdown passes, three to Woodsum (4, 26, 58 yards) who broke Larry Kelley's all-time career TD reception record in Yale's 41–14 win on a dark, drizzly afternoon at Harvard Stadium. But history focuses on Charlie Yeager, Yale's 5-foot-6, 122-pound student manager, who snared a PAT pass from Molloy for Yale's 41st point. Yeager, who enjoyed playing catch with the players, was told during the preseason by the coaching staff that if Yale had a big lead over Harvard, they would put him in the game. At halftime Yeager put on uniform No. 99.

Molloy took the snap for the extra point by Bob Parcells. But Molloy did not place the ball as usual. Instead he rose from his knees, ran to his right and floated it to Yeager in the end zone. The Harvard side viewed this as a "rubbing it in" tactic. Ironically, the game day cover program had an illustration of a generic Yale player leading the team on the field wearing No. 99.

Yale's 41 points was exceeded in the series only by the Yale team of 1884 that spanked Harvard, 52–0. Entering the 2019 season the Yale-Harvard series has produced more than 3,600 points. No doubt the point scored by Yeager was the most unique.

1953 (5–2–2) Coach: Jordan Olivar; Captain: Joe Fortunato

Yale captain Joe Fortunato is pictured against a different Yale Fence, one that captains of all sports at Yale have been photographed since 1953. At last report, the original Yale Fence was in the hands of a resident in the shoreline area of Connecticut.

The NCAA established "iron man" football that lasted for a decade. The rules prohibited a player from returning to a game in the same quarter in which he was taken out, except in the last four minutes of each half. This convoluted system resulted in players playing both ways and remaining on the field for long periods of time, thus killing the platoon system that most likely favored the larger college programs.

Oct. 16: In order to avoid the roundabout train routes to Ithaca, New York, the Yale football team traveled by air for the first time. The team departed from the Bridgeport Municipal Airport in the town of Stratford. Yale obtained the charter of a giant Pan American DC-6B, the same type of plane used by Pan Am for trans-oceanic flights. Flying time each way was approximately one hour.

Oct. 17: The shortened trip to upstate New York did not energize Yale's offense as the Bulldogs and Cornell played to a scoreless tie.

Oct. 31: Yale laid an egg as Dartmouth upset the Elis, 32–0, in the Bowl. The Elis were unbeaten though twice tied, yielding just two touchdowns in five games. Dartmouth arrived winless, having lost five in a row. But the Big Green's Bill Beagle lit up the Yale defense, throwing four touchdown passes. Leo McKenna tossed a fifth. Dartmouth established a school record with six fumbles recovered against the Blue that led to the vexing loss.

Nov. 7: Yale beat Temple, 32–6, in a game played in four inches of wet snow that held the paltry attendance to 3,500, the smallest Bowl attendance in 12 years. Yale was forced to cancel its freshman game. Fullback Connie Corelli, who totaled 69 yards, managed a 51-yard scoring run.

Larry Reno, a 5-foot-7, 160-pound junior sprinter and hurdler, who ran the 60-yard dash in 6.4 seconds and 9.9 in the 100 (Yale's SID Charley Loftus said 9.7), joined the team during the week. He had played at East Denver High School and for a season at Andover. Aware that the football team was depleted with injuries, he asked his track coach, the noted Bob Giegengack, for permission to speak to Yale football coach Jordan Olivar about helping the team. Both Giegengack and Olivar consented. Reno got in for one play against Temple, although his name did not appear in the program. Reno was not allowed to block or tackle in practice.

Nov. 14: One year after a student manager scored an extra point for Yale, Reno impacted one of the greatest Yale-Princeton games ever played. Trailing, 17–0, at the half, Yale staged a comeback for the ages. Yale QB Bobby Brink opened the scoring in the second half on a 7-yard run. The Tigers fumbled the kickoff and the ball was recovered on the Tigers' 37 yard line by Connie Corelli. Pete Shears then scored from the 2-yard line. On the kickoff, Yale tackle Phil Tarasovic forced a fumble from Art Pitts that was recovered by John Phillips on the Princeton 34. On the final play of the third quarter, Jimmy Lopez, who replaced Brink at QB, ran 25 yards for a touchdown to give Yale a 20–17 lead. Hub Pruett, who had kicked the two first extra points, missed the third. Undaunted, the Tigers regained the lead, 24–20, when Royce Flippin ran 68 yards to the end zone before Dick Martin kicked the extra point.

Reno, wearing number 88, played briefly in the first half before returning to the game with 42 seconds left. He caught a 43-yard pass from Lopez and took it down to the Princeton 12, beating Tigers captain Homer Smith on the play. Smith was aware of Reno's speed because they raced against each other twice in the low hurdles and split.

The play was called "8-Z-In." With 24 seconds left in the game, the knockout punch came when Lopez passed to Bobby Poole, who caught the ball at the 3-yard line to score the winning touchdown. Thanks to the unexpected heroics of a Yale track star, Yale ended a six-year hex of consecutive Princeton victories over Yale led by coach Charlie Caldwell's single-wing offense. The Tigers hadn't lost to Yale or Harvard since 1946.

Because of Reno's heroics, the *New York Herald Tribune* wrote, "the names of immortals like [Frank] Merriwell and [Dink] Stover sound like bit players."

Nov. 21: Yale's euphoric victory over Princeton was short-lived when they fell to Harvard, 13–0, on touchdown runs by Dexter Lewis (22 yards) and John Culver (35). Reno got into one uneventful play and earned a major "Y" letter in football since he met the requirement of playing in the Princeton and Harvard games.

Following the game, several fans, mostly from Massachusetts, reported car thefts. Among the items pilfered were a diamond ring ($200), a camera ($100), a topcoat and suit ($150), a coat ($75), a birthstone ring ($50) and $90 in cash. In each instance, police said, ventilator windows in the automobiles had been forced.

A few miles down the road a car was overturned in the West Rock tunnel shortly before kickoff. Anxious to get to the game, several motorists, who were blocked by the overturned vehicle, righted it and everybody drove away. When an investigating state trooper arrived, he could find no sign of a traffic tie-up.

1954 (5–3–1) Coach: Jordan Olivar; Captain: Thorne Shugart

The Presidents' Agreement of 1954 brought the Ivy League colleges together under a pact that covered scheduling, eligibility, scholarships, spring practice and postseason play. Informally, it was known as the "Ivy Group."

Sept. 25: Yale opened its season with a 27–0 win over UConn. Yale abandoned their white pants and unveiled gold (or mustard-colored) pants that they wore as part of their home uniform through 1959. Former Yale defensive coordinator Buddy Amendola co-captained the Huskies with John Cunningham.

Oct. 16: Yale gave Cornell a drubbing in the Bowl, winning, 47–21. Anne Morrissy, the first female sports editor of the *Cornell Daily Sun*, broke a Yale press box tradition of granting access to only male working reporters, a practice supported by sports information director Charley Loftus. Misspelling her surname, the syndicated columnist Red Smith wrote in The *New York Herald Tribune*, "Miss Morrisy is a slick little chick whose name probably will be linked in history with those of other crusading cupcakes such as Lady Godiva, Susan B. Anthony, Lydia Pinkham and Mrs. Amelia Bloomer." He continued, "the first sports writing doll to thrust her shapely foot through the door of an Ivy League press coop, she has breached the last bastion of masculinity left standing this side of the shower room." Conversely, *New Haven Register* reporter John J. Leary presented her with a corsage on behalf of the Connecticut Sports Writers Alliance.

Two decades later as Anne Morrissy Merick, she became the first female television field producer for ABC-TV and requested an assignment to cover combat in the Vietnam War. At the time, General William Westmoreland issued an edict barring women from such hazardous duty. Morrissy Merick joined forces with her colleagues and successfully lobbied the Pentagon and Secretary of Defense Robert McNamara to lift the ban. Anne Morrissy Merick, a trailblazer in her field, cracked two male preserves during her historic journalistic career.

Nov. 6: Army, No. 6 in the UP poll and No. 7 in the AP poll, ambushed Yale, 48–7, before a sellout crowd of 70,890. Army's Tommy Bell scampered 64 yards for a TD on the Cadets' first possession to begin the blowout. Bob Kyasky aded two TDs for the Cadets.

UP female reporter Faye Loyd was denied access to the Yale Bowl press box just three weeks after Morrissy was allowed access. Yale SID Charley Loftus, offered her a seat in the top row of the stands where she balanced a typewriter on her knees and filed her report with someone handing statistics to her through the scaffolding that supported the press box. There was an uproar from other journalists and publications, all critical of Yale and Loftus, who soon changed his policy and welcomed all.

Nov.13: Princeton's Royce Flippin crossed the goal line on a 1-yard plunge with 15 seconds left in the game to give the Tigers a 21–14 win over Yale.

Nov. 20: Harvard scored 13 points in the last quarter to overcome a 9–0 deficit and deliver a heartbreaking loss to Yale, 13–9. Tony Gianelly (1-yard run) and Bob Cochran (39-yard pass from Frank White) scored the Cantabs' TDs. End By Campbell accounted for nearly all of Yale's points. He scored on a 7-yard touchdown pass from Bob Brink in the third quarter and he tackled Harvard's Matt Botsford in the end zone for a safety in the first quarter after Botsford intercepted a pass and his momentum took him into the end zone.

1955 (7–2) Coach: Jordan Olivar; Captain: Philip Tarasovic

In this era, the talented backfield tandem of Dennis McGill and Al Ward terrorized opponents.

Oct. 8: McGill scored four touchdowns against Columbia in the Bowl as the Bulldogs routed the Lions, 46–14.

Nov. 5: Yale upset 19th-ranked (AP) and undefeated Army, 14–12, before 61,000 in the Bowl. Using a 6–3–2 defense to stifle Army's running game, the win knocked the Black Knights of the Hudson out of the Top 20. End Paul Lopata and halfback Al Ward scored Yale's two TDs while Dick Winterbauer kicked the two

The game day program for the November 5, 1955, Yale-Army game.

extra points that proved to be the difference. Yale's stouthearted defense stalled Army's running game with captain and tackle Phil Tarasovic and linebacker Mike Owseichik leading the way. The Cadets lost five fumbles. Following the game, Tarasovic carried the game ball into the stands and presented it to his father. Also, a fight reportedly broke out between several players but it stopped abruptly when the Army band played the national anthem.

Nov. 19: In an effort to motivate the Crimson, the words REMEMBER CHARLEY YEAGER were chalked prominently in block letters at the Dillon Field House during the week leading up to The Game. It was, however, a failed exercise as Yale beat Harvard, 21–7, in the New Haven snow that peppered the 56,000 frozen customers, some of whom wore raccoon coats reminiscent of the '20s. Red Smith wrote, "This was football's holy of holies, the 72nd presentation of THE GAME between Harvard and Yale, wet as a baptismal font and cold as the Puritan conscience."

The Elis' Gene Coker sliced through the Harvard line for 105 yards, more than the entire Harvard backfield combined. The Yale TDs were scored by Vern Loucks on a 7-yard pass toss from Dean Loucks (no relation), Al Ward on a 1-yard run and McGill, who scampered 39 yards with a pass interception.

The Crimson's only touchdown came late in the third period on an 8-yard pass from Walt Stahura to Ted Kennedy, the future United States senator, capping a 92-yard drive. Kennedy made a shoestring catch in the north end zone after the ball had been deflected by teammate Dexter Lewis. Bing Crosby, no relation to the crooner, kicked the extra point. In attendance were Kennedy's brothers John F., a future President of the United States, and Bobby, a future U.S. senator and attorney general of the United States and father, Joe, a Harvard alum who played baseball against Yale in 1911. Connecticut Governor Abe Ribicoff and New York Mayor Robert Wagner were also in the chilly crowd.

Tarasovic presented the game ball to Bob Spears, the 1951 Yale captain, who was stricken with polio the previous spring.

1956 (8–1) Ivy League Champs (outright) Coach: Jordan Olivar; Captain: John Owseichik

Yale won the Ivy League championship in the first season of formal Ivy League play and finished 17th in the UP poll. The Bulldogs scored 246 points, the most since the 1903 team and won their first H-Y-P title since 1946.

Oct. 7: Yale's touchdown twins "Dennis the Menace" McGill and Al Ward paced the Elis to a 20–2 win over Brown. Dick Winterbauer's 70-yard pass play to McGill was the Bulldogs' big play in the game. Brown captain Dick Bence and Yale QB Dean Loucks swapped punches with six minutes left to play in the third quarter and both were banished for the rest of the game.

Left to right: **Gene Coker, Dennis McGill, Dean Loucks and Al Ward.**

Oct. 27: Colgate delivered Yale's only loss of the season, 14–6.

Nov. 3: McGill, Yale's whirling dervish halfback, ran for a school-record 93-yard TD run in their 19–0 win over Dartmouth. The record would last for 57 years.

Nov. 17: Yale earned the Ivy League's first official football championship with a 42–20 victory over previously unbeaten Princeton before 68,000 in the Bowl. McGill caught two touchdown passes and threw one for the Elis, who made it a runaway by scoring five times in the first half. Yale's Charlie Griffith blocked a punt that was recovered by Steve Ackerman, who ran 50 yards for a score.

Nov. 24: The Bulldogs bashed Harvard, 42–14. Seven minutes after the opening kickoff, McGill, who racked up 116 yards, scored for the first time on a 2-yard run and the touchdown parade was on its way. In the second quarter, McGill took a pitchout from quarterback Dean Loucks and ran 78 yards to the end zone. After Jim Joslin ran 39 yards for a Harvard score in the second quarter, Ward answered when he took a Harvard kickoff and returned it 79 yards for another score. Steve Ackerman then scored on a 13-yard pass play from Loucks to give the Bulldogs a 28–7 lead at the half.

Al Ward and Dennis McGill worked together to run roughshod over Yale opponents.

In the second half Paul Lopata (8-yard pass from Dick Winterbauer) and Herb Hallas (2-yard run) both scored. John Simourian tallied Harvard's other TD in the third quarter on a 1-yard plunge. Vern Loucks kicked five extra points for the Elis, who finished undefeated in the Ivy.

1957 (6–2–1) Coach: Jordan Olivar; Captain: Jack Embersits

Oct. 5: Frank Finney's 10-yard run with 55 seconds left in the game and Marty Moran's extra- point kick gave Brown a pulsating 21–20 win over Yale.

Nov. 16: Yale beat Princeton, 20–13, before a capacity crowd of 46,000 at Palmer Stadium. Yale receiver Mike Cavallon, enjoying his finest hour, caught three touchdown passes. Before the end of the game the Yale fans waved the traditional handkerchiefs at the Princeton fans in derision.

Nov. 23: Yale unleashed a devastating offensive attack destroying a stolidly, overmatched Harvard eleven in a 54–0 uprising in the Bowl, the

THE HIGHLIGHTS   1958

largest margin of victory for either side in the series. This was Harvard coach John Yovicsin's first game against Yale and he was given a rude howdy-do. With Yale leading, 34–0, at the half, one of the Harvard classes dispatched a telegram to Yale coach Jordan Olivar to "please" take it easy on the Crimson in the second half.

Herb Hallas scored three touchdowns on runs of 4 and 3 yards and a 58-yard pass from Winterbauer, who cut Harvard into ribbons. The precision-throwing QB also connected with Cavallon for a score. The famed Red Grange, "The Galloping Ghost," and broadcaster Lindsey Nelson covered the game on TV.

1958 (2–7) Coach: Jordan Olivar; Captain: Paul Lynch

Located in the north end zone, the first electrified scoreboard appeared in the Bowl. The two-point conversion, an idea discussed during Walter Camp's lifetime, went into effect for college football.

Oct. 4: A solid Brown team led by QB Frank Finney, fullback Paul Choquette and center-linebacker Don Warburton, beat Yale in a barnburner, 35–29, in Providence.

Nov. 8: Yale's Herb Hallas set an Ivy League record when he returned a punt 94 yards in Yale's 30–6 loss to Penn. Hallas got great initial blocks from Rich Winkler and Matt Freeman.

Nov. 15: After Yale defeated Princeton in back-to-back years, the Tigers devoured the Bulldogs, 50–14. The deflating loss was only the second time that a Yale team ever surrendered 50 points in a game.

Herb Hallas' 94-yard punt return against Penn in 1958 remains the longest punt return in Yale football history.

Nov. 22: A round-trip train ticket from New Haven to Boston for the Yale-Harvard game was $7.08. Yale fans rode home glum as the Crimson beat the Bulldogs, 28–0, in the 75th playing of The Game. It was payback for Harvard after losing, 54–0, to the Elis the year before. Harvard sophomore QB Charley Ravenel, who spearheaded several scoring drives for the Cantabs, scored on a 7-yard run on the last play of the second quarter. In the second half, Ravenel lit the fuse for scoring runs of 20 and 17 yards by Chet Boulris and Larry Repsher. Albie Cullen went over from the 2 yard line to complete the rout. Harvard entered the game 3–5 while Yale was 2–6.

1959 (6–3) Coach: Jordan Olivar; Captain: Richard Winkler

Led by the running of Winkler, who started every game for three years, Yale started the season unbeaten, untied and unscored upon in its first five games but lost their last three out of four contests.

The goal post was widened from 18 feet, 6 inches to 23 feet, 4 inches to encourage kicking. The point after touchdown became virtually automatic. In 1990, the distance was restored to the current 18 feet, 6 inches. Members of the Yale Precision Marching Band gave the Bowl a facelift by painting the 17 miles of seats.

March 1: Albie Booth died unexpectedly in New York City of a heart attack after attending a Broadway play. Many ex-teammates and Army coach Earl "Red" Blaik were among the dignitaries who attended the funeral at the Our Lady of Mount Carmel Roman Catholic Church in Hamden, Connecticut.

Sept. 26: Tradition was restored when Yale wore new white pants, replacing the mustard-colored ones it had worn for five years, and rolled to a 20–0 victory over Connecticut.

Oct. 24: Yale beat Colgate, 21–0, to go through its first five games unbeaten, untied and unscored upon, something that Yale had not done since 1909 and a feat no major college team had accomplished since 1943. The Elis were ranked 15th in the nation, tied with Oklahoma.

Oct. 31: The magic carpet ride ended on this Halloween day as Dartmouth spoiled Yale's perfect season with a 12–8 win in a driving rain in the Bowl. The Bulldogs allowed its first points of the season with 10 minutes and 46 seconds remaining in the third quarter when Dartmouth QB Bill Gundy tossed the first of two TD passes for the Green.

Nov. 14: Yale QB Tom Singleton did everything but sell tickets in the Elis' 38–20 win over Princeton at Palmer Stadium. The blonde, crew cut signal caller from Illinois threw for 108 yards (completing all eight of his pass attempts) and a touchdown, ran for 26 yards and a touchdown, kicked three extra points, punted three times, intercepted a pass, and added a two-point conversion pass.

Nov. 21: Harvard halfback Chet Boulris connected with Hank Keohane for an 85-yard touchdown pass that ignited Harvard's 35–6 win. The 35 points were the most Harvard had inflicted on their rival since 1915. Boulris also scored on a 13-yard run. Crimson QB Charley Ravenel, "The Gambler," rolled up 386 yards of total offense and crossed the goal line on two short runs. Yale's only score came on a 60-yard pass from Singleton to Kenny Wolfe. The crowd of 66,053 was the largest at the Bowl since the 1954 Yale-Army game.

1960 (9–0) Ivy League Champs (outright) Coach: Jordan Olivar; Captain: Michael Pyle

The 1960 team that finished 9–0 is the last undefeated, untied eleven in Yale football history. Frank Birmingham, the sports editor of the *New Haven Journal-Courier* in 1960, met President John F. Kennedy early in 1963 at a college football induction ceremony in New York City. As Birmingham extended his hand upon being introduced, the president asked, "Was Yale's undefeated 1960 team really as good as its record?"

Yale, who finished 18th in the UPI poll, was voted a share of the Lambert Trophy, symbol of Eastern football supremacy. The Elis were ranked 14th in the season-ending AP poll ahead of 16th-ranked Penn State and 19th-ranked Syracuse.

Sept. 24: Yale, destined to go undefeated and ranked in the nation's Top 20, needed all its defensive strength to subdue UConn, 11–8. Wally Grant, an obscure fifth-string sophomore QB, kicked the deciding field goal, a 37-yarder, in the fourth quarter.

Oct. 1: In the 300th game played in the Bowl, Grant's 29-yard field goal in the third quarter gave Yale a 3–0 lead in a game the Bulldogs won, 9–0, over Brown. The Blue defense, led by Mike Pyle and AP All-American Ben Balme, also known as "The Embalmer" for his vicious hits, stopped Bears drives at the 4-yard line and the 1-yard line. Ted Hard's touchdown plunge gave Yale its final margin. Pyle played nine years with the Chicago Bears and was their offensive team captain from 1963 to 1969.

Oct. 22: Yale fullback Bob Blanchard stole the show as Yale took apart Colgate, 36–14. Blanchard not only intercepted a pass and ran 99 yards for a touchdown, he also tossed a 37-yard TD aerial to John Hutcherson.

Nov. 12: Yale completed its eight-game home schedule by blitzing Princeton, 43–22. QB Tom Singleton fired three touchdown passes, two to Kenny Wolfe.

Nov. 19: Yale scorched Harvard, 39–6, to cap its first undefeated and untied season since 1923, outscoring their opponents, 253–73. Kenny Wolfe's 41-yard TD run on Yale's first snap off a fake to Blanchard, and Hutcherson's 42-yard interception return for a TD was too much for the Crimson to overcome. Connie Shimer snared two Bill Leckonby passes (15 and 3 yards) for touchdowns. Ed Kaake added a 33-yard field goal in the second quarter. The Elis led, 39–0, before Harvard scored their lone TD on QB Charley Ravenel's 2-yard run.

Left to right: Ben Balme, Tom Singleton, Hardy Will and Bob Blanchard. The four greats from Yale's last undefeated 1960 team recall the glory days at Mory's (courtesy Bill O'Brien).

1961 (4–5) Coach: Jordan Olivar; Captain: Paul Bursiek

Oct. 14: Columbia blanked Yale in the Bowl, 11–0, busting Yale's 11-game winning streak dating back to the start of the 1960 season. The Lions under coach Aldo "Buff" Donelli, and captained by Bill Campbell, shared the Ivy championship with Harvard. It is Columbia's only Ivy crown.

The Highlights   1962

Oct. 28: Colgate downed the Elis, 14–8, beating Harvard, Princeton and Yale on successive weekends.

Nov. 11: The Elis had their way against Penn in Philadelphia, winning, 23–0. Yale back Lee Marsh, who rushed for 112 yards, was named the "Back of the Week," beating out Syracuse great and eventual Heisman Trophy winner Ernie Davis. Yale's Lyn Hinojosa suffered a broken neck when he made a cross-body block on a kickoff return for running back Hank Higdon. Hinojosa remained in a Philadelphia hospital for several weeks and never played again.

Nov. 25: Harvard trounced Yale, 27–0, in the Bowl in one of the worst performances by any Yale team against the Crimson. A Yale fumble in the early minutes was recovered by Harvard captain Pete Hart on the Yale 15. This led to Scott Harshbarger's 2-yard TD. Harvard then kicked off but the Yale return men, acting as if it was a punt, left the ball untouched on the Yale 26. The loose ball was recovered by Harvard tackle Dick Diehl. This led to robust fullback Bill Grana's 16-yard TD run.

Things didn't improve in the second half for the sluggish Bulldogs. After Bill Taylor scored on a 9-yard toss from Mike Bassett, the comedy of errors continued for Yale in the last quarter when a snap from center got away from QB Bill Leckonby and was recovered in the end zone by Harvard's Dave Nyhan.

An old-fashioned ruckus broke out near the end of the game when Leckonby attempted to block the extra point. Leckonby laid out the holder with a forearm shiver which led to the brawl and ejection of several players. Incredibly, it was the only time Leckonby's father, the head football coach at Lehigh, saw his son play at Yale.

Yale captain Paul Bursiek and Hart are pictured on the front cover of the Yale-Harvard game day program. This began the tradition of the respective captains appearing on the front cover of the Yale-Harvard game day programs that has continued ever since.

1962 (2–5–2) Coach: Jordan Olivar; Captain: Henry Higdon

Jordan Olivar, in his final season as Yale's head football coach, went with a three-platoon system—offense, defense and general utility. Defensively, the system had merit as Yale yielded no more than two touchdowns in any of its nine games yet won only two. At the end of the season, Olivar, under pressure from alumni to spend more time in New Haven, resigned to pursue his insurance business interests in California. "Ollie"'s record was an impressive 61–32–6 that included two Ivy league titles.

Oct. 20: The 130-piece Harvard band, on their way to the Harvard-Columbia game in New York City, stopped by the Yale campus, waking up some 5,000 Yale students at 4:30 a.m. by playing "Ten Thousand Men of Harvard," "Harvardiana," and a few anti–Yale blasts. Seven Harvard students were charged with disturbing the peace and parading without a license and were released on $50 bail each.

Oct. 21: Did the Harvard band awaken a sleepy Yale offense that scored a total of 34 points the first three games when the Elis went 1–1–1? Yale won its first Ivy League contest of the season, thoroughly asserting its mastery over Cornell, 26–8. Yale QB Brian Rapp threw for two touchdowns and the Elis picked off three Cornell passes to beat the Big Red for the fourth consecutive year.

Yale's pass defense limited future NFL QB Gary Wood to two completions in 13 attempts. Pete Cummings, Yale's 200-pound sophomore fullback, scored on a 19-yard TD run at the end of an 80-yard drive. Wally Grant kicked field goals of 39 and 36 yards, breaking the record of three in one season set by Billy Booe in 1947.

Nov. 3: Dartmouth downed Yale, 9–0, in adverse weather conditions that Joseph M. Sheehan in the *New York Times* described as "atrocious with chill winds and lashing rain that made the Bowl a place of acute misery. With both teams sticking mainly to the ground and only two penalties called, they got it over with in 1 hour and 52 minutes." All-America linebacker Don McKinnon led a sturdy Dartmouth defense and quarterback Bill King engineered just enough offense for a 9–0 win that moved the Green along toward a 9–0 season.

Nov. 17: Princeton edged Yale, 14–10, in the Bowl despite an illegal 6-yard pass play that was thrown for an Eli touchdown. The pass was thrown by Yale fullback Pete Cummings after he had taken a pitch from QB Ed McCarthy. Following the pitch to Cummings, McCarthy went ahead of Cummings to block and turned downfield to the end zone where he caught Cummings's pass. The play was illegal for two reasons. McCarthy had taken a hand-to-hand snapback from the center in the close-up position of a T quarterback which made him ineligible to receive the pass, and it was a violation for him to be downfield.

Nov. 24: Jordan Olivar closed his Yale coaching career with a 14–6

THE HIGHLIGHTS   1963

loss to Harvard at Harvard Stadium. Bill Taylor and Fred Bartl, subbing for the injured Bill Grana, scored Harvard's TDs on short runs of 4 and 2 yards. Jack Cirie's 59-yard punt return touchdown proved to be Yale's only score.

The game was witnessed by former Harvard players Bobby Kennedy, the attorney general of the United States, and 1941 All-American defensive lineman Endicott "Chub" Peabody, who was later inducted into the College Football Hall of Fame.

1963 (6–3) Coach: John Pont; Captain: George Humphrey

March 6: John Pont was named Yale's head football coach. He enjoyed meteoric success. His record stood at 12–5–1 before his departure to Indiana University. His 1967 team was the only Hoosiers team to play in the Rose Bowl. Joe Paterno, an assistant at Penn State, was the second choice for the job.

Sept. 28: In Pont's debut, the Bulldogs had to work for a 3–0 decision over a pesky University of Connecticut team before 30,614 in the Bowl. Chuck Mercein, who led Yale in rushing in '63 and '64, saved the bacon with a 30-yard field goal that was set up by Jim Howard's 35-yard punt return.

Oct. 12: Pont won his first Ivy League game, a 19–7 win over Columbia on a sun-drenched, steamy day in the Bowl. Archie Roberts, the ballyhooed Lions quarterback who had a cup of coffee in the AFL, completed 13 of 24 passes for 176 yards, 164 of which were in the first half. He scored Columbia's only touchdown in the first quarter on a 4-yard run to set up the Lions 7–0 lead. Randy Egloff scored twice in the second half for the Elis

Oct. 19: Pete Gogolak's 33-yard FG with 45 seconds remaining in the game gave Cornell a 13–10 win over Yale. Gogolak, who is widely considered the chief figure behind the game's adoption of soccer-style placekicking, booted his way around pro football with the AFL Buffalo Bills and NFL New York Giants. Gogolak joins Calvin Hill (Yale, Dallas Cowboys) and Ed Marinaro (Cornell, Minnesota Vikings) as the only players to play regular-season games in the Bowl as collegians and pros.

Nov. 22: President John F. Kennedy was assassinated midway in the second quarter of the Yale-Harvard freshman game. The 14–14 tie game was completed but the players were not told of the tragedy until after the contest. The varsity game scheduled for the next day was postponed until the following week. The action of Yale and Harvard set a precedent as almost 90 percent of the nation's colleges followed suit.

Nov. 23: Reportedly, President Kennedy was planning to attend the game. The November 23 game day program featuring captains George Humphrey (Yale) and William Southmayd (Harvard) was distributed the following week.

Nov. 30: The Game was played on a somber, gray day in the Bowl before an estimated 51,000 as the nation mourned the death of a president. Following two consecutive losses to Harvard, the Elis rebounded with a 20–6 victory. Harvard drew first blood when Scott Harshbarger scored on a 38-yard screen pass from Mike Bassett. Jim Groninger's 5-yard TD run in the second quarter gave Yale a 7–6 lead they would never relinquish. Randy Egloff added to Harvard's pain on TD runs of 5 and 2 yards in the second half.

1964 (6–2–1) Coach: John Pont; Captain: H. Abbott Lawrence

Sept. 26: The Bowl continued to be a temple of doom for UConn. Chuck "The Truck" Mercein ran for 166 yards on 18 carries as Yale beat the Huskies, 21–6. The UConn score came on a 23-yard TD pass from Lou Aceto to Brian Kidd. The win gave Yale a record of 86–0 against Connecticut schools dating back to 1875.

Oct. 3: Yale became the first school in the country to win 600 football games, crushing Lehigh, 54–0, in the Bowl. Captain Ab Lawrence presented the game ball to university president Kingman Brewster Jr.

Oct. 24: Yale came from behind to beat Cornell in Ithaca, 23–21. Mercein staged a memorable performance when he kicked three field goals (48, 30, 46 yards) and ran for a TD. It was the 10th field goal of his career, a Yale record.

Nov. 14: One week shy of the 50th anniversary of the Yale Bowl, Princeton, en route to an undefeated season, upended Yale, 35–14, in a game billed as the "Battle of the Fullbacks"—Cosmo Iacavazzi vs. Chuck Mercein—a matchup that drew 61,173 fans to the Bowl. Iacavazzi, the marvelous Princeton running back who played briefly with the New York Jets, scored two touchdowns (39 and 47 yards) in the fourth quarter and each time fired the ball into the stands in the north end zone. Yale's Brian Dowling would answer Iacavazzi's insulting tosses with one of his own at Princeton three years later.

THE HIGHLIGHTS   1965

Mercein, who played seven years in the NFL with the Giants, Packers and Jets, missed the second half after suffering a season-ending thigh injury.

Nov. 21: On a sunny, cold day at Harvard Stadium, John Pont coached his final game at Yale, an 18–14 loss to the Crimson. Harvard, trailing, 14–12, in the fourth quarter, took the lead on Bobby Leo's 46-yard run. Harvard senior fullback Stan Yastrzemski, cousin of Boston Red Sox Hall of Famer Carl Yastrzemski, made the first start of his varsity career.

1965 (3–6) Coach: Carmen Cozza; Captain: F. David Laidley

Jan. 29: Carmen Cozza, an assistant on John Pont's staff and his college roommate, was named Yale's 31st head football coach after Joe Paterno turned down the offer. The job paid $14,000. Cozza, whose tenure lasted for 32 years, became the winningest coach in Ivy League history. Cozza hired a quality staff in Jim Root, Bill Narduzzi, Neil Putnam and Seb LaSpina and later added the likes of Buddy Amendola, Paul Amodio, Dave Kelley and others.

Two of the stars on Cozza's early teams were defensive tackles Bob Greenlee (All-Ivy) and Glenn Greenberg, who were known as the "Jolly Green Giants," at 6'4" and 6'2" respectively and both tipping the scale at approximately 240 pounds. Greenberg was the son of baseball Hall of Fame slugger Hank Greenberg. Ironically, it was Hank who signed Cozza to a minor-league contract in 1952 while the general manager of the Cleveland Indians.

Jan. 30: Two months after he took his final snap, Yale QB Ed McCarthy lost his life in a car accident while on a ski trip. McCarthy and two other Yale students, en route to Vermont for a skiing weekend, were driving along U.S. Route 5 near Greenfield, Massachusetts, when their car hit a snow bank, went out of control and struck a tree.

Sept. 25: Cozza made an inauspicious debut when UConn beat Yale, 13–6, for the first time since the rivalry began in 1948. Gene Campbell's 35-yard touchdown on an interception with four minutes to play sunk the Bulldogs. It was the first time Yale lost to any Connecticut school after 86 straight wins. An apocryphal rumor circulated that Cozza received a telegram from a disgruntled alum who said, "There's a train leaving for New York at 4 o'clock on Monday—be under it."

Oct. 9: After starting the season 0–2, Cozza won his first game as

Yale's new head coach, a 3–0 victory over Brown in Providence. QB Watts Humphrey, who competed for the QB job with Tone Grant and Pete Doherty, came off the bench to lead a drive that set up the field goal by Danny Begel, who was an outstanding cellist. This was music to Cozza's ears. He would call this win one of his biggest Ivy League wins ever.

Oct. 16: Columbia tripped Yale, 21–7, in New York for their first victory of the season. The Lions' senior flankerback, Roger Dennis, scored on a 54-yard punt return and a 6-yard run. A total of eight female cheerleaders recruited from the Connecticut College for Women in New London shouted in vain. It was the first time that Yale ever had female cheerleaders on the sideline. "We believe it is entirely fitting that Yale have girl cheerleaders," said George Brown, Yale's chief cheerleader. "It will help in the bid to make the university co-educational." Yale athletic director DeLaney Kiphuth stated, "It was an innovation, and a welcome one, but it's out as a regular stint on football Saturdays in the Yale Bowl."

Oct. 23: Led by QB Watts Humphrey, who rushed for 93 yards and completed 7 passes in 11 attempts for 91 yards, Yale beat Cornell, 24–14, in the Bowl. For his efforts, he was voted the Ivy League Player of the Week. Humphrey had good Yale pedigree. His father, Gil, was a QB and placekicker in the mid–1930s and his brother, George, was the 1963 Yale captain.

Following graduation, Humphrey enlisted in the military and was an infantry company commander in the Marines, serving in Vietnam. In 1968 his unit was involved in operations south of Da Nang, where he was hit by a rocket round of shrapnel. He was brought to a MASH unit where Dr. Ben Balme, the 1960 Yale All-American lineman, tended to him. The former Yale QB lost one-third of the muscle in his right forearm. But if it wasn't for Dr. Balme, he might have lost the use of his arm. The two have never met.

Nov. 6: Yale and Penn unwittingly celebrated the 25th anniversary of the famous "fifth down" Cornell-Dartmouth game. With seconds remaining in the contest, the Quakers had a first down at midfield trailing, 21–19. On first down, Penn QB Bill Creeden was thrown for a 17-yard loss. On 2nd-and-27, Creeden threw an incomplete pass. He then completed a pass to put the ball on the Yale 29 where it was 4th-and-9. At this point with seconds remaining, Creeden threw the ball out of bounds, apparently thinking it was third down.

It should have been Yale's ball with a tick on the clock. But everyone, including the officials, fell asleep on the downs. On the "fifth down" Creeden threw a pass that was intercepted by Chris Beutler on the Yale 15. The game ended as Beutler was run out of bounds. Penn coach Bob Odell said, "Everyone was thinking of the time, not the down."

The game was almost a replay of the Cornell-Dartmouth game of November 16, 1940, when nationally ranked Cornell scored the winning touchdown on what was determined on film the following day as the "fifth down." Cornell officials conceded the game to Dartmouth (3–4), giving the Indians a 3–0 win which ended Cornell's 18-game winning streak. Red Friesell, one of the game officials, sent a telegram to the Dartmouth president that read, "I want to be the first to admit my very grave error on the extra down, as proven by the motion pictures of both colleges."

Nov. 20: Harvard beat Yale, 13–0, in the Bowl. Bobby Leo again proved to be a thorn in Yale's side. For the day he rushed for 61 yards, including a 4-yard TD run in the third quarter that broke a scoreless tie. He also caught three passes for 27 yards. Tom Choquette scored the other Harvard TD in the final frame on a 1-yard blast. Harvard capitalized on two picks against Yale QB Watts Humphrey in the second half.

1966 (4–5) Coach: Carmen Cozza; Captain: Robert F. Greenlee

Sept. 24: Yale legend Brian Dowling made the first varsity start of his vaunted career and threw two TD passes in the Bulldogs' 16–0 win over UConn. He would toss 30 TD passes in his Yale career.

Oct. 1: Rutgers beat Yale, 17–14, in a torrential rainstorm that drew 16,764. Broadcaster Dick Galiette said, "The rain was terrible that day. Our booth was filled with water and I was clutching a metal microphone and worrying about being electrocuted." Down, 17–0, entering the final quarter, the Elis clawed back but the Scarlet Knights thwarted the Yale comeback. Dowling suffered a season-ending knee injury in the second quarter.

Oct. 15: Yale quarterback Pete Doherty threw five touchdown passes to lead Yale to a 44–21 win over Columbia in the Bowl. Columbia quarterback Marty Domres, who later played for several different NFL teams, passed for 326 yards in a losing effort. The only other quarterbacks to throw five touchdown passes in the Bowl are Dartmouth's Greg Smith (2001) and Yale's Jeff Mroz (2005 vs. Cornell).

Nov. 5: Dan Begel's 29-yard field goal with 21 seconds to go gave Yale a 17–14 decision over Penn at Franklin Field.

Nov. 12: Princeton beat Yale for the sixth straight year and the 15th time in the last 20 years. Yale led Princeton, 7–6, with 3:02 left in the game when Tigers captain Walt Kozumbo blocked a Bob Kenney punt after a low snap. Larry Stupski grabbed the rolling ball and raced 42 yards for the touchdown, giving the Tigers a pulsating 13–7 win.

Stupski changed his stripes after his days at Old Nassau. While attending Yale Law School he played on the rugby team. Graduate students were eligible to play rugby because it was run on a club basis.

Nov. 19: Halfback Bobby Leo continued to haunt the Elis. He rushed for 106 yards, including two TDs, one a 52-yard gallop in the fourth quarter as Yale was blanked by Harvard, 17–0. Jim Babcock added a 29-yard field goal and kicked both extra points. During Leo's varsity career, he scored at least one touchdown in every game he played against Yale.

1967 (8–1) Ivy League Champs (outright). Coach: Carmen Cozza; Captain: Rodney Watson

The return of unlimited substitutions, permitting two-platoon football was welcomed by most. The tandem of Brian Dowling and Calvin Hill proved to be a joint football monarchy inextricably linked à la Larry Kelley–Clint Frank and Dennis McGill–Al Ward. Dowling was a magnetic force and Hill might have been the greatest athlete ever to attend Yale. Cozza emerged from behind the coaching curtain to exalted coaching status. Following an ignoble 7–11 record in his first two seasons, Cozza's teams would win 107 of their next 137 games (107–27–3), including 10 Ivy championships as the fortunes of Yale football rose to a peak of excellence.

Sept. 30: The Elis, playing without star quarterback Brian Dowling, suffered their only loss of the season, losing to Holy Cross, 26–14, on opening day.

Oct. 7: Yale defeated UConn on a clear, crisp day, 14–6, giving the Bulldogs an 18–1 edge in the intra-state series. The big play for the Bulldogs was produced by Calvin Hill early in the last quarter. The great halfback, who wanted to be Yale's first black quarterback, threw a surprise 32-yard touchdown pass to tight end Bruce Weinstein, giving Yale a 7–6 lead. An interception by Pat Madden set up a 3-yard TD by Hill with two minutes remaining. Dan Begel converted both extra-point attempts.

The Highlights 1968

Nov. 2: Lieutenant Woody Knapp, who lettered as a defensive back in '63 and '64, became a naval aviator and gave his life in air combat in the skies over North Vietnam.

Nov. 4: The Bulldog was ferocious on this day, devouring Dartmouth with ease, 56–15. Dartmouth was coming off a last-second win over Harvard that kept the Green undefeated. Dowling uncorked a 67-yard touchdown pass, ran 30 yards for a score and made it a Yale runaway, 35–2, at the half.

Nov. 18: Yale beat Princeton, 29–7, at Palmer Stadium to break the Tigers' six-year hex on the Elis. The win put the Bulldogs on a 14-year winning streak against the Men of Nassau. After scoring Yale's first TD on a pass from Hill, Dowling fired the ball into the Princeton stands toward the direction of the school's president, answering Cosmo Iacavazzi's humiliating stunts from the '64 game.

Nov. 25: In a game replete with several heart-stopping moments, Yale beat Harvard, 24–20, capturing the Ivy league title before 68,135 screaming fans in the Bowl and breaking Harvard's three-year hex. Dowling hit Del Marting with a 66-yard touchdown pass with 2:16 remaining for the winning score in what was one of the more seminal moments in Bowl history.

The Crimson came roaring back and were headed toward the Yale goal line when Ken O'Connell fumbled on the 10-yard line with 56 seconds left in the game. Pat Madden recovered the loose ball.

Yale opened the scoring in the second quarter when Marting recovered a Harvard fumble and carried the pigskin in for a 1-yard score. Hill then scored on a 53-yard pass from Dowling before Danny Begel kicked a 36-yard FG, giving the Elis a 17–0 lead. Crimson QB Ric Zimmerman connected with Ray Hornblower for a 14-yard TD late in the first half, pulling Harvard within 17–7. The Cantabs' Vic Gatto's 3-yard run cut the Yale lead to 17–13 in the third quarter and Harvard went ahead in the final frame after Carter Lord scored on a 31-yard pass from Zimmerman. Yale trailed, 20–17, before Dowling worked his magic. The large throng had witnessed one of the greatest games ever played in the historic saucer.

1968 (8–0–1) Ivy League Champs. Coach: Carmen Cozza; Captain: Brian Dowling

Oct. 12: Yale's offensive machine racked up a school-record 614 yards in a 35–13 win over Brown.

1968

Nov. 2: Yale vanquished Dartmouth, 47–27. Dowling set two Eli records. He gained 324 yards of total offense—295 by passing. The masterful QB completed 14 of 22 passes, three good for touchdowns, to Hill (38 yards), Marting (15) and Lew Roney (20). Hill gained 102 yards rushing and snared five passes for 122 yards. He also completed two of four passes, one for a touchdown to tight end Bruce Weinstein.

Nov. 9: Hill tipped a high pass away from a defensive back, caught the ball as it came down and scored on a 52-yard play as Yale stayed unbeaten by crushing Penn, 30–13, at Franklin Field. Hill also rushed for 126 yards and a touchdown on 19 carries.

Nov. 16: Yale won its 16th consecutive game by barreling Princeton, 42–17, in the Bowl.

Nov. 23: For the first time since 1909, both Yale and Harvard entered The Game undefeated and untied. One writer billed the game as "Mr. Magic" (Brian Dowling) vs. the "Boston Stranglers" (Harvard's defense). Tickets were scalped for as high as $160. Yale's allotment of 15,000 tickets sold out immediately. To pacify those excluded, the Yale Club of New Haven sponsored a closed-circuit television broadcast of the contest at the New Haven Arena.

But Yale's quest for a perfect season was stymied by a Harvard comeback that defied belief and continues to resonate. It was the third time the Crimson had spoiled a Yale perfect season (1921, 1938 and 1968). Down, 22–0, Frank Champi replaced George Lalich at QB in the second quarter and put the Crimson on the board with a 15-yard pass to Bruce Freeman. Harvard trailed, 22–6, at the half and 29–13 with 42 seconds remaining in the game before Champi connected with Freeman for a 15-yard TD pass, making the score 29–19. Champi then threw an incomplete pass to Pete Varney trying for the two points but Yale was called for pass interference. Fullback Gus Crim then carried the ball in from the 1 to make the score 29–21. Yale subsequently fumbled an onside kick from Harvard's Ken Thomas that was recovered by Harvard's Bill Kelly on the Yale 49. The game clock reportedly never started, and 42 seconds still remained on the clock following the recovery. Champi then ran for 14 yards to the Yale 35 and a face mask penalty against the Elis advanced the ball to the 20 with 32 seconds left in the game. Three plays later Crim ran 14 yards up the middle on a draw play to the Yale 6. Following a loss of two yards, Champi tossed an 8-yard TD pass to 5'6" captain Vic Gatto, the first back in Harvard history to rush for 2,000 yards. With no time left on the clock, Harvard now trailed, 29–27, before Champi connected with Varney for the two-point conversion as the game ended at 29–29. Yale's 22-point blown lead was second in team history to the 23-point blown lead vs. Dartmouth in 1931 that ended in a 33–33 tie.

One might blame the loss on Yale's six lost fumbles or its inability to use the clock effectively, but It was Champi's day. The two teams shared the Ivy title and the *Harvard Crimson* bannered, "Harvard Beats Yale, 29–29." To that, former New York governor George Pataki (Yale '67), answered, "Like all Yale fans, I take some solace in the knowledge that Harvard considers a tie with Yale to be its greatest 'victory,' while Yale considers the tie with Harvard to be its worst 'defeat.' How appropriate."

Hill rushed for 92 yards and scored one touchdown, passing the fabled Albie Booth for most points (144) in a Yale career. He also scored 24 touchdowns and passed for six in his Yale career before playing 12 seasons in the NFL, mostly with the Dallas Cowboys, and one season in the World Football League.

Dowling, who closed his career with eight Yale records, ran for two touchdowns and passed for two. He completed 13 of his 21 passes for 116 yards. For the season, he ran for 313 yards and passed for 1,554, a net total of 1,867 yards. He went on to a modest career in the NFL with the Patriots and Packers and also played for the New York Stars/Charlotte Hornets franchise in the WFL.

It wasn't until Hill read the *Yale Daily News* the following Monday in New Haven that he realized the game had ended in a tie. He thought Harvard won the game based on their wild celebration.

Yale did win the Rhodes Scholars battle. The Yale roster included two, Kurt Schmoke and Tom Neville, who would

Brian Dowling and Calvin Hill worked magic for the Bulldogs in 1967 and 1968 (courtesy Bill O'Brien).

later captain a Yale football squad. The Harvard roster included Paul Saba.

John T. Downey, a Yale football letter winner in 1950 before joining the CIA, was a prisoner of war in 1968. His Chinese captors allowed correspondences from home while he endured solitary confinement. Downey received from a friend who left the game early, a postcard announcing Yale had won, 29–13. Months later he learned of the "loss."

1969 (7–2) **Ivy League Champs. Coach: Carmen Cozza; Captain: Andy Coe**

The "Improbable 69ers" rose above the competition to gain a share of the Ivy league title with Dartmouth and Princeton. Only three times has there been a three-way tie for the Ivy title. From 1967 to 1969, Yale went 23–3–1 to win or share three Ivy titles.

"Yale went co-ed in '69, to the delight of the undergraduates and the dismay of the old Bourbons," wrote Tom Bergin.

Sept. 27: Don Martin, the ICAA 100-yard sprint champion, dramatically ran back the opening kickoff of the season 85 yards for a touchdown. But when the day ended, UConn had defeated Yale, 19–15, ending Yale's 17-game unbeaten streak. UConn running back Vin Clements, who would go on to play for the New York Giants in the NFL, carried the ball 27 times for 87 yards and made three catches for 43 yards.

Oct. 4: Sophomore receiver Bob Milligan caught three touchdown passes in Yale's 40–21 win over Colgate in the Bowl.

Oct. 25: Yale beat Cornell, 17–0, holding the Big Red to 60 yards. Cornell's All-American running back Ed Marinaro, averaging 211 rushing yards per game, was held to 29 yards on 11 carries before retiring for the day with a bruised hip.

Nov. 1: The Bulldogs' only Ivy loss came at the hands of Dartmouth, 42–21.

Nov. 8: Yale's Jack Ford intercepted a Penn pass and ran 77 yards for a TD in the Bulldogs' 21–3 win over the Quakers in the Bowl. Ford went on to an Emmy Award-winning career in TV news.

Nov. 15: Harry Klebanoff kicked a 23-yard field goal in the closing minutes for a 17–14 Yale victory at Princeton. That result, combined with Princeton's defeat of Dartmouth the next week, put the Bulldogs in a three-way tie for the Ivy League title.

THE HIGHLIGHTS 1970

Nov. 22: The Elis gained a share of the Ivy League title with a 7–0 win over Harvard. Fullback Bill Primps scored Yale's touchdown in the third quarter to complete an 80-yard scoring march directed by QB Joe Massey. Don Martin's 36-yard run was the big play in the drive. Klebanoff, Primps's high school teammate at Ossining High School in New York, kicked the extra point. Three plays later Harvard had the ball on the Yale 10 only to be driven back to the 32, where a failed field-goal attempt occurred moments before time expired. Captain Andy Coe led the defense.

1970 (7–2) Coach: Carmen Cozza; Captain: Tom Neville

Among a halo of stars produced by Yale in the '70s, running back Dick Jauron was the dominant force of the Yale offense from 1970 to 1972. Quiet confidence was his hallmark. He was the first Yale player to be selected to the All-Ivy first team three times. "If you were in a phone booth with him for 20 minutes, you still couldn't catch him," said Cozza of Jauron, who was inducted into the College Football Hall of Fame on December 8, 2015, at the 58th NFF Annual Awards Dinner at New York City's Waldorf Astoria.

Sept. 26: On a 90-degree day in the Bowl, sophomore fullback Jauron burst onto the varsity scene, rushing for 116 yards and a touchdown on 22 carries as Yale blanked UConn, 10–0. He also caught six passes for 81 yards.

Oct. 24: Jauron led a Yale uprising in Ithaca where the Bulldogs shredded Cornell, 38–7. The great running back rushed for 176 yards, the third-best single game performance in Yale history behind Clint Frank (190; 1937) and Levi Jackson (177; 1948).

Oct. 31: A crowd of 60,820 packed the Bowl where Dartmouth continued its Halloween jinx by spoiling Yale's undefeated season, 10–0. Both teams were ranked in the United Press International Top 20, the last time two nationally ranked teams from the Ivy League faced each other.

This was the last time Bob Blackman faced Yale as Dartmouth's coach. His 16-year record against the Elis was 8–7–1. The Big Green finished 9–0, its third undefeated season in the last nine years. Blackman won his seventh Ivy League title before coaching at the University of Illinois and Cornell. His record at Dartmouth was 104–37–3.

Nov. 21: Harvard quarterback Eric Crone, celebrating victory an instant too soon, took the game's final snap and ran back into his end zone, holding the ball aloft. Time hadn't expired, but Crone hung onto the ball and gave up only a safety when tackled by Yale's Ron Kell. Luckily for him, Harvard still won, 14–12, allowing coach John Yovicsin to win his final game at Harvard. During his tenure the Crimson went 78–42–5 that included three Ivy championships. Yale's 10 third-quarter points resulted from Don Martin's 62-yard run and Harry Klebanoff's 31-yard FG.

1971 (4–5) Coach: Carmen Cozza; Captain: Rich Maher

Sept. 25: Dick Jauron rushed for 186 yards and a touchdown to lead Yale past UConn, 23–0. Because of circumstances, Jauron ran out of the fullback position in '71.

Oct. 23: Cornell buried Yale, 31–10, in the Bowl. The star of the game was future actor and NFL back Ed Marinaro, who rushed for 230 yards.

Oct. 30: Dartmouth beat Yale in Hanover, 17–15, when Ted Perry kicked a 40-yard FG with 53 seconds left in the game. It was the first time Yale played at Dartmouth since the 1884 inaugural contest. The two schools played in New Haven 46 consecutive times from 1924 until 1970 because of the added revenue the Bowl would generate and the fact that there was no major highway connecting the two schools until Interstate 91 was constructed. The Bulldogs and the Big Green also played in Springfield, Massachusetts (1894), Providence, Rhode Island (1896), and in Newton Centre, Massachusetts (1899 and 1900).

Nov. 6: Roly Purrington made his first start at QB and led the Bulldogs to a 24–14 win over Penn. Captain Rich Maher caught three passes for 64 yards.

Nov. 13: Thanks to great runs by Jauron, the second-half passing of Purrington and Brian Clarke's seventh field goal of the season, Yale edged Princeton, 10–6, at Palmer Stadium. The Tigers' formidable backfield with the likes of Hank Bjorklund, Walt Snickenberger and Doug Blake had no answer for Yale's defense on this day.

Nov. 20: Harvard coach Joe Restic, who played two years with the Philadelphia Eagles, made his first appearance in the Yale-Harvard series a successful one as the Crimson tripped the Bulldogs, 35–16. Restic's well publicized "multiflex" offense, directed by QB Eric Crone, led to a 28–2 halftime lead, the largest lead the Crimson ever had at intermission of any previous Y-H game. Crone's 4-yard TD toss to Rich Gatto and 27-yard TD pass to Dennis Sullivan gave the Crimson a 14–0 lead in the first quarter and they never looked back. Jauron, who scored twice on runs of 4 and 14 yards, racked up 85 yards but fell just short of the 1,000-yard mark for the season, finishing with 930.

1972 (7–2) Coach: Carmen Cozza; Captain: Bob Perschel

Sept. 30: Yale opened the season with a 28–7 win over UConn. Jauron continued to be a Huskies killer, carrying 17 times for three TDs on runs of 80, 64 and 18 yards. For the day he totaled 194 yards, a Yale single-game record. In his three games against UConn, the running back from Swampscott, Massachusetts, collected 496 yards.

Oct. 21: Thanks to key blocks from Tyrell Hennings and Paul Sortal, Jauron scampered for 87 yards against Columbia for the deciding score in Yale's 28–14 win.

Nov. 4: In what Cozza called as close to a flawless performance as he could remember, Yale manhandled Dartmouth, 45–14, in the Bowl. Sophomore QB Tom Doyle ran the ball 12 times for 160 yards.

Nov. 25: Yale overcame a 17–0 first half deficit to beat Harvard, 28–17, on a sunny day in Boston. Jauron, who rushed for a series-record 183 yards, scored two touchdowns including a 74-yard TD run early in the fourth quarter. For the season, Jauron rushed for a record 1,055 yards. Roly Purrington and Tyrell Hennings also crossed the goal line for Yale. Harvard's Ted DeMars rushed for 153 yards, including an 86-yard first-quarter touchdown.

The Elis won the Big Three title, having defeated Princeton the week before, 31–7.

Jauron, who finished his career with 27 rushing TDs and 3,555 all-purpose running yards, went on to a eight-year career in the NFL as a defensive back and defensive back with the Lions and Bengals. He served as a head coach with the Bears, Lions and Bills. Among a myriad of awards, Jauron won the Gridiron Club of Greater Boston George H. "Bulger" Lowe award and was the Ivy League's MVP.

1973 (6–3) Coach: Carmen Cozza; Captain: Gary Wilhelm

Oct. 6: Mark van Eeghen, destined to play 10 years in the National Football League, scored three touchdowns for Colgate, but Yale hung on to win, 24–18, in a fumble-filled game in the Bowl. Elvin Charity (10 tackles, four pass breakups) and Rich Fehling, who blocked a punt, led Yale's defense.

Nov. 10: Yale QB Tom Doyle was benched in the third quarter because of a sluggish offense vs. Penn. The Quakers, down 17–0 at the half, took a 21–17 lead on the passing of Marty Vaughn. But Doyle returned to the game and caught a halfback pass from Don Gesicki in the fourth quarter to give the Bulldogs a 24–21 win. Brent Kirk set up the deciding score with a 22-yard interception that he returned to the Penn 8.

Nov. 17: Doyle ran for two TDs as Yale defeated Princeton, 30–13, in the 100th anniversary of Yale's longest rivalry.

Nov.24: Yale QB Kevin Rogan, who battled an injury-plagued career, made his first varsity start and graded high as the Elis put away Harvard, 35–0, in the Bowl on a cloudy, drizzly day. Rogan threw for 128 yards, including a 36-yard TD pass to Gary Fencik. Rudy Green, who led the team in rushing in 1973 and 1974, scored on TD runs of 6 and 4 yards. Tyrell Hennings and John Donohue also scored on short runs. Brian Clarke was perfect, kicking five extra points. Clarke, Yale's effervescent kicker, booted a Yale-record 21 field goals. He gained fame in the acting world on TV's *Eight is Enough* and *General Hospital* series.

1974 (8–1) Ivy League Champs. Coach: Carmen Cozza; Captain: Rudy Green

June 29: Charley Loftus, Yale University's director of sports information from 1943 to 1968, died of an apparent heart attack at the age of 55 in New Haven. During his tenure he was responsible for the coverage of more than 3,000 Yale athletic events and the preparation of more than 1,500 publications, many of which won national recognition. He was the first to provide written play-by-play accounts of football games to newsmen and is said to have developed the joint long-distance telephone press conference with opposing coaches. An eccentric man, he never attended out of town contests and invariably arrived at the Yale Bowl with a police escort.

Nov. 2: Yale needed a big defensive play from end Scott Keller and tackle Rich Feryok in the next-to-last minute to secure a 14–9 triumph over Dartmouth to stay unbeaten. On a fourth-down play from Yale's 10 yard line, Keller chased Big Green passer Mike Brait into Feryok's bear hug for an 11-yard loss. Yale got 16 tackles from linebacker Brent Kirk.

Nov. 16: Led by Rudy Green's two TDs and 138 yards rushing, Yale won its 11th straight game and fourth Ivy title under Cozza with a 19–6 victory over Princeton. The Bulldogs trailed when the Tigers' Scott Morrison booted an 18-yard FG with 6:54 remaining in the first half. Yale answered with two quick TDs by Green to push them ahead at the half, 13–3. Princeton climbed to within seven points after Morrison kicked another FG in the third quarter. The Bulldogs locked up the Tigers early in the final stanza when Yale's Rick Lawrence pounced on a poorly tossed pitchout on the Princeton 16-yard line that led to a Tyrell Hennings TD. Yale defensive end Brian Ameche, the son of Heisman winner Alan "The Horse" Ameche, formerly of the Baltimore Colts, starred defensively along with such stalwarts as tackle Rich Feryok, and linebackers John Smoot, John Cahill, and Tim Knowles.

Ten of the 11 1934 Yale Ironmen attended the contest and were photographed in front of the Walter Camp Memorial Gateway.

Nov. 23: Harvard Stadium again proved to be Yale's Kryptonite as Harvard deprived Yale of a perfect season for the fourth time and tied for a share of the Ivy championship after driving 95 yards to score with 15 seconds left to win, 21–16. Harvard's Hawaiian QB, "Pineapple" Milt Holt, groggy but still standing, curled around left end from the 5 for the game-winner. Alki Tsitsos kicked the extra point.

Yale wasted a landmark performance by wide receiver Gary Fencik, who caught 11 passes for 187 yards, both Bulldog records at the time. Fencik lobbied coach Carm Cozza to play defense the following year but this performance against Harvard might have cemented his future at Yale. The highlight play of the game occurred just before the end of the first half when Harvard end Pat McInally took a lateral from the lefty Holt and fired a 56-yard flea flicker to Jim Curry, who took it down to the Yale 2 yard line, setting up a 1-yard scoring pass to tight end Peter Curtin.

Legendary coach Carm Cozza is seen here with player Gary Fencik, who would enjoy a solid career with the Chicago Bears from 1976 to 1987.

1975 (7–2) Coach: Carmen Cozza; Captain: John Smoot

Nov. 1: In one of the most pulsating finishes in Yale Bowl history, Randy Carter's 47-yard field goal in the final seconds repelled Dartmouth, 16–14. The Big Green took a 14–13 lead when Harry Wilson nabbed a fumble in Yale's end zone with 44 seconds left in the game. But Dartmouth penalties for celebrating an interference call plus a Stone Phillips to Al Barker pass positioned Yale for Carter's walk-off field goal, his third of the day. Phillips went on to an Emmy Award–winning career in television that included his role as co-anchor of *Dateline NBC*.

Nov. 8: Don Gesicki ran for 164 yards and two touchdowns, leading Yale over Penn, 24–14. The victory gave Carm Cozza his 68th win at Yale, passing Walter Camp as the winningest head football coach in Yale history.

Nov. 15: Ironically, Yale's longest pass play in school history was executed by a running back when Gesicki, who played QB in high school, completed a 97-yard aerial to Gary Fencik in the Blue's 24–13 win at Princeton. Gesicki received a pitch from QB Stone Phillips. He ran to his left and fired the pass from his own 3-yard line to Fencik, who caught the ball on Yale's 35 and outran the Princeton defense for the touchdown. In 2012, Yale QB Eric Williams threw a 98-yard TD pass, eclipsing Gesicki's record toss.

Nov. 22: It appeared that Yale, Harvard and Dartmouth were headed for a three-way share of the Ivy title before Mike Lynch's "wounded duck" 26-yard field goal with 33 seconds remaining gave Harvard a 10–7 win over Yale and sole possession of the Ivy title, the Crimson's first undisputed league championship. The game featured future Chicago Bears teammates Dan Jiggetts, the Harvard captain, and Fencik. Fencik, who was a member of the Bears' Super Bowl XX team, spent 12 years as a defensive back in the NFL with the Bears. At Yale, Fencik had 86 career receptions for 1,435 yards and seven touchdowns.

1976 (8–1) Ivy League Champs. Coach: Carmen Cozza; Captain: Vic Staffieri, Yale's 100th captain

Yale flourished from 1976 to 1981, recording an impressive 45–9–2 mark during this six-year golden period in which Yale lost only six Ivy League games and either won or shared five Ivy titles.

Sept. 18: Yale lost to Brown, 14–6, at Providence, then won their final

THE HIGHLIGHTS   1977

eight games of the season to gain a share of the Ivy title with the Bears. The scenario was duplicated 23 years later when the Brown beat the Bulldogs in the season opener before Yale ran the table.

Oct. 2: With Ronald Reagan, the future 40th U.S. president in the crowd, John Pagliaro rushed for 193 yards and two TDs in Yale's 21–6 win over Lehigh in the Bowl. End Greg Hall scored the only TD of his Yale career and was introduced to Reagan at Mory's following the game. Reagan was visiting his son, Ron, who was a Yale student.

Oct. 23: Yale beat Penn, 21–7, at Franklin Field. The Elis established an existing school record for most total first downs in a game (32), most rushing first downs (30) and most rushing plays (84). Pagliaro enjoyed his finest day, gaining 187 yards on 33 carries, including three TDs. He also accounted for 13 first downs.

Nov. 13: Yale defeated Harvard, 21–7, on a sunny, crisp day in Boston to win a share of the Ivy title with Brown. Mike Southworth crossed the goal line twice for the Bulldogs on runs of 7 and 2 yards. Pagliaro added the other Yale TD on a 5-yard sprint. Randy Carter kicked the three extra points. This was supposed to be Carm Cozza's final game since he was scheduled to become the school's athletic director. The players carried him off the field and in the locker room everyone sang "Bulldog, Bulldog," and chanted, "One more year!"

Nov. 20: The players got their wish. Cozza, after retiring as coach to become Yale's full-time athletic director, decided that coaching is what he wanted and quit the AD job. He would coach another 20 years.

1977 (7–2) Ivy League Champs (outright). Coach: Carmen Cozza; Captain: Bob Rizzo

Sept. 17: Clinging precariously to a 10–7 margin, the Bulldogs staged an epic goal-line stand with 2:27 remaining that halted Brown four times inside the 2-yard line as Yale escaped with a gut-wrenching 10–9 victory in the season opener for the two defending Ivy League champions. Monster back Kevin Gardner, with help from linebacker George Rapp, felled Brown fullback Wally Shields two inches from the goal line on fourth down with 36 seconds left as the 27,196 standing fans in the Bowl roared hoarsely. Ends Clint Streit and Dan Goodfriend, tackle Bob Skoronski, linebacker Scott McKenzie, middle guard Dave Humphreville and tackle Frank Paci all played key roles thwarting Brown's drive to the goal line.

With 30 seconds to go, Yale QB Bob Rizzo attempted a sneak to move the ball and kill the clock, but he fumbled the snap and was piled on for a safety that gave Brown its last two points.

"That was the greatest goal-line stand I've ever seen," said Cozza to the *Yale Daily News*. "While it was going on I was only thinking of what we would do after the next kickoff."

Skoronski is the son of former Green Bay Packers tackle Bob Skoronski, who was the offensive captain on Vince Lombardi's five championship teams.

The historic goal-line stand was only part of the story. Dave Schwartz was a first-string sophomore forward on the soccer team that was defeated by Brown, 1–0, earlier in the day. A few hours later Schwartz got a measure of revenge against the Bears. He switched from soccer to football and kicked a 34-yard field goal for the Bulldogs in the third quarter that proved to be the difference.

After the game, Schwartz was quoted in the *New York Times*, "I know this means a lot to a lot of people, but I just wish we had won the soccer game."

Sept. 24: John Pagliaro set a Yale record with 35 carries in a 23–12 win over UConn on a rainy day in the Bowl.

Oct. 1: Yale played host to Miami of Ohio and lost, 28–14. The game had special meaning for Cozza who played at the Ohio school known as the "Cradle of Coaches" for producing many future head coaches. The Elis led, 14–6, at the half but three fumbles in the second half led to Yale's demise.

Oct. 8: Trailing, 3–0, the Bulldogs were headed to the Dartmouth goal line following a Bob Rizzo to John Spagnola 81-yard pass play. With 66 seconds remaining in the game, Dartmouth's Don Rutishauser broke up a fourth-down Yale pitchout from Rizzo to Pagliaro from the 4-yard line, forcing Pagliaro to fall on the ball at the Dartmouth 9. Nick Lowery, the future Pro Bowl NFL placekicker, nailed a 24-yard field goal early in the third quarter that gave the men from Hanover the victory.

Nov. 5: Yale dismantled Princeton, 44–8, before a homecoming crowd of 23,000 at Palmer Stadium. Yale used all 86 players, including five quarterbacks.

Nov. 12: The Bulldogs handled Harvard in New Haven, 24–7, before 64,685 fans. The highlight of the game was Mike Sullivan's 66-yard TD run from punt formation. Leading, 10–7, early in the fourth quarter, Yale had the ball on their own 34 in a 4th-and-20 situation. Sullivan, standing on the 20, took the eye-level snap from center Jim Browning. The ball sailed to Sullivan's right. Harvard's big defensive end Russ Savage took a hard slant in, making it virtually impossible for Sullivan, a left-footed punter, to execute the punt. Sullivan took off toward the right sideline and thanks to a block from Steve Carfora, headed untouched into the Harvard end zone. Rich Angelone (5-yard run) and John Pagliaro (2-yard run) also crossed the goal for the Elis. Dave Schwartz put the Elis on the board in the first quarter with a 22-yard field goal.

"Pags," who closed his career scoring Yale's final TD, rushed for 172 yards on 30 carries. He was selected the Ivy league's MVP in 1976 and 1977. He joins Harvard's Carl Morris as the only players to twice receive the Asa A. Bushnell Cup as the Ivy League's MVP. In '77 "Pags" ran for 1,159 yards, breaking Dick Jauron's single-season mark of 1,055. He also had 14 rushing touchdowns. The first team Walter Camp All-American

Left to right: Dick Jauron, John Pagliaro and Kevin Czinger. This trio of Yale royalty led the Elis in the 1970s. Pagliaro was a two-time Ivy league MVP (courtesy Bill O'Brien).

rushed for 2,476 yards in his career and was the first Yale running back to have back-to-back 1,000-yard seasons.

1978 (5–2–2) Coach: Carmen Cozza; Captain: Bill Crowley

Sept. 23: Yale opened the season at Brown with a 21–0 win. The big play was Mike Sullivan's 56-yard TD run in the second quarter. Kevin Czinger posted his first two varsity sacks in a career that totaled an incredible 27.

Nov. 4: An electrifying 100-yard kickoff return by running back Kenny Hill, the longest in school history, highlighted Yale's 42–14 win over Cornell in the Bowl. QB Pat O'Brien had three touchdown runs in the first half and his backup, Dennis Dunn, scored on a 63-yard sprint in the third quarter.

Nov. 18: Yale pulled a razzle-dazzle play titled, "Downtown Left" when end John Spagnola drifted back a few feet from his left end spot as soon as the ball was snapped and received a lateral from QB Pat O'Brien. Spagnola then threw a 77-yard touchdown pass to right end Bob Krystyniak, who jogged slowly down the right side then took off deep. It proved to be the longest TD pass by a Yale player in the history of the Y-H series and was the only pass Spagnola threw in his football career covering high school, college and his 11-year NFL career spent mostly with the Philadelphia Eagles. "Spags" later hauled in Pat O'Brien's 59-yard pass from a Harvard defender for the deciding score in Yale's 35–28 victory at Harvard Stadium. Crimson QB Larry Brown tossed four touchdown passes in a losing effort. Yale's Kenny Hill rushed for 154 yards including an 18-yard TD run. The Bulldogs' Rich Angelone (93 yards) and Mike Sullivan (51), rounded out a well-

Left to right: Chris Heatherington and John Spagnola. Both Yale stalwarts pictured here enjoyed lengthy NFL careers after Yale (courtesy Bill O'Brien).

balanced running attack. The two teams combined for a Y-H series-record 42 points in the first half—28 by Yale and 14 by Harvard.

1979 **(8–1) Ivy League Champs (outright). Coach: Carmen Cozza; Captain: Tim Tumpane (Ivy League MVP)**

The 1979–80 Yale teams won the Ivy League title outright. It's the only time the Bulldogs won back-to-back undisputed Ivy titles. This period might be classified as the "Czinger Era" in relation to middle guard Kevin Czinger, who handled his position with unmatched bravado.

Sept. 22: Just recovering from a bout of mononucleosis and 10 pounds under his regular weight of 185, Czinger set up both Yale touchdowns by blocking punts in a 13–12 victory over Brown in the Bowl. Mike Sullivan scored the winning touchdown, holding the ball out across the goal line on a fourth-down plunge with less than 2 ½ minutes to play.

Oct. 13: Yale's stingy defense held Dartmouth to three first downs—none in the second half—to subdue the Big Green, 3–0, before 26,000. Dave Schwartz kicked the deciding field goal, a 24-yarder, in the second quarter that was set up by Sullivan's 36-yard punt return to the Big Green 11. Dave Shula, son of ex–Miami Dolphins coach Don Shula, was a split end on the Dartmouth team that was quarterbacked by Jeff Kemp, son of Jack Kemp, the former U.S. senator, vice-presidential candidate and Buffalo Bills QB.

The defensive unit of sophomores Pat Conran, Fred Leone, Serge Mihaly, Jim Dwyer, Dennis Tulsiak, juniors Dave Novosel, Jeff Rohrer and Czinger plus seniors Tim Tumpane, Arnie Pinkston and Skip Porter might have been the gold standard during the Cozza years. Dwyer's fumble recovery ended the Green's deepest penetration at the Yale 19.

Nov. 3: Yale recorded its 700th football victory by beating Cornell in Ithaca, 23–20. Sophomore QB John Rogan tossed a 12-yard touchdown pass to Bob Rostomily with 47 seconds left for the victory. It was their second scoring hookup of the day, keeping Yale undefeated and on track toward the Ivy League title.

Nov. 9: Princeton students posing as Yale cheerleaders dognapped Handsome Dan XII, a.k.a. "Bingo," under the eyes of its owner, Rollin G. Osterweis, Yale history professor emeritus. Osterweis was told by the imposters that they wanted to photograph the bulldog. "Bingo" was the only female Yale mascot in the line of 17 bulldogs.

Nov. 10: Led by running back Kenny Hill, who gained 129 yards on 19 carries, Yale won its 13th straight game over Princeton by defeating the Tigers in New Jersey, 35–10, to clinch a tie for the Ivy championship. Hill's 64-yard dash on a muddy field launched the scoring parade. Dennis Dunn ran for a TD and passed for another. Yale's defense secured the last two touchdowns when Dave Conrad returned a fumble in midair and Arnie Pinkston returned an intercepted pass for 40 yards.

Between halves the Princeton band marched out and Handsome Dan XII, dressed in Tiger stripes, was carried in the arms of the Princeton Tiger to a reunion with the real Yale cheerleaders. Professor Osterweis was notified by phone at his Hartford, Connecticut, home that Dan "Bingo" had been well cared for. The next day's *New York Times* game story was headlined, "Yale Takes Game, Ivy Crown and Purloined Mascot Home."

Nov. 17: The largest crowd in 25 years (72,000) packed the Yale Bowl hoping see the Bulldogs and College Football Hall of Fame head coach Carm Cozza climax a perfect season with a win over archrival Harvard. Yale, a 13 ½ point favorite, was unbeaten and untied and led the nation in defense against the rush while Harvard was an anemic 2–6. But when the sun set and the late November shadows covered the Bowl, it was Harvard 22, Yale 7, marking the fifth time Harvard had spoiled a perfect Yale season.

Yale's Kenny Hill fumbled five times and Harvard recovered two of them. Crimson quarterback Burke St. John threw a 39-yard touchdown strike to Jim Callinan and ran for a 2-yard score in the fourth quarter. Despite the loss, Yale won the Ivy League with a record of 8–1.

1980 (8–2) Ivy League Champs (outright). Coach: Carmen Cozza; Captain: John Nitti

Ivy League teams were allowed to play 10 games in a season for the first time since 1922.

Sept. 27: Yale disposed of UConn, 20–10, thanks to a storybook performance by running back Rich Diana, who rushed for 91 yards, scoring on a 6-yard run and a 5-yard pass reception. He also returned a punt for 77 yards and made a touchdown-saving tackle. On the other end of the ball Kevin Czinger, the Ivy MVP, made 14 unassisted tackles.

Oct. 4: Diana grabbed a pass intended for teammate Bob Burkitt and turned it into a third-quarter touchdown that carried Yale to a 17–16 decision over visiting Air Force, who had tied Big Ten Illinois, 20–20, the week before. It was the Bulldogs' 100th victory under coach Carm Cozza and their 14th win in the last 15 games. The crowd of 23,000 was treated to a barn burner. Czinger, one of the toughest players in Cozza's 32-year tenure, came out of a hospital bed, played with ferocity and indomitable spirit while recovering a key fumble. Air Force holder Bob Renaud failed on a fake conversion run that cost the Falcons the game.

Oct. 11: Yale lost to Boston College on the road, 27–9, in the first night game Yale ever played. Backup quarterback Phil Manley took over for John Rogan in the last quarter and ignited Yale's offense when he directed a drive for Yale's only touchdown, a 5-yard run by captain John Nitti and a 37-yard FG by Tony Jones. Because of Manley's performance against BC (5 completed passes in 12 attempts for 62 yards), he earned a starting shot against Columbia the following week. Despite the loss, the Bulldogs hung tough.

BCs massive line did not overpower the outmanned Yale defense, gaining only 88 yards on 47 carries. Czinger applied pressure on Eagles QB John Loughery throughout the game. The *Register*'s Jon Stein wrote, "He was all over Loughery like fleas on a hound dog."

Oct. 18: Phil Manley became the first black quarterback to start a game for Yale in the Elis' 30–10 win over Columbia. Manley and John Rogan rotated every other quarter until Manley suffered an injury. It would be the only start of Manley's varsity career.

Nov. 1: Yale dismantled Dartmouth, 35–7, in the Bowl. Diana rolled with 124 yards on the ground. Fred Leone intercepted a Jeff Kemp pass and returned it 39 yards for a TD. Offensive tackle Bob Regan played exceptionally well on the pitch-sweep play. But the Elis lost Jeff Rohrer, the future Dallas Cowboys linebacker, with a broken ankle.

Nov. 8: After pounding Dartmouth in Hanover the week before, the Elis were upset by a 2–5 Cornell team, 24–6, in the Bowl, their only Ivy League loss of the season.

Nov. 15: Yale kept their thumb on Princeton for the 14th straight time by taming the Tigers, 25–13, which assured the Bulldogs of a share of the Ivy championship.

Nov. 22: Yale beat Harvard, 14–0, in Boston on a sunny, cold day. Both teams brought 7–2 records into the game. The Elis opened the scoring in the first quarter on a 25-yard TD pass from John Rogan to Curt Grieve. Defensively, Yale held Harvard's multiflex offense to minus 11 yards rushing and 130 total yards.

John Nitti, who gained 69 yards, added another six points on a 1-yard plunge in the third quarter. Tony Jones kicked both extra points. This allowed Yale to win the Ivy title outright, the last time this would happen until 2017.

After coaching at Yale for 33 years, many as the freshman coach, assistant coach Harry Jacunski retired after this game. Jacunski, an end who co-captained Fordham in 1938, played alongside Vince Lombardi and was one of the "Seven Blocks of Granite." He played six seasons in the NFL with the Green Bay Packers.

1981 (9–1) Ivy League Champs. Coach: Carmen Cozza; Captain: Fred Leone

Yale won its third consecutive Ivy title, the second time they had done so.

Ivy League MVP Rich Diana rushed for 2,576 yards in his career.

THE HIGHLIGHTS   1981

The Ivy League selected a Silver Anniversary All-Star team. Seven Yale players were named to the first team—Ben Balme, Mike Pyle, Dick Jauron, Calvin Hill, Jim Gallagher, Tom Neville and Kevin Czinger.

Sept. 19: Rich Diana broke Dick Jauron's single-game rushing record of 194 yards when he ran for 196 in the Eli's season-opening 28–7 victory over Brown.

Oct. 3: In what was arguably Cozza's greatest non-league win, Yale upset Navy, 23–19, before 38,000 in the Bowl. The Middies were a 10- to 13-point favorite after losing to Michigan the week before (21–16).

Yale, down, 12–0, within the first seven minutes, never quit. A 45-yard Tony Jones field goal and a TD pass to tight end Tom Kokoska cut Navy's lead to 12–9 at the half. Elis quarterback John Rogan (16-for-30, 202 yards) pitched three touchdown passes, two to Curt Grieve and one to Kokoska.

Early in the fourth quarter Yale went up, 16–12, on the first of Grieve's two TD catches. Navy regained the lead after Travis Wallington blocked a Yale punt that was recovered on the Yale 16. Rich Clouse then scored, putting Navy on top, 19–16. After a Jones punt pinned Navy on its 2-yard line, the Middies punted from their end zone and reached only their own 24—setting up Rogan's 24-yarder to Grieve with 3:19 remaining for the game-winner.

Jon Stein wrote in the *Register*, "The good ship Navy was scuttled." Yale defensive end, captain Fred Leone, was named *Sports Illustrated*'s Defensive Player of the Week for his three fumble recoveries. Tackle Serge Mihaly also starred on defense with 13 tackles. Napoleon McCallum, Navy's star running back, was knocked out of the game in the second quarter with a hip pointer after being hit hard by end Greg Burkus.

The game was televised on ABC with Al Michaels and Ara Parseghian in the booth. Parseghian coached Cozza at Miami of Ohio. The win was arguably the most significant win by an Ivy League team since the league was formed in 1956 as Navy had wins over Boston College, Syracuse and Georgia Tech that year. The Yale victory was magnified at the end of the season since Navy finished 7–4–1 and narrowly lost to Ohio State in the Liberty Bowl.

Oct. 10: Tony Jones kicked a 32-yard field goal with 35 seconds left that gave Yale a nail-biting 29–28 decision over Holy Cross at Worcester.

Nov. 14: Rich Diana, Yale's linchpin, rushed for a then school-record

QB John Rogan led Yale in the Bulldogs' big win over Navy in 1981.

222 yards on a record 46 carries in a 35–31 loss to Princeton that spoiled Yale's perfect season and its 14-year hex over the Tigers. The devastating loss, in which Yale blew a 21–0 lead against the 3–4–1 Tigers, created co-Ivy champs in Yale and Dartmouth.

Tigers QB Bob Holly threw for an Ivy League-record 501 yards (36 of 57) with receiver Derek Graham accounting for 278 yards. Holly scored with four seconds on the clock on a left rollout after a Yale pass interference penalty in the end zone put the ball on the 1-yard line. The game is considered Princeton's "Game of the Century."

Nov. 21: Yale rebounded from its critical loss to Princeton with a 28–0 whipping of Harvard before 72,440 in the Bowl. Diana scored on a 39-yard pass from John Rogan and a 4-yard run. Grieve tallied on a 25-yard pass from Rogan and a 7-yarder from Joe Dufek. All-Ivy linebacker Jeff

In 1981, Curt Grieve caught a then Yale record 51 passes for 791 yards and 12 TD receptions.

Rohrer, who played eight seasons with the Dallas Cowboys, led the team with 136 tackles. During his Yale career he had 130 solos.

Following the 1981 season, Cozza was offered the University of Virginia football coaching job but turned it down. The Cavaliers then hired Navy coach George Welsh, who headed the Virginia football program for 19 years.

1982 (4–6) Coach: Carmen Cozza; Captain: Pat Ruwe

The Ivy League went to Division I-AA and Yale suffered its first losing season in 11 years. This would be a harbinger of things to come. Cozza's next 15 years would produce a humbling 65–81–2 mark, that included only one Ivy title.

Oct. 2: For the first time in Yale football history, the Bulldogs lost their first three games of a season. Following losses to Brown and UConn, Yale was nipped by Holy Cross, 10–6.

Oct. 9: The hungry Bulldogs won their first game of the season, defeating Boston University in the Bowl, 27–24.

Nov. 6: Two Ivy League coaching legends Carmen Cozza (Yale) and Bob Blackman (Cornell) faced each other for the last time in a game won by the Big Red, 26–20, in the Bowl. Blackman and Cozza finished a symmetrical 6–6 against each other. Blackman was 4–2 vs. Cozza while at Dartmouth and 2–4 while at Cornell.

Nov. 13: Bill Moore booted a 52-yard field goal in the Bulldogs' 37–19 win over Princeton. From 1982 to 1984, Moore made 53 extra points in 56 attempts for a remarkable .946 percentage. In the first quarter with Yale leading, 13–0, Yale punter Jim Nottingham, set to punt from his end zone with the ball on Yale's 8 yard line, ran instead and reached the Princeton 19. According to Cozza in his book, *True Blue*, Nottingham had made a bet with his roommate that he was going to take off with the ball sometime during the game.

Nov. 20: Yale completed a disappointing 4–6 season on a losing note at the hands of Harvard on the road, 45–7. After a second-quarter Crimson score, thanks to a twisted stunt engineered by MIT students, a large black weather balloon marked MIT suddenly rose from the turf at midfield, inflating and exploding in a cloud of smoke.

1983 (1–9) Coach: Carmen Cozza; Captain: Tom Giella

Yale wallowed in futility. Its 1–9 mark was the Bulldogs' worst record in 111 years of football. It was the first season the Elis would go winless in the Bowl until the 1997 team suffered the same humiliation. Disgruntled alums pointed fingers at Yale President A. Bartlett Giamatti and Athletic Director Frank Ryan for the decline in the football program after Giamatti cut back on football admissions in '79. But coach Carm Cozza took the high road saying, "I don't want anyone but myself to be blamed for a losing season." After 37 years of service, Yale ticket manager Jack Blake retired.

Sept. 24: Matt Latham thrilled UConn fans with TD punt returns of 76 and 64 yards in UConn's 38–12 win over Yale.

Oct. 1: Yale lost, 26–14, to William & Mary in Norfolk, Virginia. Both teams showed up wearing white jerseys. William & Mary was distinguished by their yellow helmets.

THE HIGHLIGHTS   1983

Oct. 8: Boston College, bound for the Liberty Bowl, blew away the Bulldogs, 42–7, behind the passing of 1984 Heisman winner Doug Flutie, who completed 18 of 26 tosses for 325 yards and four touchdowns. Flutie is one of six Heisman Trophy winners to play collegiately in the Bowl including Larry Kelley and Clint Frank (Yale), Tom Harmon (Michigan), Glenn Davis (Army) and Dick Kazmaier (Princeton).

Nov. 12: After getting crushed by Cornell, the Bulldogs re-huddled and won their only game of the season defeating Princeton, 28–21. Yale fullback Jeff Bassette scored three touchdowns on short runs including a 1-yard burst with 6:05 left to play for the winning score. The Tigers tied the score, 21–21, on Doug Butler's 9-yard touchdown pass to Ralph Ferraro early in the fourth quarter, but the Elis marched 61 yards in 12 plays to set up Bassette's winning TD. Paul Andrie gained 165 yards on 29 carries and scored on a 12-yard run in the first quarter for the Bulldogs. Kevin Guthrie caught seven passes for 142 yards, giving him 77 catches for the season, a new Princeton record.

Nov. 19: The 100th game in the Yale-Harvard series drew 70,097 fans to the Bowl, including Yale Heisman winners Larry Kelley and Clint Frank. They saw an underdog 1–8 Yale team stay even for three quarters before succumbing to the Crimson. In the fourth, a Steve Ernst touchdown and Rob Steinberg's field goal lifted the Harvards to a 16–7 victory and a two-way tie with Penn for the Ivy League title. Captain, linebacker and later Bulger Lowe Award winner Joe Azelby led the Crimson.

Following the game, Harvard students climbed the aluminum goal posts of the north side (scoreboard side) of the field. The post toppled and fell on Meg Cimino, an 18-year-old Harvard freshman. Paramedics found her amid the tumult bleeding heavily from her mouth, ears and nose, and her heart soon stopped. She had no vital signs according to a report by the *New York Times*. She suffered a fractured skull and damage to her brain stem and cerebellum.

The paramedics, with the help of a doctor who ran to the scene, revived Cimino. The Harvard co-ed was on a respirator for 10 days and hospitalized several weeks. She reportedly received a $925,000 settlement from Yale and the city of New Haven. After a long recovery, she graduated from Harvard and subsequently earned a law degree from the University of Pennsylvania.

1984 (6–3) Coach: Carmen Cozza; Captain: Marty Martinson

Sept. 22: Brown's Keiron Bigby intercepted three Yale passes, returning them for an NCAA-record 216 yards and two touchdowns as the Bears won at Providence, 27–14. The killer was a 100-yard return in the fourth quarter after Yale had driven to Brown's 6-yard line.

Oct. 6: Starved for a victory after losing 12 of its previous 13 games, Yale turned things around in a hurry in a 41–0 rout of Morgan State. Nose guard John Zanieski led Yale's defense with a blocked punt and two sacks. Yale went on to win five of its next six, finishing the year 6–3.

Oct. 13: Sophomore backup Tim Macauley scored two touchdowns—one on a 71-yard dash—to lead Yale past Dartmouth, 28–18, before 25,372 in the Bowl.

Oct. 20: Backup quarterback Mike Cyr, replacing injured Mike Curtin, threw three touchdown passes as Yale outlasted Columbia, 28–21. Tom Kotkiewicz batted down a Lions pass on the last play of the game to prevent a tie.

Oct. 27: Yale played its 1,000th intercollegiate game, losing at Pennsylvania, 34–21. From 1982 to 1986, Penn won or shared the Ivy title five straight years,

Nov. 3: Mike Curtin's game-winning pass rallied the Blue from a 14–6 third quarter deficit to beat Cornell. 21–14.

Nov. 9: The Yale freshmen, behind the passing of Kelly Ryan and the running of Troy Jenkins, beat Princeton, 41–21. Dean Cain, who played Superman in the TV series *Lois and Clark*, played defensive back for the Tigers. Not even Superman could help the Tigers on this day.

Nov. 10: Curtin's 14-yard pass to Kevin Moriarty in the northwest corner of the end zone with five seconds left brought Yale a 27–24 victory over Princeton in the Bowl. The pass capped a 12-play drive that covered 98 yards in 86 seconds, starting after Yale had stymied the Tigers on a 4th-and-goal play.

Nov. 17: On a windy day at Harvard Stadium, Yale overcame an early 14-point deficit and beat the Crimson, 30–27, to tie for second place in the Ivy League. Bill Moore kicked three field goals and Paul Spivack, a senior fullback who had been injured most of his career, carried 26 times for 103 yards and two touchdowns.

The Highlights 1985

1985 (4–4–1) Coach: Carmen Cozza; Captain: Carmen Ilacqua

Sept. 28: On a sunny Saturday everybody lost. Yale and UConn had expected a crowd close to 35,000, but Hurricane Gloria struck New Haven at midday Friday, leaving a jumble of fallen trees and downed power lines and disabling the city's traffic light system. As a matter of public safety, New Haven mayor Biagio DiLieto ordered the game called off.

"Amazing" Grace Lewis, Yale's football matriarch retired. Grace was the secretary in Yale's football office for 34 years, serving four head coaches—Herman Hickman, Jordan Olivar, John Pont and Carm Cozza.

Oct. 5: Army routed Yale, 59–16, at West Point. Never had a Yale team allowed so many points. "It was the poorest defensive effort since I've been here," lamented Cozza. The 43-point deficit matched the 50–7 beating Yale took against Penn in 1940. Craig Stopa kicked a 54-yard field goal, the longest in Army history.

Army officials prevented the Yale Precision Marching Band from performing at halftime after Army's athletic director Carl Ulrich found the script "offensive and indecent."

Oct. 25: The last non-varsity game ever played in the Yale Bowl took place on this Friday afternoon when the Army JV team defeated the Yale freshmen, 33–22.

Nov. 22: The Bullpups played Harvard in the inaugural game at Clinton E. Frank Field at the Dewitt Cuyler Complex and came out a winner, 18–15. Two passes from Mark Lesko to Tom Szuba, the second with 30 seconds left, produced the winning score.

Nov. 23: Yale fullback Rich Koze twice smashed off right tackle for first downs in 4th-and-1 situations during a time-consuming last-quarter drive that preserved Yale's 17–6 victory over Harvard. The outcome cost the Crimson a share of the Ivy League title and allowed Penn to win the title outright for the second year in a row.

Captain Carmen Ilacqua, who had 299 tackles in his career (167 solo), made 15 tackles (seven solo) as the Blue held Robert Santiago, Harvard's All-Ivy runner, to 28 yards on 18 carries. The defensive play of the game was made by Yale defensive end John Quinn, who laid a vicious hit on Santiago at the Yale 9 early in the second quarter, causing a fumble that was recovered by the Elis' Derek Kay, terminating Harvard's 82-yard drive.

Yale became the first Ivy League member that declined to permit one of its games to be televised. The Yale-Harvard game was originally scheduled to be carried as the PBS *Ivy Game of the Week*. But AD Frank Ryan said, "We felt that if it was on PBS, it would erode the live attendance." The Game that normally averaged 62,000, drew 57,647, most likely to Ryan's dismay. The Cornell-Princeton game was substituted.

1986 (3–7) Coach: Carmen Cozza; Captain: Ken Lund

Ken Lund captained the Yale team to a 3–7 mark. His brother, Don, was bestowed the honor in 1988, making the Lund duo the only brothers to captain the Yale football team. In '88, Don led the Bulldogs in solo tackles (113) and total season tackles (176).

Oct. 4: Junior QB Kelly Ryan, throwing from a shotgun formation to protect an injured knee, passed for a Yale-record 426 yards, but Army outlasted Yale, 41–24, in the Bowl. Despite his knee injury, Ryan passed for 1,739 yards that season. He netted more yards of total offense than any Yale quarterback before him except Brian Dowling.

Oct. 11: Colgate back Kenny Gamble racked up 220 yards on 36 carries but the Blue beat the Raiders, 28–23.

Nov. 2: The old wooden Yale press box went up in flames. The cause of the fire was faulty wiring in an electrical box.

Nov. 15: An onside kick, nudged along by Jose Egurbide and recovered by Buddy Zachery, set up John Duryea's 17-yard field goal with 62 seconds left as Yale, trailing, 13–3, in the final 2:30, beat Princeton, 14–13.

Nov. 22: Harvard entered The Game with only two wins and three consecutive losses but turned on the Bulldogs and won, 24–17. The big play of the contest was made by Harvard's sophomore QB Tom Yohe, who completed a 53-yard touchdown pass to fullback George Sorbara in the third quarter that put the Crimson ahead for good, 21–17. The ancient rivals both finished the season at a dismal 3–7, the first time since 1958 that both teams ended the year with losing records. Dr. Harold Sedgwick, Harvard Class of 1930, attended his 47th Y-H game in a row.

1987 (7–3) Coach: Carmen Cozza; Captain: Kelly Ryan

The Yale Bowl was declared a National Historic Landmark and was chosen by *The Sporting News* as one of the 40 best college football stadiums in its 2005 book, *Saturday Shrines*. This was one of Yale's greatest comeback teams, led by quarterback Kelly Ryan, the Ivy League MVP.

The Highlights 1987

Sept. 26: Ryan's fourth touchdown pass of the day, an 11-yarder to Tom Szuba with 18 seconds left, gave Yale a thrilling 30–27 victory over Connecticut before 34,068. Yale had trailed, 27–17, after UConn's George Booth scored with 4:38 left. For the season, Ryan totaled 2,120 net yards.

Oct. 3: Yale made its longest trip ever, playing Hawaii in a Saturday night game (Sunday morning New Haven time) in Honolulu. Heikoti Fakava, Hawaii's short-yardage back, scored five times as the Rainbow Warriors won, 62–10, at Aloha Stadium. The 52-point loss proved to be the largest deficit in Yale football history. The score is a bit deceiving in that Yale was only six points behind with eight minutes to play in the third quarter. The undaunted Elis would win their next six games.

Oct. 10: Kelly Ryan threw a pitchout to Mike Stewart, whose pass to Dean Athanasia with 23 seconds to go brought Yale a 40–34 comeback victory over William & Mary in the Bowl. Stewart also ran for 188 yards.

Oct. 24: Trailing, 22–21, with 32 seconds to play and facing the abyss of defeat, Yale pulled off perhaps its most unlikely miracle win in the annals of the football program dating back to 1872. Penn QB John Keller, instead of taking a knee made a colossal blunder and fumbled the snap. Yale's Mike Browne recovered the ball at midfield.

The unflappable Ryan then completed three passes, all to Bob Shoop. With the ball on the Penn 32, Kelly connected with Shoop, who instead of stepping out of bounds to set up a field goal try for Dave Derby, cut toward the goal posts and scored with six seconds remaining in the game. If he was tackled, Penn would have won. But Yale won the incredible contest, 28–22. WELI Radio play-by-play broadcaster Bill Gonillo correctly yelled into the microphone that it was one of the greatest moments in the history of Yale sports.

Nov. 14: Yale shot down the Princeton Tigers, 34–19, behind the gun of "Cool Hand Kelly," who completed 21 of 30 passes for 329 yards and three TDs with no picks. The opposing quarterback that day was Jason Garrett, the ex-coach of the Dallas Cowboys.

Nov. 21: Harvard iced Yale, 14–10, in the Bowl to win the Ivy championship. The game was played in severe frigid conditions in what has become known as the "Freeze Bowl." Some said the wind chill reached between 10 to minus 20 degrees during the game. Yale coach Carm Cozza said it was the worst weather conditions he had ever coached in. It was reported that half the crowd of 66,548 left by the fourth quarter, missing

From his QB position, "Cool Hand Kelly" Ryan orchestrated a season of miracle comebacks in 1987.

Yale's last drive that was thwarted by a Troy Jenkins fumble when he was hit by Harvard's Tom Aubin. Tony Hinz (161 rushing yards) scored both Harvard touchdowns as the Crimson finished 8–2 overall and 6–1 in the Ivy to win the league title.

1988 (3-6-1) Coach: Carmen Cozza; Captain: Don Lund

Sept. 13: Yale announced that Joel E. Smilow, a 1954 Yale graduate and president, chairman and chief executive officer of Stamford-based Playtex Inc., had donated $1 million to endow the head football coach's job, the first endowed position in the athletic department.

Sept. 17: Yale wrestled Brown to a 24–24 tie at Providence but at a big price. Bob Verduzco, the Blue's starting quarterback, suffered torn knee ligaments. He didn't take the field again until two years later.

THE HIGHLIGHTS   1988

Sept. 26: Because of multiple injuries to the corps of Yale quarterbacks, Yale freshman football coach and varsity baseball coach Joe Benanto suggested that Cozza call Darin Kehler, a baseball player, who was an All-State high school QB in Valley View, Pennsylvania. Kehler joined the team and made a remarkable impact.

Oct. 1: Navy and its strong wishbone offense had their way with Yale at Annapolis, winning, 41–7. Kehler dressed for the game but did not play.

Oct. 8: On a field soaked by rain, Mike Mayweather ran for 155 yards and Ben Barnett for 92 out of the wishbone as Army, a 30-point favorite, rolled over Yale, 33–18, before 17,898 fans in the Bowl. Keith Walker added two field goals for the Cadets. Yale's senior tailback, Buddy Zachery, scored early in the fourth quarter on an 82-yard run from scrimmage. Linebackers Jon Reese and Don Lund sparked a strong defensive effort. Reese (395) and Lund (386) rank one and two in career tackles for Yale.

Oct. 15: Yale, 0–3–1, clipped Columbia, 24–10, for their first win of the season. The week before, Columbia had snapped a 44-game losing streak at the hands of Princeton. Kehler, taking advantage of his rainbow of opportunity, emerged as the team's quarterback with a strong performance off the bench. Entering the game with the score tied, 10–10, in the third quarter, the double-threat Kehler moved the chains. Zachery had touchdown runs of 34 and 32 yards and garnered 138 yards in 18 carries.

Oct. 29: The Darin Kehler era began in earnest as Yale beat Dartmouth, 22–13. With Yale trailing, 13–12, Kehler engineered an 89-yard drive from the Yale 11 that concluded with a 24-yard field goal by Scott Walton that gave the Bulldogs a 15–13 lead. Zachery, who rushed for 174 yards, subsequently ran 57 yards for an insurance TD.

Nov. 12: QB Jason Garrett, captain of the 1988 Princeton team and the Asa S. Bushnell Award winner as the Ivy League Player of the Year, quarterbacked a 24–7 victory over Yale. It was the Tigers' first win in New Haven since 1966. Garrett completed 21 of 26 passes for 259 yards, five of them to his brother Judd, who also ran for 76 yards.

Nov. 19: In a game televised nationally on ESPN, Kevin Callahan scored on a 1-yard run and caught a pass for another as Yale beat Harvard in the 105th meeting, 26–17. Brian Hennen scored on a 47-yard run after a punt was blocked by Rich Huff. It was Yale's fourth blocked punt of the year, and the first time a punt had been blocked and returned for a touchdown in the history of the Yale-Harvard series.

Kehler ran for a touchdown. Kevin Brice carried 19 times for 98 yards while Buddy Zachery had 20 carries for 97 yards to complete the Bulldogs' well-balanced attack. With 2:22 left in the half, backup QB Mark Brubaker, who had lost the job early in the season because of an injury, entered the game. Brubaker, operating out of the shotgun, drove the team 64 yards to pay dirt, hitting Callahan for the go-ahead touchdown just 29 seconds before the half. For his outstanding play, linebacker Jon Reese was carried off the field by his teammates, a rare sight for a defensive player.

1989 (8–2) Ivy League champs. Coach: Carmen Cozza; Captain: Jon Reese

To take advantage of Kehler's running ability, Yale switched to a modified wishbone offense. Kehler would rush for 903 yards for the season, the best single-season total of any Yale quarterback in history. He also passed for 870 yards in a season that Yale and Princeton would share the Ivy League title.

Yale captain Jon Reese rebounded the same week after he was seriously injured in a car accident on Halloween night.

Sept. 16: Kehler ran for 107 yards as the Bulldogs opened the season with a 12–3 win against Brown.

Sept. 23: Kehler kept the ball rolling, rushing for 186 yards in Yale's 33–17 win over Lehigh. It was the highest rushing total ever by a Yale QB. He also completed 11 of 15 passes for 130 yards. For the day, he accounted for 316 yards of total offense.

Oct. 28: Yale defeated defending Ivy League champion Penn, 23–22, on sophomore Ed Perks's 28-yard field goal with 10 seconds remaining. The outcome positioned Yale to earn a share of the Ivy League title for the first time since 1981.

Jon Reese, the intimidating linebacker, is Yale's all-time leader in solo tackles with 257.

The Highlights 1989

Oct. 31: Yale captain Jon Reese, a first team All-Ivy player, was seriously injured when the car he was driving and carrying five other Yale players was in a terrible accident while on the way to dinner following practice. The accident was caused by a drunk driver who ran a red light on Edgewood Avenue. Reese, who was sent to the Hospital of Saint Raphael, broke his jaw in two places. He also broke his nose, tore ligaments in his elbow, lost several upper teeth, and had multiple stitches on his upper lip. It appeared that Reese, who had started every game since his sophomore year, would never play again.

Nov. 2: Jon was recuperating in the Yale infirmary when he showed up for practice and barely able to talk spoke to his teammates about the importance of the Ivy League title. The next day he led the team in calisthenics. Dr. Robert Parker, who had done the surgery on Reese, cleared him to play against Cornell as long as he wore a special mouthpiece and face mask. Joe Levatino, who was on the equipment staff, trainers Bill Kaminsky and "Sweet Lou" Scigliano designed a special Darth Vader–looking helmet with a black visor.

Nov. 4: Early in the game, sophomore Kevin Skol, Reese's replacement at middle linebacker, was injured. Cozza reluctantly put Reese into the game. In one of the most courageous performances any Yale football player has ever had, he made nine tackles and caused a fumble in helping Yale to a 34–19 win over Cornell. It was the only game that Reese did not start during his Yale career.

QB Darin Kehler rushed for 89 yards and passed for 158, including two touchdowns. Defensive back Rich Huff intercepted two passes, his six and seventh of the season, tying him with 1937 Heisman Trophy winner Clint Frank and Mark Wallrapp (1995).

Nov. 11: Carm Cozza enjoyed his 150th win at Yale and his 10th and final Ivy League championship as Yale downed Princeton, 14–7, allowing the Bulldogs to share the title with the Tigers. Maurice Saah scored on a 30-yard run in the third quarter to tie the score, 7–7. Both teams entered the game 5–0 in the conference. Yale's final score was set up by Huff, who got a hand on a Princeton punt that caused the ball to go out of bounds at the Tigers' 17. The Bulldogs then scored three plays later.

Judd Garrett, the third of the Garrett brothers to play for Princeton, gained 149 yards on 33 carries. All three Garrett brothers transferred from Columbia when their father, Jim, departed as the Lions' coach.

Nov. 18: Harvard, 4–2 in the Ivy and 4–5 overall, deprived Yale of the outright Ivy title, handing the Elis a 37–20 loss. Crimson halfback Silas Myers scored two touchdowns in the second quarter for a 14–0 halftime lead. The Bulldogs, trailing, 21–0, in the third quarter, came within a point of tying the score but the conversion kick after the third TD was partially blocked and the quarter ended with Harvard ahead, 21–20. The Cantabs then scored 16 unanswered points on a day they would collect 412 yards (230 rushing and 182 passing) in coach Joe Restic's "multiflex" offense.

1990 (6–4) Coach: Carmen Cozza; Captain: Chris Gaughan

Sept. 15: Yale opened the season at Brown with a 27–21 win. Kehler connected on 9 of 18 passes for 205 yards and two touchdowns.

Sept. 22: The Bulldogs beat Lafayette, 18–17, in a game played in a torrential rainstorm that Carm Cozza called the worst of his Yale coaching career. An announced crowd of 6,458 had diminished to fewer than 500 by the time Lafayette missed a field-goal attempt on the final play of the game. In the fourth quarter Yale pulled to within 17–16 when Nick Crawford crossed the goal line. Cozza gambled for the win instead of the tie. Rather than kicking the tying extra point, Kehler hit Chris Warner in the end zone with 5:29 to go for a two-point conversion to give Yale the lead. A missed Lafayette field goal try by Jim Hodson from 38 yards sailed wide with seven seconds left.

Nov. 3: Scott Oliaro ran for a Cornell school-record 288 yards to lead the Big Red past the Bulldogs, 41–31, in the Bowl. Yale had a school-record 214 kickoff return yards on eight runbacks. The Elis' Maurice Saah returned five kickoffs for 166 yards and Ed Perks kicked a 52-yard field goal in a losing effort. (Perks was 27-for-27 in PATs in 1990.)

Nov. 10: Kevin Callahan rushed for 104 yards on 22 carries and tossed a touchdown pass to Chris Warner as Yale wore down Princeton, 34–7, in a driving rainstorm.

Nov. 17: Kehler rushed for 92 yards and passed for 113 yards in leading Yale past Harvard, 34–19. The multi-dimensional quarterback finished his career seventh on Yale's all-time passing list with 1,816 yards and eighth on the all-time rushing list with 1,643 yards. With five minutes remaining in the game, Cozza removed Kehler, who leaped into the arms of his coach.

Quarterback Darin Kehler led Yale to many victories after being recruited off the baseball team.

1991 (6-4) Coach: Carmen Cozza; Captain: Chris Kouri

June 22: Yale coach Carmen Cozza and Harvard coach Joe Restic coached Japanese teams at Harvard Stadium. Cozza piloted Waseda, dressed in crimson and Restic directed Keio, dressed in blue. The coaches wore their respective school colors. Keio won the contest, 21–19, on a 22-yard TD pass with 38 seconds remaining.

Oct. 19: Dartmouth's Jay Fiedler, who played for four NFL teams, tossed a 10-yard TD pass to Mike Bobo with 23 seconds left in the game to give the Big Green a 28–24 win over Yale.

Nov. 2: Nick Crawford rushed for a Yale QB-record 204 yards in Yale's 31–12 win over Penn.

Nov. 23: Yale captain Chris Kouri, pulled from the game after taking a hit that caused internal bleeding, returned in the second half to complete a 112-yard rushing day as Yale beat Harvard, 23–13, before 40,091 in the Bowl. He scored once and blocked for Jim Gouveia on the go-ahead touchdown. Kevin Skol led Yale's defenders with 14 tackles and Eric Drury blocked two punts.

1992 (4–6) Coach: Carmen Cozza; Captain: Dave Sheronas

July 7: Yale's 1937 Heisman winner Clint Frank passed away at age 76.

Oct. 3: UConn beat Yale. 40–20. at Storrs. In the 49-game series played between Yale and UConn, this was the only game played at UConn's home field.

Oct. 10: The only wedding ceremony in Yale Bowl history was held at halftime of the Yale-Fordham game, won by Yale, 31–12. Two former Yale Precision Marching Band members, Rori Smullen and Jim Lockman, tied the knot. The couple renewed their 20th anniversary vows at the Bowl at halftime of the Yale-Lafayette game in 2012.

Oct. 17: Dartmouth, led by the passing arm of Fiedler, whipped Yale, 39–27, in Hanover. Fielder passed for a school-record 419 yards.

Nov. 14: Princeton humiliated Yale, 36–7, outgaining the Bulldogs, 565 yards to 125. Yale's defense got the Blue's only touchdown on a fumble return near the end of the game.

Nov. 20, 1992: The Yale Bullpups beat the Harvard freshmen in Boston, 26–6, in the last freshman game Yale has ever played.

Nov.21: Harvard blanked the Bulldogs, 14–0, in Boston to finish 3-7. The star of the game was Crimson defensive back Rob Santos, who intercepted a Yale pass in the end zone early in the fourth quarter, and with 3:58 remaining swatted the ball from Yale's elusive Keith Price on a 4th-and-1 at the 2, causing a fumble. Harvard QB Mike Giardi scored on short runs in the first and third quarters. Price finished his career with 1,141 rushing yards.

At the time, an article in the *Harvard Independent* was calling for Harvard coach Joe Restic to retire. Entering the game, Harvard was 18–30–1 in their last 49 games, including back-to-back losses against dreaded Yale. Following the game, Restic said to the *Boston Globe*, "Joe Restic will leave when Joe Restic decides to leave." He would coach just one more season.

1993 (3–7) Coach: Carmen Cozza; Captain: John Saunders

Spring practice was reinstated for the Ivy League schools for the first time since 1953.

Sept. 18: The multi-purpose Lapham Field House used by male and female athletes was renovated and renamed the Joel E. Smilow Field Center following a generous gift of $5.37 million from Mr. Smilow (class of '54) and another $1.7 million from other alumni, including the Humphrey family (George, Watts, and their mother, Louise Ireland Humphrey). The day did not end on happy note as Brown defeated Yale, 12–3.

Oct. 2: Yale battled Central Florida in the shadows of Disney World. Tied, 28–28, with 42 seconds remaining in the game, David Rhodes's 10-yard run with a recovered Yale fumble gave the Knights a 35–28 lead before Richard Blake's 42-yard interception TD return with two seconds left sealed UCF's 42–28 win.

Nov.19: In response to Yale's dismal 2–7 season, Theo Epstein, the editor of the *Yale Daily News*, wrote an editorial stating that coach Carm Cozza should step down after 29 years.

Nov. 20: Possibly inspired by Epstein's story, Yale's injury-battered team upset Harvard, 33–31. Perhaps because of the teams' anemic records (Yale 2–7; Harvard 3–6), only 33,776 showed up for the annual Y-H joust played in the old crater on 81 Central Avenue in New Haven.

Harvard QB Mike Giardi had a career-high 279 yards passing and set an all-time Harvard career record for total yards, running and passing, with 5,057.

The Yale hero was Dave Iwan, who caught seven passes for 175 yards and scored touchdowns on plays of 45 and 26 yards. His single-season total of 873 yards eclipsed the record of 791 set by Curt Grieve in 1981. It should be noted that many brothers have had the honor of playing in the Bowl, but only two sets have the distinction of scoring touchdowns in the venerated saucer. That goes to Herb Hallas (1956–58) and brother Hank (1960–62) and the Iwan sibs, Dave (1991–93) and Dan (1993–95).

Following the game, Cozza joked that the game ball should go to Epstein and the *Yale Daily News*. Epstein, the current President of Baseball Operations for the Chicago Cubs, told the *New York Times* in November 2016 that that he wished he had handled the situation differently.

This was also Harvard coach Joe Restic's final game. The winningest coach in Harvard football history, Restic finished with a 117–97–6 mark that included five Ivy championships during his 23-year tenure. Tim Murphy has since eclipsed Restic in wins (178) entering the 2020 season. Restic was 10–13 vs. Yale.

1994 (5–5) **Coach: Carmen Cozza; Captain: Carl Ricci**

Sept. 17: Rob Masella scored on a 95-yard kickoff return at Brown in Yale's 27–16 victory.

Sept. 24: Tony Mazurkiewicz blocked a punt in the second quarter, setting up the first of five unanswered touchdowns as Yale surged past Holy Cross, 47–22. Rob Nelson rushed for 117 yards and a TD.

Oct. 1: A Dan Mellish fumble recovery and Mark Wallrapp's capture of an onside kick paved the way for two early Keith Price touchdowns and a 28–17 victory over UConn. Rain held the crowd to 9,314. The victory was Yale's last in its 49-game series with its intra-state rival.

Oct. 8: There would be no celebration for Yale's 500th game in the Bowl as Lehigh QB Rob Aylsworth set a single-game Yale Bowl passing mark with 454 yards (30-for 41), including three touchdowns, in the Engineers' 36–32 win. It was Lehigh's first victory in 13 tries against Yale.

Nov. 5: Rob Nelson ran for three touchdowns as Yale stopped a four-game losing streak by beating Cornell, 24–14, in the Bowl. The victory also ended a skein of four losses to the Big Red. Wallrapp's interception in the end zone kept Cornell from taking the lead in the third quarter.

Nov. 19: Yale coach Carm Cozza beat Harvard for the record 16th time as the Blue closed out the Crimson, 32–13, in Boston. Cozza's 16 wins in the Y-H series was surpassed by Harvard's Tim Murphy in 2015. Tight end Dave Prybyla made a miraculous over-the-middle catch on a 4th-and-13.

1995 (3–7) **Coach: Carmen Cozza; Captain: Tony Mazurkiewicz**

Sept. 16: Yale kicked off the season by defeating Brown, 42–28, in the Bowl. The star of the show was QB Chris Hetherington, who rushed for 166 yards and passed for 223.

Nov. 11: The Elis spoiled the Tigers' undefeated season by winning at Princeton, 21–13. Yale QB Chris Hetherington's 229 total yards led the way for the Bulldogs. That season he passed for 1,169 yards and was the team's second-leading rusher, with 540 yards. Hetherington played for six different NFL teams, the most of any Yale player.

Nov. 18: Harvard's Eion Hu scored from two yards out with 29 seconds left to give the Crimson a 22–21 win. It's the last time a Y-H game was decided by a single point. In attendance was 89-year-old Al Ostermann, who attended the first game ever in the Yale Bowl in 1914 and has been at every other one since but one, a total of 507. For many years Ostermann was present in the Bowl in an official capacity operating the electronic scoreboard. In 1993, *USA Today* scoured the nation for college football fans with attendance streaks, and no one came within a decade of Ostermann, who died at age 95 in 2001.

1996 (2–8) Coach: Carmen Cozza; Captain: Rob Masella

Carmen Cozza closed out his legendary 32-year tenure as Yale's head football coach. He exited with an overall 179–119–5 career record, a .599 winning percentage. His Ivy League mark stands at 135–84–5, making him the winningest coach in Ivy League history. His 10 Ivy League championships are the most of any coach. The overtime rule was introduced throughout college football.

Oct. 5: Army beat Yale at West Point, 39–13. Yale's first touchdown came on a pass interception by defensive back and captain Rob Masella, who picked off a pass on Army's 34 yard line and raced into the end zone with 48 seconds left in the first half. The other Bulldogs score was made by linebacker Todd Scott. who jumped on a fumble in the Army end zone. The Cadets kicked three field goals in the first half.

Nov. 2: Carm Cozza coached his 300th game at Yale, but there was no cause for celebration as the Bulldogs were defeated by Penn, 20–3, at Franklin Field.

Nov.16: Cozza coached his final game in the Yale Bowl, a 17–13 loss to Princeton. That day, 31 of his 32 captains were on the field to honor their beloved coach. Yale presented Cozza with a new tractor.

Nov. 23: Cozza ended his 32-year reign as head football coach with a 26–21 loss to Harvard. He was inducted into the College Football Hall of Fame in 2002.

Dec. 19: Yale hired Jack Siedlecki as its 32nd head football coach. Siedlecki was the head coach at Amherst before coming to Yale.

1997 (1–9) Coach: Jack Siedlecki; Captain: Todd Scott

Siedlecki inherited an undernourished Bulldog, hungry for victory. The Bulldogs hadn't had a winning season since 1991 and was 17–33 in its last 50 games.

Sept. 20: In the most lopsided opening day defeat in Yale football history, Brown pummeled Yale, 52–14, spoiling Siedlecki's head coaching debut for the Bulldogs. Saddled with injuries, Yale was forced to start freshman Mike McClellan at quarterback, the first frosh QB to start a game for Yale since Art Dakos in 1945. Brown's 629 yards gained were the most by any opponent since the Bowl opened in 1914. Sophomore QB James Perry threw four first-half touchdowns for the Bears and passed for 333 yards for the game.

Oct. 3: Yale beat Valparaiso, 34–14, under the lights at Soldier Field in Chicago to give coach Siedlecki his first win.

Jack Siedlecki succeeded Carm Cozza in 1997.

Nov. 1: Penn beat Yale, 26–7, but forfeits the game to Yale because Penn player Mitch Morrow dropped some courses and thus did not meet the Ivy standard of reasonable progress toward a degree. However, according to the NCAA, the 1997 Yale-Penn game remains a Penn victory.

When it discovered the ineligible player, Penn said it was forfeiting the game. The Ivy League office went along with that and lists Penn's Ivy record for 1997 as 0–7. But both Penn and the Ivy office ignored Article 31.10.5 of the NCAA Manual, which specifies who has power to change a result and under what circumstances. Neither Penn nor the Ivy office has that power, although the NCAA allows conferences to award forfeitures for purposes of conference standings. Therefore, according to the NCAA, the game is listed as a Penn victory since it did not meet the criteria for changing the result. It only met the criteria for changing a conference standing. Basically, the NCAA changes a result only in circumstances that fall just short of requiring the "death penalty" that it imposed on SMU in the late 1980s. Thus, Yale counted the game as a Penn victory and does not count it toward Yale's 800 wins. Otherwise the 1999 Harvard game would have been the 800th victory, but by NCAA rule, it wasn't.

Nov. 15: Princeton, ending a three-game losing streak, beat Yale, 9–0, at Giants Stadium on a blustery and cloudy day before a crowd of 6,503. The Big Three rivals played for the 120th time. The game was played at Giants Stadium because Princeton Stadium was being constructed.

Nov. 22: This Yale edition matched the 1983 team as the losingest team in school history, finishing 1–9 after Harvard beat them in the Bowl, 17–7.

1998 (6–4) Coach: Jack Siedlecki; Captain: Corwynne Carruthers

Cozza joined the WELI broadcast booth and served in the role of color commentator until 2016 working with Dick Galiette and later Ron Vaccaro.

Sept. 19: Yale opened the season with a thrilling 30–28 win over Brown in Providence. Wide receiver Jake Borden scored on a 27-yard pass from QB Joe Walland with six seconds remaining in the game.

Sept. 26: UConn trounced Yale, 63–21. The 42-point loss is the worst Bulldogs loss in terms of margin of defeat in the team's history in the Yale Bowl. It was the final game in the 49-game series between the two schools. Yale has the edge, 32–17.

Oct. 17: Despite Mike Murawczyk's four field goals, the Elis lost to Dartmouth for the ninth straight time, 22–19. Walland completed a 34-yard pass to Ken Marschner in the final seconds. As Murawczyk was about to attempt a game-tying 23-yard field goal, referee William Gosselin marked the ball and then lifted it, marking the end of the game. Yale had used its final timeout with 11 seconds to play.

Nov. 21: Murawczyk made the most of a second chance. After his extra-point was blocked, leaving Harvard ahead with five minutes left,

Yale got the ball back on a Jeff Hockenbrock fumble recovery. Murawczyk then kicked a 27-yard field goal with 3:04 to go, giving Yale a 9–7 victory in Boston.

1999 (9–1) Ivy League Champs. Coach: Jack Siedlecki; Captain: Jake Fuller

Sept. 18: Yale suffered ill fortune when Brown won, 25–24, on a fluke play in the opening game of the season. The Bears scored with 14 seconds left in the game to pull within one point of the Bulldogs, 24–23. It appeared for a moment that Yale had won the contest when Ben Blake blocked the extra point but Brown's Mike Powell picked up the free ball and tossed it to Rob Scholl, who rambled it into the end zone for a two-point conversion. Yale missed a 47-yard field goal try on the last play of the game. This would be Yale's only loss of the season.

Oct. 2: Yale beat San Diego, 17–6, at Torero Stadium at night. Following the game, many of the Yale players crossed the border into Tijuana, Mexico. According to defensive end Peter Sarantos, "Dan Searle and a drunk Mexican guy got into a verbal altercation, and friends of the Mexican guy pulled him away and in doing so, the guy fell off a small bridge which turned into a 10-foot fall." Head coach Jack Siedlecki and most his coaching staff were not aware of the caper because they flew home early to prepare for the Holy Cross game the following week.

Oct. 16: Following nine straight losses to Dartmouth, the Bulldogs levied an assault on Big Green, winning, 44–3. Eric Johnson caught nine passes for 117 yards and a touchdown; Rashad Bartholomew ran for 109 yards and a TD; and QB Joe Walland piled up 329 total offensive yards

Nov. 20: Just two years after going an abysmal 1–9, the Bulldogs reversed their record by beating Harvard, 24–21. Yale wide receiver Eric Johnson caught a 4-yard Joe Walland pass inches off the ground with 29 seconds left for the winning touchdown that gave the Bulldogs a share of the Ivy League championship with Brown, the first Ivy title for Yale in 10 years.

Johnson's snare has been celebrated in Ivy circles as "The Catch." For the day he had 21 catches for 244 yards, both Yale single-game records. The great Yale receiver, who married singer Jessica Simpson, went on to have a successful career with the San Francisco 49ers.

Yale, down, 14–3, in the third quarter, was led by Walland, who threw

Above: Eric Johnson makes "The Catch" against Harvard in 1999. *Below:* Joe Walland and Eric Johnson are still smiling about "The Catch" (both photographs courtesy Bill O'Brien).

a Division I AA-record 51 passes and had a record 33 completions in the second half. For the day he was 42 of 67 for 437 yards. Except for the first play of the second half when Walland handed off to Rashad Bartholomew, every play was designed to be a pass play as the Bulldogs used four wide receivers (Johnson, Jake Fuller, Jake Borden and Tom McNamara) to keep the Harvard defense busy. Walland was in the infirmary the night before the game with a 103-degree temperature.

2000 (7–3) Coach: Jack Siedlecki; Captain: Peter Mazza

Walland's 67 attempts and speed-up offense in the Harvard game was a preview of things to come in the 21st century for Yale football. The no-huddle offense, visible play clock, along with pace of game, the spread offense, including the run-pass option off the spread and rules favoring the offense have led to the shattering of long-standing offensive records. Teams this century average approximately 75 plays each game. Back in the day, 55 to 60 might have been the norm. In a 10-game schedule teams run perhaps 200 more plays each season then what was run in the distant past.

June 27: Larry Kelley, Yale's 1936 Heisman winner, died at age 85 of a self-inflicted gunshot wound at his home in Hightstown, New Jersey. His Heisman trophy was auctioned in December 1999 for $328,110.

Sept. 16: Yale defeated Dayton, 42–6, and became America's first football program, high school, college or pro, to win 800 games. Yale beat Michigan to the milestone by two weeks.

Sept. 23: Led by Cornell QB Ricky Rahne, whose two fourth-quarter touchdown passes overshadowed Rashad Bartholomew's 180-yard game, the Big Red nipped Yale, 24–23, in Ithaca. Yale's Mike Murawczyk, who already had booted three field goals, missed a 32-yarder as time ran out.

Sept. 30: Yale edged Holy Cross in the Bowl, 33–27. Todd Tomich returned five punts for 99 yards, a team record.

Oct. 28: Defensive back Ryan LoProto twice scored on interceptions, one a 67-yard TD, as the Elis trounced Columbia, 41–0.

Nov. 11: With 16 seconds left on the clock in the fourth quarter, Princeton's Chisom Opara scored on a 32-yard pass from Jon Blevins to give the Tigers a 19–14 lead which proved to be the final score.

Nov. 18: Led by Bartholomew's 119 rushing yards, Yale downed Harvard, 34–24, the third straight season the Bulldogs won The Game. Harvard's Chuck Nwokocha's 94-yard kickoff return was the longest kickoff return in the Y-H series. Bartholomew finished the season with 1,232 yards and 3,015 yards for his career.

Dec. 7: Levi Jackson, Yale's first black captain, died in Detroit, Michigan at age 74.

2001 (3–6) Coach: Jack Siedlecki; Captain: Tim Penna

Sept. 15: Yale cancelled its game at Towson because of the terrorist attacks of 9/11. Former Yale defensive lineman Rich Lee lost his life in the World Trade Center tragedy.

Sept. 22: P.J. Collins set the modern school mark with seven punt returns and Billy Brown scored three TDs in Yale's 40–13 win over Cornell in the Bowl.

Sept. 29: Justin Davis kicked a 28-yard field goal with four seconds left as Yale, after trailing for much of the game, edged Holy Cross, 23–22, in Worcester, Massachusetts. Keith Reams caught two touchdown passes from Peter Lee for the Bulldogs.

Oct. 7: In the only Sunday college game ever played in the Yale Bowl, Dartmouth beat Yale, 32–27, before a free admission crowd of 19,996. Dartmouth quarterback Greg Smith ripped apart the Yale defense, passing for 407 yards while completing 38 passes in 54 attempts. Robert Carr rushed for a Yale freshman-record 185 yards in a losing cause.

The game was originally scheduled for October 6 but was rescheduled for the next day to accommodate for cleanup of Yale's Tercentennial celebration the previous day.

Nov. 3: Yale's Jay Schulze scored four touchdowns, but the Elis defense couldn't stop the big play as Brown, who trailed, 20–7, in the second quarter, rallied to win, 37–34. Bears QB Kyle Rowley threw touchdown passes of 28, 58 and 37 yards. Yale backup QB T.J. Hyland rushed for 141 yards and passed for 146 in a losing cause.

Nov. 17: Led by Neil Rose's four touchdown passes, Harvard beat Yale, 35–23, ending Yale's three-game win streak in the series. The win sealed the Crimson's first perfect season since 1913. Coach Percy Haughton had last led Harvard to undefeated and untied seasons in 1912 and 1913.

2002 (6–4) Coach: Jack Siedlecki; Captain: Jason Lange

Sept. 28: Yale lost quarterback Alvin Cowan to a leg fracture on its second offensive play of the game and turned to sophomore running back

Robert Carr, who led the Bulldogs to a 50–23 victory over Cornell at Ithaca. Carr had 18 carries for a Yale sophomore-record 235 yards and scored four touchdowns. Yale's Mark Patterson had three quarterback sacks.

Oct. 5: Carr recorded his second successive 200-yard game, carrying 38 times for 219 yards and a touchdown as Yale silenced Holy Cross, 28–19, in the Bowl. Jeff Mroz tossed two TD passes and Pat Bydume reeled off a 51-yard scoring run.

Oct. 12: Dartmouth clipped Yale at Hanover, 20–17, when Yale's last-second 35-yard field-goal attempt was blocked.

Oct. 26: Penn breezed by Yale, 41–20, in the Bowl. The highlight of the day for Yale was David Knox's four kickoff returns for 179 yards.

Nov. 9: Quarterback Jeff Mroz passed for 281 yards and four touchdowns as Yale came from behind three times to beat Brown, 31–27, in Providence. Ralph Plumb's ninth catch of the day with 1:46 left capped a 70-yard, nine-play drive for the winning score.

Nov. 23: Harvard got by Yale, 20–13, on a biting, cold day with temperatures in the 30s and a swirling wind gusting to 50 mph at Harvard Stadium before a sellout crowd of 30,323. Because of the elements, Harvard coach Tim Murphy replaced QB Neil Rose in the second half with sophomore Ryan Fitzpatrick, more of a running threat. "Fitz" finished with 72 yards rushing and 135 yards passing. In the third quarter Fitzpatrick scored twice and Nick Palazzo crossed the goal line for the Crimson. Robert Carr (3-yard run) and Ron Benigno (24-yard pass) scored for the Blue.

2003 (6–4) Coach: Jack Siedlecki; Captain: Alvin Cowan

Sept. 20: Carr ran for three touchdowns and Benigno caught three scoring passes as Yale shredded Towson, 62–28, in the Bowl. Don Smith, with three tackles for losses, led a Yale defense that forced six turnovers.

Oct. 18: Yale tight end Nate Lawrie garnered 16 catches in a 52–40 loss to Colgate at Hamilton, New York. Lawrie played with five different NFL teams.

Oct. 25: Yale's 28-point fourth-quarter rally tied the game at 31–31 before Penn won this heartbreaker in overtime, 34–31, on a Peter Veldman field goal. It was the first time Yale played an overtime game in 122 years. Three TD passes by Alvin Cowan—the last to Ralph Plumb with 32 seconds left—rallied Yale from a 21-point deficit to a 31–31 tie in regulation after John Troost's kick tied the score. Penn's Sam Mathews rushed for 204 yards.

Nov. 8: Brown beat Yale in the Bowl, 55–44, in front of 15,442 fans. The combined 99 points established a Yale Bowl record for most combined points scored in a game. The nerve-racking contest saw a Bowl-record eight lead changes. Bears wide receiver Lonnie Hill caught a 17-yard touchdown pass from Kyle Slager to give Brown a 47–44 lead with 26 seconds left. Nick Marietti's extra point made it 48–44. Then James Gasparella ended Yale's final drive, intercepting a pass and returning it 32 yards for a touchdown in the final seconds. Hill finished with 13 catches for 183 yards and four touchdowns. Cowan completed 22 of 34 passes for 381 yards and three touchdowns in a losing cause.

Nov. 15: Chandler Henley's catch of a Cowan pass on the last play of regulation time tied the score at Princeton, and John Troost's field goal in the second overtime brought Yale a hard-fought 27–24 victory after Yale recovered a fumble. Cowan passed for all three Yale touchdowns.

Nov. 22: At 7:45 a.m., several hours before the start of the Yale-Harvard game, a facilities worker at the Yale Bowl discovered a Harvard banner that seemingly carried a not-so-friendly message attached to the scoreboard on the north end of the Bowl. Yale officials viewed this as a bomb threat and the New Haven bomb truck was brought in. Traffic in the sur-

Alvin Cowan passed for 6,024 yards in his career.

rounding streets of the Bowl was at a standstill as the crowd of 53,136 was delayed entry. The incident proved to be a hoax unlike the Harvard football team that blew up the Bulldogs, 37–19. Junior QB Ryan Fitzpatrick, who would go on to a lengthy NFL career, completed four touchdown passes to Corey Mazza, Rodney Byrnes, Kelly Widman and Brian Edwards.

This game ended the Dante Balestracci era. The intimidating Harvard linebacker known as "The Disrupter," made eight tackles and had two sacks. He also had a blocked PAT attempt, and an 8-yard first down run from punt formation. Balestracci was the first player in Ivy League history to earn first team All-Ivy honors all four years.

2004 (5–5) Coach: Jack Siedlecki; Captain: Rory Hennessey

Oct. 2: Yale beat Colgate, 31–28, on Andrew Sullivan's 37-yard FG with seven seconds remaining in the game.

Nov. 6: Despite Ralph Plumb's 18 receptions, good for a school-record 258 yards, Yale lost to Brown in Providence, 24–17. Plumb ranks third in all-time receiving yards with 2,396.

Nov. 20: Harvard, a team that eight times scored at least 30 points against an opponent during the season, completed the program's seventh undefeated and untied season by cruising past Yale, 35–3. Ryan Fitzpatrick, who captained the Harvard team, earned the season's Frederick Greeley Crocker award as team MVP and the Asa Bushnell Cup as Ivy League Player of the Year. Harvard's Ricky Williams picked off an Alvin Cowan pass and returned it for a 100-yard touchdown. It stands as the only 100-yard play in the Y-H series.

Harvard won the battle on the field, but Yale won the war of pranks. The scheme was conceived by Yale students Michael Kai and David Aulcino. About 20 Yale students, costumed as a Harvard pep squad, handed out white or crimson placards to about 1,800 Harvard fans. The fans were told when they lifted the placards on cue they would spell GO HARVARD. Instead, when raised on high, the placards spelled, WE SUCK. The "Mother of all Pranks" gained national press coverage including the *Jimmy Kimmel Live!* show.

2005 (4–6) Coach: Jack Siedlecki; Captain: Jeff Mroz

The Abare twins (Bobby and Larry) emerged on the scene. The two outstanding defensive players were a double dose of poison to opposing offenses. Bobby was a first team All-Ivy and All–New England selection for three years.

Sept. 24: Jeff Mroz tied a Yale record by throwing five touchdown passes as the Bulldogs mowed down Cornell, 37–17, in the Bowl. Ashley Wright caught three of the scoring missiles while Todd Feiereisen grabbed two.

Oct. 8: Yale defeated Dartmouth, 13–0, in a rain-drenched Yale Bowl. Mroz clicked on scoring passes to Alex Faherty and Feiereisen. Yale's defense was led by Matt Handlon (13 tackles), Lee Driftmier (12) and Brandon Dyches (11) including four for losses.

Oct. 21: Broadcaster Dick Galiette died at age 72. Galiette was the steady welcoming, soundtrack of Yale football for 33 years. He worked his final game the week before at Goodman Stadium in Bethlehem, Pennsylvania, where Lehigh beat Yale, 28–21, in overtime.

Nov. 12: Yale trailed until the last two minutes, then scored twice in 27 seconds to beat Princeton, 21–14, in the Bowl. After Feiereisen caught a Mroz pass for a tying touchdown with 1:14 left, Bobby Abare's 27-yard return of a Tiger fumble positioned Mroz to score the deciding TD on a quarterback sneak with 47 seconds left on the clock. Alan Kimball kicked the extra point.

Nov. 19: With dusk falling on New Haven, Harvard's Clifton Dawson ended Yale's longest game in the modern era in the third overtime with a 2-yard TD run to give Harvard a 30–24 win at the Bowl. It was the first triple-overtime Ivy League game on record. Yale squandered a 21–3 lead and was undone in the overtimes by two fumbles and an interception. The Bulldogs have played five overtime games in the Bowl and are 4–1, their only loss to Harvard.

Dawson is the Crimson leader in career rushing attempts (958), rushing yards (4,841), single-season rushing yards (1,302), career rushing touchdowns (60), and single-season rushing touchdowns (20).

2006 (8–2) Ivy League Champs. Coach: Jack Siedlecki; Captain: Chandler Henley

The Mike McLeod era (2005–2008) returned Yale among the Ivy elite. The New Britain, Connecticut, native holds numerous Yale records including career rushing yards (4,514) and touchdowns (55). In 2007, he established a Yale single-season record 23 rushing touchdowns.

Sept. 23: Yale rebounded from an opening day loss to San Diego by beating Cornell, 21–9, on the road. McLeod rushed for 104 yards and two touchdowns while the defense limited the Big Red to three field goals.

Oct. 14: McLeod ran for 204 yards on 40 carries and scored twice as Yale edged Lehigh in a 26–20 overtime decision in the Bowl. He tallied the game-winner from 1-yard out in the first overtime after the Mountain Hawks missed a field-goal attempt.

Oct. 21: Yale won back-to-back overtime games in the Bowl. Alan Kimball's 35-yard field goal in OT gave Yale a 17–14 win over Penn.

Nov. 4: Bobby Abare, with three interceptions, led Yale to a 27–24 win over Brown in Providence.

Left to right: The Abare twins, Larry and Bobby. Bobby was a three-time All-Ivy League First Team selection.

Nov. 11: Led by quarterback Jeff Terrell, Princeton rallied from a trio of 14-point deficits to take a 34–31 decision in the Bowl that led to the two teams sharing the Ivy League title. The win gave Princeton its first H-Y-P title since 1994.

Nov. 18: The Bulldogs bounced back from their loss to Princeton and smashed rival Harvard, 34–13 in Boston. McLeod's three touchdowns and a 38-yard fumble return by safety Steve Santoro handed the Elis their biggest win at Harvard since a 39–6 victory in 1960.

2007 (9–1) Coach: Jack Siedlecki; Captain: Brandt Hollander

The Bulldogs came out of the gate with vigor, winning their first nine games before falling to Harvard. McLeod, who was voted the Ivy League Player of the Year, was hobbled over the final four games by a toe injury suffered against Penn.

Sept. 29: At Worcester, McLeod rushed for five touchdowns, tying the modern Yale record, as the Bulldogs crushed Holy Cross, 38–17. McLeod also vanquished a 76-year Yale rushing mark with 256 yards on 40 carries. The Bulldogs racked up 412 rushing yards, including a 48-yard sprint by Rocky Galvez, McLeod's backup. Jay Pilkerton picked off two Crusaders passes.

Mike McLeod is Yale's all-time leader in rushing TDs (54) and rushing yards (4,514).

Oct. 13: McLeod broke his own single-game rushing record, netting 276 yards on 40 carries, including two TDs, as the Bulldogs ran over Lehigh, 23–7.

Oct. 20: McLeod's third touchdown of the day, coming in the top half of the third overtime at Philadelphia, gave Yale a 26–20 victory over Penn and kept the Bulldogs undefeated. In the bottom half of the third overtime the Quakers had a first down one yard from Yale's goal line, but the Big Blue defense held. The win came with a heavy price when it was determined that McLeod had fractured a bone in his right toe, causing him to play the remainder of the season in pain.

Oct. 27: Yale beat Columbia in New York, 28–7. Tom Mante punted five times for 239 yards, an average of 47.8 yards per punt, a Yale school record.

Nov. 17: Again, Harvard spoiled Yale's march on history. In one of the most disappointing losses in the annals of Yale football, the Crimson pummeled Yale, 37–6, in the Bowl before 57,248, the largest crowd in 18 years. The blowout spoiled Yale's perfect undefeated and untied season.

The sons of John Harvard set the tone early when Harvard QB Chris Pizzotti connected with 6-foot-6 receiver Matt Luft for a 40-yard TD 68 seconds into the first quarter. Pizzotti would toss three more touchdown strikes. Luft caught more passes in the first quarter (five) than Yale completed (3-fo-22) all day; two went for touchdowns. He finished with eight catches for 160 yards.

Harvard took a commanding 27–0 lead at halftime and never looked back. The Cantabs' Steven Williams intercepted a Yale pass in the third quarter, the 16th of his career, a Harvard record. McLeod, the nation's leading rusher playing injured, was held to 50 yards on 20 carries. Yale's only score came on an 87-yard punt return by Gio Christodoulou with 4:15 remaining in the game.

Yale's celebrated defense, anchored by captain Brandt Hollander, had allowed just over 11 points per game, the fewest in the country entering the Harvard game, but had no answer for the Crimson on this frustrating day.

The game determined the Ivy championship and was the only time in the history of FCS football that a team had lost at home in a season-ending game while vying for a perfect season.

THE HIGHLIGHTS   2008–2009

2008 (6–4) Coach: Jack Siedlecki; Captain: Bobby Abare

Jack Siedlecki ended his 12-year run as Yale's head football coach with a 70–49–0 mark that included a share of two Ivy League titles. He had one year left on his contract. His departing words were, "I'm tired of Yale and Yale is tired of me."

Oct. 4: Yale beat Holy Cross, 31–28, in two overtimes in the Bowl. Tom Mante's 34-yard FG in the second overtime was the difference.

Oct. 18: Fordham QB John Skelton led the Rams on an 85-yard drive to set up Adam Danko's 20-yard field goal with 14 seconds left, to lead Fordham past Yale, 12–10, before 6,873 at Jack Coffey Field.

Nov. 8: The Elis played the role of spoiler against unbeaten Brown, winning, 13–3, on the road. The big play was a 78-yard pass play from Brook Hart to Peter Balsam.

Nov. 22: Mike McLeod and coach Jack Siedlecki ended their Yale careers on the same day in a dismal 10–0 loss at Harvard. Twins Bobby and Larry Abare played their final game together. Larry had one more year of eligibility.

2009 (4–6) Coach: Tom Williams; Captain: Paul Rice

Jan. 7: Tom Williams was named Yale's 33rd head football coach, succeeding Jack Siedlecki. Williams was the first African American to hold the position at Yale. A former linebacker at Stanford, Williams had been a defensive assistant for the Jacksonville Jaguars before coming to Yale.

Sept. 26: Tom Mante tied a 104-year-old school record for longest field goal (54 yards) and broke the Ivy League record but the Bulldogs lost to Cornell, 14–12, in the Bowl, spoiling Williams's home debut as Yale's head coach. The Elis almost pulled it out after time had expired. On the final play of regulation time, Yale QB Patrick Witt ran it into the end zone to cut the Big Red lead to 14–12. But Witt's attempted two-point conversion pass was incomplete.

Oct. 17: Lehigh beat Yale, 7–0. Yale senior Larry Abare, a standout safety, broke his arm and missed the next four games with the Elis losing three of them.

Nov. 21: The Game provided what may very well have been the most controversial coaching play call in the history of the Y-H series. The Crimson, trailing, 10–0, scored twice against an exhausted Yale defense in the final 6:46 to win, 14–10, before a stunned 52,692 fans.

The Bulldogs, nursing a 10–7 lead late in the fourth quarter, faked a punt on a 4th-and-22 on their 28 yard line despite having the best punter in the league (Mante) and Harvard having no timeouts. But the gamble was thwarted by the Harvard defense when Yale's John Powers was stopped at the Yale 40, seven yards short with 2:25 remaining in the game.

Harvard capitalized on the mind-boggling call by Yale coach Tom Williams, who at this point had little confidence in his tired defense, the reason he took the fatal gamble. Three plays later Crimson QB Collier Winters connected with Chris Lorditch for a 32-yard TD. Earlier in the last quarter, Winters had thrown a 41-yard scoring strike to Matt Luft. Harvard linebacker Jon Takamura, a native of Honolulu, intercepted a pass by Yale QB Patrick Witt in the final minute to seal the game.

In grand Hawaii fashion, Takamura passed out bright pink leis in celebration of the victory. Alex Thomas rushed for 125 yards in a losing cause for the Bulldogs. Larry Abare returned and played with a cast that covered almost his entire right arm.

Mante averaged 51.3 yards on three punts, including a soaring 69-yard kick that wowed the Bulldog fans. Following the game Williams addressed the fake punt play before anyone asked. "I was trying keep momentum on the blue side," he said. The play was reportedly the idea of an assistant coach, but the buck always stops with the head coach.

2010 (7–3) Coach: Tom Williams; Captain: Tom McCarthy

Oct. 9: Sophomore Philippe Panico's 19-yard field goal, his first ever, gave Yale a pulsating 23–20 win over Dartmouth on the road. The drive for the game-winner was set up by Yale senior cornerback Chris Stanley, who stripped the ball away from Dartmouth tailback Nick Schwieger at the Dartmouth 47 after he had received a screen pass from QB Conner Kempe. With the score tied, 20–20, this set up the Yale offense at the Dartmouth 47 with 1:06 to play. Two plays later Yale junior quarterback Patrick Witt completed a 28-yard pass to senior wide receiver Jordan Forney that got the ball to the 7. With 26 seconds to play, the Bulldogs sent sophomore tailback Mordecai Cargill up the middle for five more yards. With a timeout still in hand, Yale allowed the clock to tick down to four seconds in order to bring Panico out for the final play of regulation. It ended a back-and-forth game that saw four lead changes and 780 yards of total offense.

Nov. 6: Chris Smith became the first Ivy League player to return two kickoffs (83, 79 yards) for TDs in a game during Yale's 27–24 win over Brown at Providence. Junior tailback Alex Thomas ran for 121 yards on 27 carries, including a 27-yard touchdown. Brown came back from a 24–10 deficit to tie the score in the fourth quarter. With 9:30 left in the game, Panico kicked a 36-yard field goal which proved to be the game-winner. It was his second 36-yard FG of the game.

Nov. 13: Forty-two members of the 1960 team, the last undefeated and untied Yale football team, gathered for a 50th reunion celebration in the Yale Bowl before the Yale-Princeton game won by Yale, 14–13.

Nov. 20: Despite Alex Thomas's three touchdowns, the Bulldogs fell on the sword of Harvard Stadium in a 28–21 loss to the Crimson. Yale's final drive ended up nine yards short of a first down with 42 seconds to play, enabling Harvard to run out the clock in front of a sellout crowd of 31,398.

On the same day, The Lapham Field House was renamed the Smilow Field Center because of the donation of Joel E. Smilow '54, to renovate the facility.

2011 (5–5) Coach: Tom Williams; Captain: Jordan Haynes

Sept. 17: Chris Smith caught two touchdown passes and Mordecai Cargill also scored twice as Yale beat Georgetown, 37–27, in New Haven. Yale QB Patrick Witt completed 23 of 31 passes for 280 yards and three touchdowns.

Oct. 8: Yale beat up Dartmouth, 30–0, in the Bowl on a day the Yale defense limited tailback Nick Schwieger, the 2010 Ivy League co-MVP, to 39 yards on 16 carries. The Bulldogs' rushing attack stole the show behind its two tailbacks, senior Alex Thomas and junior Mordecai Cargill. That duo combined for 213 yards and a pair of touchdowns. Thomas's 74-yard TD run early in the game proved to be the big play of the day.

Oct. 22: Penn ate up 522 yards against Yale sending Yale to defeat, 37–25. The Bulldogs led, 20–10, entering the fourth quarter but Penn scored 27 points in the final 13 minutes to ice the game. Chris Smith, Yale's talented receiver, racked up 148 yards before leaving the game with an injury in the third quarter. Penn QB Billy Ragone threw for 236 yards and Witt tossed for 258 yards while Thomas ran for 204 yards for the Bulldogs in a losing cause.

Patrick Witt passed for 37 TDs in his career.

Oct. 29: Playing without running back Alex Thomas and receiver Chris Smith, Yale edged Columbia, 16–13, in New York on a snow-covered field that some estimated to be four inches deep. The Bulldogs' Mordecai Cargill plowed his way to a career-high 242 yards on 42 carries with TD runs of 19 and 4 yards. The Lions roared back from a 16–0 deficit but came up short in the "Snowtober" contest.

Nov. 5: Brown beat Yale, 34–28. The Bears' Mark Kachmer made the longest run from scrimmage in Yale Bowl history when he scampered for a 95-yard touchdown. It broke the record of 94 yards set by another Brown player, Bob Flanders, in 1968.

Nov. 19: Harvard trounced Yale, 45–7, duplicating the score of the 1982 game, also won by Harvard. Yale opened the scoring when Witt threw a 24-yard touchdown to Jackson Liguori midway through the first quarter. But it was all downhill after that for the Bulldogs. Harvard QB Collier Winters carved up the Yale defense, completing 27 of 42 passes for 355 yards, including a 60-yard toss to Kyle Juszczyk that made the score 38–7. Witt was taken out of the game with a little more than five minutes remaining after he threw his third interception, which was returned 32 yards by Alex Gedeon for Harvard's final score.

Gio Christodoulou ended his Yale career (2007–11) as the all-time punt return leader with 834 yards and 3 TDs.

The Game took a back seat to the tragedy that occurred in the morning at Parking Lot D when Brendan Ross, a 21-year-old Yale student driving a keg-laden U-Haul truck, struck three women. Nancy Barry, 30, was killed and her friend, Sarah Short, was injured along with Elizabeth Dernbach, a Harvard employee. Ross was originally charged with negligent homicide, a charge later reduced with the Barry family's agreement to driving unreasonably fast and unsafe. The agreement did not rule out civil suits.

Dec. 21: Head coach Tom Williams resigned after coming under fire for allegedly stating that he, like Yale QB Patrick Witt, was faced with a decision while a Stanford player whether or not to interview for a Rhodes Scholarship or play in a game. The story drew scrutiny in the *New York Times* when an official of the Rhodes Trust said there was no record that Williams had ever applied. Williams told the *New Haven Register* that a faculty advisor at Stanford had encouraged him to apply for the Rhodes, but he never did and did not intend to misrepresent that. In addition, published biographies of Williams stated that he had been on the practice squad of the San Francisco 49ers. The scenario that emerged was that he had taken part in a three-day tryout camp but never signed a contract with the 49ers or took part in their summer training camp.

2012 (2–8) Coach: Tony Reno; Captain: Will McHale

Jan. 12: Former Yale and Harvard assistant Tony Reno was named the 34th head Yale football coach, replacing Tom Williams. Reno was a Yale assistant under Jack Siedlecki from 2003 to 2008 before going to Harvard as special teams coordinator and defensive secondary coach under Tim Murphy. Tailback Tyler Varga, a 5-foot-11, 225-pound running back transfer from the University of Western Ontario, emerged as one of the greatest backs in Yale history. "He was built like a nuclear warhead with a bodybuilder's physique," wrote Zach Schonbrun in *The New York Times*.

May 15: Yale captain Will McHale had his captaincy suspended following his arrest by Yale police. McHale, who had a fight with another male student, faced charges of creating a public disturbance. McHale did remain an important part of the team.

Sept. 15: Tony Reno launched his head coaching career at Yale with a 24–21 win over Georgetown on the road. The Bulldogs won despite turning the ball over five times on three fumbles and two picks.

Sept. 29: Colgate QB Gavin McCarney ran for four touchdowns and passed for two in Colgate's 47–24 win in the Bowl. His 79-yard TD toss to Chris Looney late in the first quarter was the big play of the game.

Oct. 6: Dartmouth had their way with Yale, winning, 34–14. Several days before the Dartmouth game, an anonymous phone call to the NCAA was made questioning Varga's instant eligibility as a transfer from Canada, causing him to sit out the Dartmouth game. After nearly two weeks of deliberation, the NCAA cleared him to play the rest of the season.

Oct. 27: Because of multiple QB injuries, Yale coach Tony Reno used Varga as the QB running out of the wildcat formation. He rushed for a QB-record 220 yards on 25 carries, passed for 18 yards and scored three touchdowns but Yale lost to Columbia, 26–22, in New York. The win snapped Columbia's 10-game losing streak against the Bulldogs. Sean Brackett passed for 328 yards for the Lions, who racked up 429 total yards for the day.

Nov. 10: Princeton won its 25th Big Three with a 29–7 win over Yale in the Bowl. The Tigers were aided by an electrifying 100-yard TD interception in the north end zone (scoreboard side) by cornerback Trocon Davis that broke a 7–7 tie late in the second quarter. With all three quarterbacks injured, including Tyler Varga who was used in the wildcat formation, junior wide receiver Henry Furman started at QB. Furman, who had converted from quarterback prior to the start of the season, got the start and threw for 184 yards (18-for 28).

Nov. 17: Harvard beat Yale for the sixth consecutive time. Following a 3–3 first-half stalemate, the Bulldogs took the lead with just 7:07 left, but the Crimson scored twice to win the game, 34–24, in Boston. Furman replaced Derek Russell at QB during the game and engineered comebacks from 13–3 and 20–17 deficits. Yale's Grant Wallace led all receivers with 11 catches and 118 yards, including a 12-yard TD pass that gave Yale a 17–13 lead.

Harvard QB Colton Chapple rushed for 128 yards and was 22-for-32 passing for 209 yards and two touchdowns. Chapple's 61-yard run that led to a 9-yard TD pass to Cameron Brate put Harvard ahead, 27–24, before Treavor Scales's 63-yard touchdown run with 1:08 remaining sealed the victory for the Crimson.

THE HIGHLIGHTS   2013–2014

2013   (5–5) **Coach: Tony Reno; Captain: Beau Palin**

Sept. 21: QB Henry Furman scored three TDs and Tyler Varga rushed for 236 yards on 39 carries as Yale smoked Colgate, 39–22, to open the season.

Sept. 28: After being sidelined for the entire 2012 season, wide receiver Deon Randall made up for lost time when he scored four TDs to help lead Yale to a 38–23 win over Cornell in its Ivy opener. Randall, who had an 11-catch, 148-yard reception day, scored three times on passes from Furman, who threw for 353 yards (29-for-36).

Oct. 5: Yale upset 18th-ranked FCS power Cal Poly, 24–10, at San Luis Obispo, California. Bulldogs DB Cole Champion picked off two passes, recovered a fumble and made 13 tackles. Furman passed for 199 yards and two TDs while Varga added 115 yards on 26 carries. Derek Russell scored on a fake field goal. Hampered by an injury, Varga missed four games during the season.

Oct. 19: Sam Ajala broke Fordham's receiving yards record for a game with 282 and tied the record for TD catches with four as FCS No. 8-ranked Fordham handled Yale, 52–31, at the Yale Bowl, rolling up 614 total yards. Ajala caught 10 passes, including a pair of 68-yard scoring plays. QB Mike Nebrich threw for four TDs and ran for another.

Nov. 2: Yale crushed Columbia, 53–12. Kahlil Keys scored his first career touchdown with a school-record 94-yard run from scrimmage late in the third quarter that eclipsed Denny McGill's mark of 93 yards in 1956.

Nov. 9: Deon Randall's 32-yard TD run with 39 seconds left gave Yale a dramatic 24–17 win over Brown in the Bowl.

Nov. 23: In the 130th meeting between the two schools, Harvard dismissed Yale, 34–7, before 50,934 in the Bowl. Harvard's Paul Stanton scored four TDs (two rushing and two passes), matching Harvard's Eddie Mahan's series-record four TDs in the 1915 Y-H game. Harvard kicker David Mothander booted a 48-yard field goal, the longest Harvard FG in the history of the Y-H series.

2014   (8–2) **Coach: Tony Reno; Captain: Deon Randall**

Yale celebrated its 100th season in the Yale Bowl with an offensive explosion and a historic win over Army that had Yale fans bubbling with euphoria. The team's spread offense contributed to new modern Yale school records including scoring (411 points), touchdowns (53), total plays

(836) and total offense (5,715 yards). The Bulldogs finished 22nd among the 124 FCS teams in the country.

Sept. 20: Yale opened the season by beating Lehigh, 54–43. The Bulldogs overcame their largest deficit ever in a victory at the 100-year-old Yale Bowl by erasing a 21–0 score in the first quarter. The Mountain Hawks scored the first three TDs and later led, 28–7 and 35–23, before the home team reeled off four of the game's final five scoring plays. The largest deficit overcome in the Bowl prior to this was a 19-point effort against Virginia in 1941 when the Blue trailed, 19–0, at halftime against the Cavaliers and won, 21–19.

Junior QB Morgan Roberts completed 30 of 39 passes for 356 yards and three scores. Thirteen of those tosses went to senior captain Deon Randall, who had 152 receiving yards and a 68-yard scoring play. Sensational running back Tyler Varga, who would become a magnetic force, rambled for 152 yards on 19 carries, while sophomore backup Candler Rich totaled 104 yards on 11 runs. Both had a rushing TD.

Sept. 27: Varga tied a Yale school record when he took it to the house five times as Yale shocked Army in overtime, 49–43, at the Bowl in front of 34,142 fans. Varga carried the ball 28 times for 185 yards, scoring on runs of 2, 15, 18, 10 and 3 yards. His final TD came in overtime to give the Bulldogs the walk-off victory after a missed 25-yard field-goal attempt by Army kicker Dan Grochowski, who also missed a 42-yard attempt in the final seconds of regulation play.

QB Morgan Roberts scored Yale's first touchdown on a 13-yard run in the first quarter. Yale's other TD came on a 22-yard pass from Roberts to Ross Drwal in the third quarter. Twice Yale recovered from 14-point deficits.

The high-powered Bulldogs offense racked up a total 525 yards (335 rushing and 290 passing). Yale's 36 first downs eclipsed the old school record of 32 in Yale's win over Penn in 1976. Wide receiver Grant Wallace snared six passes from Roberts for 101 yards. Linebacker Andrew Larkin and free safety Foyesade Oluokun led the Elis with eight solos and 10 overall tackles.

The Football Writers Association of America named Yale its "Big Game National Team of the Week." Yale became the first Ivy League team to earn the honor that was first awarded in 2002. The last time the Bulldogs beat a FBS/1-A opponent was Navy in 1981.

This was the 46th time Yale and Army met dating back to 1893 when the Bulldogs beat the Cadets at West Point, 28–0. Yale is 13–5–4 at Army but only 9–11–4 in New Haven. The Elis lead the series, 22–16–8. The last time Yale beat the Black Knights of the Hudson was in 1955.

The pregame pageantry started on Friday night with a concert featuring bands from both schools at Woolsey Hall. Then Saturday at noon 1,000 cadets marched in rows of four from Marginal Drive across Derby Avenue through the Walter Camp Memorial to the Yale Bowl and onto the field. A group of bagpipers led the way. Five paratroopers dropped in from a helicopter with game balls. Instant replay was used in the Yale Bowl for the first time. Army supplied the equipment at a cost of about $5,000.

Tyler Varga scores the winning touchdown in overtime vs. Army in 2014 (courtesy Bill O'Brien).

Oct. 4: Yale's juggernaut offense totaling 585 yards was too much for Cornell in its 51–13 thrashing over the "Big Red" at Schoellkopf Field. Roberts tied a Yale record with five touchdown passes (Jeff Mroz vs. Cornell in 2005 and Pete Doherty vs. Columbia in 1966). Roberts completed 26 of 30 throws for 312 yards with no picks. His 87 percent completion percentage was a school record. Yale captain Deon Randall scored twice on passes of 33 and 16 yards while wide receiver Grant Wallace scored on passes of 13 and 19 yards.

Quarterback Morgan Roberts passed for 6,182 yards, second only to Kurt Rawlings.

Oct. 11: Yale's 3–0 start to begin the season was halted the second year in a row by Dartmouth as the Big Green defeated the Elis, 38–31. Dartmouth quarterback Dalyn Williams dazzled the Bulldogs, passing for 388 yards including three touchdown tosses. Ryan McManus was on the receiving end with 12 catches for 188 yards and a touchdown.

Oct. 18: Matching his output against Army, Varga found the end zone five times for the second time this season and again tied the single game school record for touchdowns in the Yale Bowl while rushing for 184 yards (168 in the second half) as Yale downed Colgate, 45–31, to end Colgate's four-game winning streak.

Oct. 25: Yale's high voltage offense continued in the Bulldogs' 43–21 victory over Penn in the Bowl. With seven receptions for 78 yards, Deon Randall shattered the all-time Yale receptions record with 196 career catches. With Yale leading, 8–0, in the first quarter, linebacker Charles Cook blocked a field-goal attempt. Linebacker Matt Oplinger, who caught the two-point conversion, scooped up the ball and returned it 48 yards. Cornerback Spencer Rymiszewski suffered a season-ending spinal concussion late in the second quarter.

Penn coach Al Bagnoli, who headed the Quakers program for 23 years, made his final visit to the Bowl as Penn's head coach. Bagnoli's record against Yale was an impressive 16–7. He is the only coach in Ivy League history to win nine outright titles. Bagnoli would return to the Bowl the following season as the mentor of the Columbia Lions.

Deon Randall ranks fourth in receiving yards and TD receptions.

Nov. 1: Yale beat Columbia in New York, 25–7, on a damp, overcast day. Kyle Cazzetta spooked the ghosts of Eli on this Halloween weekend when he kicked four field goals (31, 25, 25, 33 yards), one shy of tying the school record held by Wyllis Terry (1883) and George Watkinson (1885). Cazzetta was Yale's first left-footed kicker since Justin Davis who lettered from 1998 to 2001.

Nov. 8: In this 119th Yale-Brown game, the Bulldogs upended the

Bears, 45–42, at Brown Stadium. Down, 20–7, in the second quarter, the Bulldogs scored 24 unanswered points and never trailed again. Varga electrified the opposition with his 204-yard, two-TD (5, 23 yards) performance. The play of the game occurred in the third quarter when Yale linebacker Darius Manora picked off a flea-flicker pitchback and raced 34 yards for a score to give Yale an 11-point lead after the extra point.

Nov. 15: The Bulldogs closed out the Yale Bowl's 100th anniversary season with a 44–30 win over Princeton. Down, 14–10, early in the second quarter, Yale sophomore defensive end Marty Moesta blocked Tyler Roth's punt and Jaeden Graham recovered the ball in the end zone for the touchdown. The 23,260 fans were treated to another explosive offensive show as the Bulldogs churned out 568 yards of total offense and in the process set a new school record in that category for a season with 5,285 yards, eclipsing the old mark of 4,781 set in 2003. Yale's 387 points on the season also set a new school record, surpassing the 2003 squad's 354 points. Varga continued his dynamic running, scoring three touchdowns on runs of 30 and 6 yards and on a 13-yard pass from Roberts, who completed 27 of 42 passes for a career-high 405 yards. Grant Wallace made 10 catches for 149 yards and captain Deon Randall snared six for 112 yards.

At halftime the Yale All-Era teams were honored on the field. A total of 67 players were selected to one of the Bowl's five All-Era teams in this year's 100th anniversary season.

Nov. 22: Harvard closed out a perfect season, beating Yale, 31–24, in Boston before a sellout crowd of 31,062. It was the third time in Harvard coach Tim Murphy's tenure that the Crimson ran the table. It was Harvard's eighth straight win in the series, including 13 of the last 14, the first time either school accomplished the feat.

The Bulldogs, trailing, 24–7, in the fourth quarter staged an incredible comeback to tie the score, 24–24, but lost the game when Harvard QB Conner Hempel connected with Andrew Fischer with 55 seconds to play for a 35-yard game-winning touchdown.

One of the Crimson's touchdowns came on a bizarre play when Harvard linebacker Connor Sheehan stripped an apparent completed pass from the grasp of Robert Clemons III and raced 90 yards for a touchdown. Varga, who carried for 127 yards on 30 carries and scored three touchdowns, finished the season with a school record 26 TDs (22 rushing), placing second to Mike McLeod's 23 in 2007. Varga averaged 6.1 yards per carry and 142 yards per game. He led the FCS in TDs and scoring average.

Roberts shattered multiple school records, passing for a record 3,220 yards including a 66.8 percent completion mark. He tied the school mark of 22 TD throws.

Deon Randall (Yale) and Norm Hayes (Harvard) captained the teams, the first time African American athletes represented each rival at the opening coin toss. Both were voted first team All-Ivy.

There was added buzz to "The Game" as ESPNs *College GameDay* visited Harvard for the first time and drew an estimated 1.9 million viewers.

2015 (6–4) Coach: Tony Reno; Captain: Cole Champion

Sept. 19: Trailing, 21–7, at the half and 28–14 with 10:05 remaining in the game, Yale opened its 143rd campaign with a 29–28 victory over Colgate at Andy Kerr Stadium before a homecoming crowd of 7,343. Yale QB Morgan Roberts, who tied the school mark with 22 touchdown passes in 2014, completed 29 of 41 (293 yards) including three TD tosses, two to sophomore WR Michael Siragusa (4 and 13 yards) and Robert Clemons III (30 yards). Siragusa's 13-yard catch with 3:39 left in the game tied the score before the successful extra point try by Bryan Holmes. Junior free safety Foyesade Oluokun blocked field-goal attempts of 36 and 34 yards in the first and third quarters. Sophomore receiver Bo Hines, who transferred from North Carolina State, had six catches. Hines led the Wolfpack with 45 catches and 616 yards in 2014. It was the ninth straight opening day win for the Elis.

For his efforts against the scholarship Raiders, Roberts shared offensive Ivy League Player of the Week honors with Harvard signal caller Scott Hosch.

Sept. 26: Yale came back from a 26–7 deficit to defeat Cornell in the Bowl, 33–26. The Bulldogs thrilled the crowd of 15,926 by scoring twice in the last 72 seconds of the game. Robert Clemons III scored on an 8-yard pass play with 1:25 to go and Sebastian Little scored on a 52-yard pass play from Roberts with 32 seconds left in the game for the winning touchdown. J. Hunter Roman blocked Zach Mays's 42-yard field-goal attempt with 3:27 remaining.

Oct. 10: Dartmouth QB Dalyn Williams passed for a career-high 435 yards and four touchdowns to lead the Big Green past Yale, 35–3. Williams became Dartmouth's career leader in total offense (7,525 yards), passing former NFL QB Jay Fiedler (1991–93).

Oct. 17: Trailing, 10–9, in the last quarter, the Bulldogs beat the University of Maine, 21–10, to spoil the Black Bears' homecoming on chilly Morse Field at the Harold Alfond Sports Stadium in Orono, Maine. It was the first meeting between the two schools since 1937 and the first time the Elis traveled to the Pine Tree State.

Oct. 23: Yale played its fourth straight road game and suffered an uninspiring loss to Penn. 34–20 at historic Franklin Field. It was the Bulldogs' first Friday night game ever against an Ivy League opponent. The Quakers erased a 10-point deficit in the first quarter. All-Ivy QB Alek Torgersen picked apart the Yale defense, throwing for 350 yards and four touchdowns.

Oct. 31: Columbia defeated Yale in the Bowl for the first time since 1996. It was also the Lions' first Ivy League win since November 10, 2012, when they beat Cornell at Wien Stadium. On this Halloween day of trick or treat, the Lions tricked the Bulldogs with a fake field goal early in the fourth quarter. With 13:28 left in the fourth quarter, Columbia set up for a 30-yard FG. Instead, kicker Cam Nizialek took an option pitch from Trevor McDonagh and ran 13 yards for the touchdown, giving the Lions a 17–7 advantage which proved to be the final score. Yale scored on Jason Alessi's 80-yard punt return in the first quarter. The injury-riddled Bulldogs collected only five first downs and totaled 120 yards for the day.

Columbia coach Al Bagnoli became the first coach since Earl "Red" Blaik to bring different opposing teams into the Yale Bowl in back-to-back years. Blaik led Dartmouth and Army into the Bowl in 1940 and 1941 while Bagnoli took Penn and Columbia in 2014 and 2015.

Nov. 14: The Bulldogs overcame a 14–0 first quarter deficit and also battled from 21–14 and 28–24 deficits to beat Princeton, 35–28, in a game that proved to be one of the all-time Yale-Princeton classics. Yale's Dale Harris ran for 177 yards on 30 carries that included a 71-yard run in the first quarter to put Yale on the board. Yale QB Morgan Roberts was 20-for-29 (185 yards) that included two TD passes and a 1-yard TD run. Robert Clemons III scored the go-ahead TD on a 19-yard grab with 4:31 left in the game that was set up by Spencer Rymiszewski's pick of a Chad Kanoff pass with a little over eight minutes remaining. Darius Manora intercepted a Kanoff pass from the Yale 47 with 3:24 remaining which enabled the Elis to run out the clock.

Nov. 21: Harvard, playing with cocksure spirit, continued its domination over Yale in its hoary series with a 39–19 victory over the Bulldogs in the 132nd playing of The Game before 52,126 fans in the Bowl. It was the first time in the 101-year-old history of the Yale Bowl that Yale played a football game under artificial lighting. Although lighting was not needed until later in the day, the contest that started at 2:30 and finished at 6:00 p.m. was played under the lights from start to finish and was televised on NBCSN. By 5:00 p.m., complete darkness had engulfed the elliptical shaped Bowl.

The Elis got lit up as well as the lamps. Harvard QB Scott Hosch, the Ivy League's Offensive Player of the Year, finished with 320 yards on 23 of 37 passing to set the Harvard single-season record of 2,827 yards. He threw four touchdown passes, two to freshman Justice Shelton-Mosley, the Ivy League Rookie of the Year, that covered 53 and 35 yards. The win gave Harvard a share of the Ivy title with Penn and Dartmouth, the third consecutive title for the Crimson, a school record.

Yale QB Morgan Roberts was 38 of 65 in passing that included TD tosses to Chris Williams-Lopez (28 yards) and Stephen Buric (8 yards). Williams-Lopez caught 13 passes for 169 yards. Roberts, a transfer from Clemson, passed for 410 yards. He finished his career as Yale's all-time leader in total offense with 6,494 yards (6,182 passing and 312 rushing). Robert Clemons III had seven receptions for 86 yards for the Elis.

The win gave the Crimson nine straight wins over Yale, a series record. Harvard won seven straight in the Bowl and 14 of the last 15 games against its ancient rival. Harvard coach Tim Murphy beat Yale for the 17th time, surpassing Carm Cozza for the most wins of any coach in the Y-H series.

2016 (3–7) Coach: Tony Reno; Captain: Darius Manora

The Ivy League used an experimental rule for conference matchups with kickoffs from the 40-yard line, instead of the 35, and touchbacks placed at the 20-yard line in an effort to reduce concussions and further promote the safety and welfare of its student athletes.

The Ivy League formally adopted another policy originating with the league's eight head football coaches to eliminate to-the-ground ("live") tackling in practices during the regular season. The Bulldogs floundered with only three wins but beat Harvard after nine straight losses.

May 23: Former Yale great running back Calvin Hill received an honorary doctorate of humane letters during Yale University's 315th Commencement. "This was more shocking than getting drafted [by the NFL]," said Hill.

July 21: Under Armour unveiled the new Yale football uniform in New York as part of a public relations event celebrating the 20-year anniversary of the company's entry into college football. The uniform remained basically the same aside from the popular Under Armour logo under the neck and just below the belt. A plain "Y" adorned the left hip.

Aug. 11: Handsome Dan XVII, a.k.a. Sherman, passed away at age nine in Quonochontaug, Rhode Island. The English bulldog was appointed a midshipman by the United States Naval Reserve with the title of Midshipmen Captain in 2015. Sherman met former presidents George H.W. Bush and Jimmy Carter as well as Sir Paul McCartney.

Sept. 17: Yale's nine straight opening day wins mark was erased as Colgate trampled over the Bulldogs, 55–13. The 42-point deficit equaled the worst loss that Yale suffered in the Bowl since UConn hammered the Bulldogs 63–21, 18 years earlier. Colgate QB Jake Melville threw for 315 yards, including a school-record five touchdowns.

Oct. 1: Lehigh sophomore QB Brad Mayes, subbing for senior QB Nick Shafnisky, set a Yale Bowl record with 524 passing yards in the Mountain Hawks' 63–35 smashing of Yale. The first-half total of 70 points (42–28) set a Yale Bowl mark for most points scored in a half. The 98 total points was one shy of the 99 points scored in Brown's 55–44 win in 2003.

The Elis, minus three injured cornerbacks, were down, 35–7, in the second quarter before scoring 21 unanswered points to pull within seven but were stalled thereafter. Yale's Jason Alessi had a dazzling 82-yard TD punt return, the third longest in school history.

Oct. 3: Dave Laidley, Carm Cozza's first captain in 1965, passed away unexpectedly at age 72 in Libertyville, Illinois.

Oct. 8: In the 100th meeting between the two schools, Yale defeated Dartmouth, 21–13. The Bulldogs, who entered the game 0–3, trailed, 10–0, in the first half before freshman running back Alan Lamar, making his first start in the backfield, ran for a 7-yard TD with 3:09 left in the second quarter. The Elis took the lead with 22 seconds remaining in the half when freshman Reed Klubnik made a diving one-handed catch of a Tre Moore toss in the corner of the end zone that capped a six-play, 75-yard drive. David Smith's 32-yard field goal pulled Dartmouth within a point late in the third quarter but Lamar, who ran for 180 yards, added a 43-yard scoring run with 11:36 to play to make it 21–13. The win gave Yale a 54–40–6 edge in the series.

Oct. 15: Despite Dale Harris's four touchdowns and 136 yards rushing, the Fordham Rams defeated the Bulldogs, 44–37, in front of 4,671 fans at Jack Coffey Field in the Bronx, New York. Fordham QB Kevin Anderson threw for 270 yards including five touchdowns while Chase Edmonds rushed for 121 yards on 18 carries.

Oct. 21: In the first true night game ever played in the Yale Bowl, Penn lit up the Bulldogs, 42–7, in front of an announced crowd of 8,674. Penn QB Alex Torgersen and Justin Watson, who had 10 catches for 166 yards, connected on three scoring passes. The Elis ran for 136 yards thanks to rookie Alan Lamar's 118-yard effort. Penn continued its domination over Yale with their 19th win in the last 25 meetings.

Oct. 28: For the second week in a row, the Elis played under the lights. This time things were brighter as Yale upended Columbia, 31–23, at Wien Stadium in New York despite the Lions scoring 23 unanswered points in the final quarter. The play of the game was executed in the second quarter by Yale junior defensive tackle John Herubin, who scooped up a fumble forced by Foye Oluokun from the hands of Columbia back Tanner Thomas and raced 61 yards for a touchdown to put Yale on the board early in the second quarter. Freshman QB Kurt Rawlings came off the bench in the second quarter and threw three touchdown passes. He also ran for 46 yards. The Bulldogs defense forced five turnovers. Senior Marty Moesta had three sacks.

Nov. 10: The dining hall at Calhoun College was named in honor of former lineman Roosevelt Thompson, a former Rhodes Scholar recipient, who lettered from 1981 to 1983. The Arkansas native was killed in a car crash in 1984, in the last semester of his Yale career

Nov. 12: Princeton's A.J. Glass set the pace with a 46-yard touchdown run early in the game followed by three John Lovett rushing TDs to give the Tigers a 31–3 win over Yale in front of 15,321 fans in the Bowl.

Nov. 17: Yale University announced its new mascot, Handsome Dan XVIII. The Olde English Bulldog was born on September 23 in Maine, six weeks after Handsome Dan XVII passed. Its keeper is Kevin Discepolo, a 2009 Yale grad and former lacrosse player who is now Yale's assistant athletic director of facilities, operations and events. Handsome Dan XVIII was named "Walter" in honor of Walter Camp.

Nov. 19: On a day that Walter made its debut as the Yale mascot and Yale coach Tony Reno quieted his skeptics, the Bulldogs pulled off a stunning upset by defeating heavily favored Harvard, 21–14, at Harvard Stadium. The win ended a string of nine straight losses to the Crimson. Yale entered the game 2–7 while Harvard was 7–2. A Harvard win would have clinched at least a share of the Ivy League title for an unprecedented fourth consecutive year.

Harvard got on the board in the second quarter when Charlie Booker scored on a 27-yard run. Freshman Alan Lamar scored Yale's first TD just before the half on a 1-yard run which tied the score, 7–7.

The Bulldogs, playing like a heavy underdog, started the second half with an onside kick that was recovered by kicker Blake Horn. This led to the next Yale score that broke a 7–7 tie when Yale freshman QB Kurt Rawlings connected with freshman wide receiver Reed Klubnik for a 28-yard TD toss. Harvard came back on the next possession to tie the score when QB Joe Viviano III hit Ryan Halvorson on a 1-yard pass.

Rawlings led the Bulldogs rushing for 74 yards on 10 carries while throwing two TD passes to Klubnik, the game-clincher coming in the last quarter with 6:47 remaining to break a 14–14 tie.

2017 (9–1) Ivy League Champs (outright). Coach: Tony Reno; Captain: Spencer Rymiszewski

The Ivy League eliminated two-a-day practices during preseason and Yale won its first Ivy League championship in 11 years and first outright title in 37 years. The 11 years was the longest drought between championships for the Bulldogs, who earned their first national ranking in 10 years, taking No. 24 in both FCS polls.

Sept. 16: After losing to Lehigh by 28 points the year before, it was payback for the Bulldogs, who kicked off their 145th season with a convincing 56–28 win over the Mountain Hawks at Goodman Stadium in Bethlehem, Pennsylvania. Sophomore QB Kurt Rawlings completed 20 of 26 passes for 308 yards and four touchdowns, two to freshman Melvin Rouse II (37, 31 yards).

Sept. 23: Yale continued their offensive assault, accounting for 342 yards on the ground as they defeated Cornell, 49–24, in their Ivy League opener in the Bowl. The game was highlighted by Deshawn Salter's 82-yard touchdown run midway in the fourth quarter after the Big Red crept within 11 points (35–24). Salter ran for 143 yards and Zane Dudek gained 173, 12 yards short of Yale's single-game freshman rushing record set by Robert Carr in 2001 against Dartmouth.

Sept. 30: Yale cruised past Patriot League power Fordham, 41–10. The barking Bulldogs carved up the Fordham defense for 472 yards. It was the first loss suffered by the Rams against an Ivy League opponent in 10 years.

Oct. 7: Dartmouth QB Jack Heneghan threw a 15-yard scoring strike to Drew Hunnicutt on fourth down with 34 seconds left to lift Dartmouth to a historic 28–27 victory over Yale, thrilling the homecoming crowd of 8,114 at Memorial Field. David Smith added the extra point to break the tie and provide the winning margin as the Big Green, down, 21–0, in the second quarter and 24–7 at the half, enjoyed its largest comeback victory in 136 years of varsity football. Conversely, Yale equaled its largest blown lead (21 points) in team history that led to a loss when Princeton upset the Bulldogs, 35–31, in 1981.

Midway in the third quarter it appeared that tight end Jaeden Graham caught a TD pass from Rawlings in the end zone that would have given the Bulldogs a 34–14 lead, but it was waved off by the official, who ruled that Graham's foot was out of bounds. Replays, however, indicated otherwise. The Ivy League and the Pioneer League were the only two leagues in the country that did not use the replay system at the time.

Oct. 14: The Bulldogs bounced back by defeating Holy Cross, 32–0, in the Bowl. It was the first shutout registered by a Yale defense since beating Dartmouth, 30–0, in 2011. The blowout led to the firing of Holy Cross coach Tom Gilmore.

More than a dozen members of the Yale football team joined a national protest movement at the intersection of sports, politics and race when they kneeled during the national anthem while some teammates stood beside them to show support.

Yale field goal and extra point kicker/punter Alex Galland played the trumpet during the anthem. Galland has played his horn at numerous basketball and hockey games but it was his first time prior to a football game. He was hoping to play before the Cornell game but forgot to take his trumpet to the Bowl.

Oct. 21: With 4:52 left in the game, Kurt Rawlings found Christopher Williams-Lopez in the corner of the end zone on a 4-yard toss to give the Elis a hard-fought come-from-behind win over Penn, 24–19. Linebacker Foye Oluokun and safety Jason Alessi both had 10 tackles. Alex Galland's 35-yard FG in the second quarter tied the game at 10–10.

QB Kurt Rawlings is Yale's all-time leader in pass completions, pass TDs and total offense.

Oct. 28: Freshman running back Zane Dudek propelled the Bulldogs to a 23–6 win over Columbia in the Bowl when he scampered for 173 yards, tying his season high.

Prior to the game, there was a malfunction in the Kenney Center elevator that leads to the press box. Entrapped in the elevator car for 45 minutes was former Yale football coach Jack Siedlecki, who was about to work his first game on WELI radio as a color analyst.

Nov. 3: Yale won its 900th game by defeating Brown under the lights at the Bowl, 34–7. Dudek, making his first varsity start, scored on runs of 68, 36 and 7 yards.

Nov. 11: In a wildly entertaining game, Yale clinched at least a share for the Ancient Eight crown with a heart-stopping come-from-behind 35–31 victory over Princeton in New Jersey before 11,229 on a clear, cold day.

The Tigers came out of the gate growling, scoring on an 88-yard TD pass from prolific QB Chad Kanoff to Jesper Horsted with 4:24 remaining in the first quarter. Midway in the second frame Princeton went ahead 14–0 when Kanoff tossed an 18-yard TD pass to Stephen Carlson. Less than a minute later, Dudek, Yale's wunderkind freshman running back, answered with a 47-yard run to pull the Bulldogs within seven (14–7). Following a 21-yard field goal by Travis Rice, Princeton piled on with another TD when Kanoff, who passed for a school-record 454 yards and four touchdowns, hit Tiger Bech with a 58-yard scoring strike. The Bulldogs, who trailed, 24–7, with 1:51 left in the first half, closed to 24–14 just before the intermission when Rawlings connected with Jaeden Graham for a 58-yard touchdown less than 30 seconds later.

Early in the second half Yale defensive end Earl Chism hit Princeton running back Collin Eaddy, causing a fumble that was recovered by the Elis' Spencer Matthaei on the Tigers' 35. Four plays later, Rawlings fired a 33-yard TD pass to Ross Drwal, making the score 24–21. Yale took the lead (28–24) after a 1-yard run by Dudek with 3:58 left in the third quarter. But the Tigers bounced back with 1:53 remaining in the quarter when Kanoff combined with Horsted on a 12-yard pass allowing Princeton to regain the lead, 31–28. Playing with fiber and steel, the Bulldogs promptly marched down the field when Dudek delivered the death blow, scoring on a 4-yard run early in the fourth quarter, giving Yale a 35–31 lead which proved to be the final score.

The game that saw four lead changes came down to a final Yale defensive stand. The Tigers, down by four with just over a minute to play, had a 4th-and-8 on the Eli 43 when Matt Oplinger (10 tackles) blitzed Kanoff. The senior linebacker, who closed out the win at Harvard the previous November on a similar blitz, wrapped up the Tiger as he got rid of the ball. The pass ended up in the hands of senior Foye Oluokun, who ran around for 20 yards before he was tackled.

For the day, Dudek rushed for 180 yards on 35 carries that included three touchdowns. Rawlings continued to rack up milestone outings with a 26-for-34, 304-yard afternoon that included TD tosses of 58 and 33 yards.

Nov. 18: Playing with unflagging zeal, Yale won the Ivy title outright by defeating Harvard, 24–3, before 51,426 in the Bowl that included Paul McCartney of the Beatles who had a grandson at Yale. It was also the first time in 17 years that the Bulldogs beat the Crimson in back-to-back years. Yale's dominating defense sacked Harvard QBs six times and held the Crimson to 164 yards.

Harvard got on the board first when Jake McIntyre kicked a 29-yard field goal. In the second quarter the Bulldogs answered with 17 points on touchdowns by JP Shohfi (9-yard pass from Kurt Rawlings), Malcolm Dixon on a 19-yard fumble return and a 25-yard FG by Alex Galland, who converted both extra points. Dixon raced to the goal line after Harvard freshman QB Jake Smith made an errant pitch to Aaron Shampklin. Dudek's 2-yard run completed Yale's scoring in the final frame. Dudek, the Ivy Rookie of the Year and the first freshman to ever lead the league in rushing, finished with 64 yards on 25 carries. Oluokun, the talented Yale linebacker who went to play for the Atlanta Falcons, starred defensively. Rawlings became the first sophomore QB to lead the Bulldogs to any Ivy title since John Rogan in 1979.

Foye Oluokun, an outstanding linebacker, went on to play for the Atlanta Falcons after his Yale career.

Following the game, the field became a sea of humanity, the likes of which may have never been seen before as thousands of fans stormed the field.

Nov. 20: Kyle Mullen, Yale's All-Ivy League defensive end, was named captain of the 2018 team. But he left the team for personal reasons prior to the 2018 season.

Nov. 26: Tony Reno, Yale's Joel E. Smilow '54 Head Coach of Football, was rewarded for the team's success with both the New England Football Writers and the Gridiron Club of Boston naming him Division I Coach of the Year.

In 2017, Zane Dudek was the Ivy League rookie of the year and the first freshman to ever lead the league in rushing.

2018 (5–5) Coach: Tony Reno; Captain: Nick Crowle

Jan. 4: Longtime Yale head football coach Carm Cozza died at age 87. He was elected to the College Football Hall of Fame in 2002. Dr. Pat Ruwe, Yale's 1982 football captain and president of the Yale Football Association said, "Today we Men of Yale Football, the Yale Football Family, Yale University, and America herself lost a piece of our foundation. For over 50 years, legendary coach Carm Cozza represented Yale Football and his Community with unmatched honor, dignity, and class. Ferociously competitive yet humble and unfailingly loyal, Coach was once called Yale's greatest teacher and was the ultimate role model to those young men fortunate enough to play for him."

Of the 2,000 or so players who played for Cozza, five became Rhodes Scholars and only seven, who remained in his program, failed to graduate. Fifteen of his players went on to play in the NFL. Writer Bob Barton once called Cozza "the pastoral counselor who deals with players one on one."

Sept. 15: After taking a commanding 21–0 lead in the opening minutes of the game, Yale started the season with a harrowing 31–28 loss in overtime to Holy Cross in Worcester, Massachusetts. It was the Crusaders' first-ever win over the Bulldogs at Fitton Field after losing the first seven meetings. Yale scored on the opening kickoff as Melvin Rouse II tied Kenny Hill's (1978) school record with a 100-yard return for a score. Yale's J. Hunter Roman then intercepted an Emmett Clifford pass on the Crusaders' first drive and one play later Alan Lamar broke free on a 42-run yard TD run. The Elis extended their first quarter lead to 21–0 when Patrick Conte threw a 23-yard touchdown pass to JJ Howland on a muddle-huddle field-goal situation.

Holy Cross put its first points on the board with a 30-yard scoring run by junior tailback Miles Alexander. After recovering the ensuing onside kick, the Crusaders marched 48 yards in six plays to make the score 21–14 on a 1-yard touchdown run by senior quarterback Geoff Wade.

The Bulldogs responded with a 20-yard touchdown pass from Kurt Rawlings to Reed Klubnik early in the second quarter and led 28–14 at halftime. The score remained the same until the fourth quarter, when Wade hit senior wide receiver Martin Dorsey with a 29-yard scoring strike to trim the deficit to 28–21 with 4:32 left. After the defense forced Yale to punt on its next possession, Wade found freshman wideout Spencer Gilliam for a 30-yard touchdown with 52 seconds left to play, forcing overtime. Freshman placekicker Derek Ng booted a 45-yard field goal in overtime to break a 28–28 tie.

The Bulldogs were led by Dudek with 217 rushing yards on 22 carries. The loss gave Yale a record of 6–4 in overtime games.

Sept. 29: Behind the passing of Kurt Rawlings (22 of 34 for 306 yards), Yale had its way with Maine, the 16th-ranked FCS team. Junior Reed Klubnik had six catches for 85 yards and three touchdowns. Junior receiver JP Shohfi had 10 receptions for 124 yards. "We got outplayed, out-coached and out-everything," said Maine coach Joe Harasymiak.

Oct. 5: Dartmouth's ground game sank Yale under the lights at the Bowl. Led by 6-foot-4, 225-pound QB Jared Gerbino, the Big Green ate up the Bulldogs, 41–18. Gerbino accounted for 169 of the Big Green's 347 rushing yards.

Oct. 13: In the first meeting ever between Yale and Mercer, the Bulldogs triumphed over the Bears by a score of 35–28. The Bulldogs held a commanding 28–7 lead before the school from Macon, Georgia, scored just before the half. Yale led, 35–28, with just over three minutes remaining in the game when QB Kurt Rawlings, named the Ivy League Player of the Week (23-for-35; 344 yards passing), connected with JJ Howland for a 14-yard gain that iced the contest.

Oct. 19: Alan Lamar ran for 179 yards and two touchdowns and Yale beat Penn, 23–10, under the lights at Franklin Field. But the Bulldogs paid an expensive price when Rawlings, who passed for 137 yards (11-of-14), suffered a season-ending injury with multiple fractures above the ankle in the third quarter. At the time he was leading the Ivy League with 1,562 yards passing and was second in total offense with 1,650 yards.

Oct. 27: Yale won the battle of statistics, outgaining Columbia, 428–160, and held a 238–51 advantage in passing yards, but the Lions won the war, 17–10, on a windy and rainy Robert K. Kraft Field at Lawrence A. Wien Stadium. Columbia running back Ryan Young rushed for 91 yards, including a 30-yard touchdown run that gave the Lions a 17–10 early lead in the fourth quarter that they never relinquished.

Nov. 3: In the most spectacular debut of any quarterback in Yale football history, Griffin O'Connor put on an aerial show for the ages as the Bulldogs routed Brown, 46–16. The freshman signal caller threw four touchdown passes and completed 30 of 38 throws for 436 yards, two yards shy of the single-game record held by Alvin Cowan (vs. Harvard, 2003). His 452 total yards ranks second to Cowan's 466 yards (vs. Colgate, 2003.) Wide receiver JP Shohfi had a game-high nine catches for 104 yards and two touchdowns. In the third quarter, O'Connor connected with Reed Klubnik, who made an amazing over-the-shoulder catch for a 60-yard TD. For the day, Klubnik had six catches for 153 yards and two touchdowns. Sophomore Alan Lamar had two TDs and Spencer Alston ran for 67 yards and a score.

The defense was stellar as well, holding Brown to a school-record minus 27 yards rushing. LB Ryan Burke had seven sacks and DB Rodney Thomas II had a pick.

Nov. 10: O'Connor passed for a school-record 465 yards on just 20 completions in 39 attempts, but it was not enough as undefeated Princeton rolled to a 59–43 win over Yale. The 102 combined points were the most ever in a Yale-Princeton game and the most total points scored in the 104-year history of the Yale Bowl. Despite O'Connor's record-breaking day, he was picked off four times, including on Yale's first two possessions that led to Princeton touchdowns which gave the Men of Nassau a 21–0 lead in the first 4:38 of the game. The Tigers scored on their first play from scrimmage on a 75-yard run by Collin Eaddy, who rushed for 266 yards, including three touchdowns. Princeton QB John Lovett ran for 110 yards (2 TDs) and passed for 145. For the day, the Tigers accumulated 634 total yards. Alan Lamar (102 yards rushing, 2 TDS) led Yale on the ground. The Bulldogs outscored their opponents, 29–17, in the second half but it was not enough to overcome the early deficit.

A tribute to Carm Cozza, the legendary 32-year former coach who died earlier in the year, was held at the Coxe Cage in the morning. The celebration of life was attended by an estimated 800 including Cozza's family and a large number of former players. There were remembrances from Pat Ruwe, Dick Jauron, Jon Reese, Calvin Hill, Brian Dowling, Steve Skrovan and Gary Fencik. The Whiffenpoofs sang a medley of Yale football songs, including "I'll Be Seeing You."

Nov. 17: The Yale-Harvard game was played at Fenway Park. It was the first time in 124 years that The Game was played at a neutral site, the last time being in 1894 in Springfield, Massachusetts. The Crimson walked away the winners, 45–27, in the highest combined scoring output (72 points) in the history of the series. Harvard's 579 total offensive yards (266 on the ground) would be its most in the history of The Game and its point total would be its highest.

The Bulldogs erased three deficits in the first three quarters to take a 24–21 lead and trailed, 28–27, early in the fourth quarter following Alex Galland's 25-yard field goal but the Harvards scored 17 unanswered points down the stretch as they wore down a young Yale defense.

Yale freshman QB Griffin O'Connor, the 2018 Ivy League Rookie of the Year, continued to percolate as he threw for 328 yards in a losing cause. Reed Klubnik (five catches for 91 yards) broke the school's receiving yards record for a season with 1,143. Crimson QB Tom Stewart threw for 312 yards and three touchdowns before leaving the game with a hip injury late in the fourth quarter. Tyler Adams, whose 62-yard TD run gave Harvard a 14–7 lead in the second quarter, gained 125 yards rushing for the winners.

QB Griffin O'Connor, was the 2018, All-Ivy Rookie of the Year. O'Connor passed for a school-record 465 yards against Princeton.

Entering the 2019 season, Yale and Harvard have met 135 times. Yale leads the series 67–60–8. Home field has not been a particular advantage for either team. Yale stands 31–29–3 in New Haven (23–27–1 in the Bowl) while on the road the Blue is 29–29–5 (26–26–3 at Harvard Stadium) and 7–2–0 at neutral sites.

Nov. 18: JP Shohfi was named captain of the 2019 Yale football team—team No. 147.

2019 (9–1) Ivy League Camps. Coach: Tony Reno; Captain: JP Shohfi

Yale won their 16th Ivy League title and finished No. 22 nationally in the FCS. The prolific passing trio of QB Kurt Rawlings and wide receivers Reed Klubnik and JP Shohfi shattered several team records. The explosive Bulldogs led the league in total offense, passing offense and scoring offense averaging 38.7 points per game. The resilient Elis bounced back from 20 and 19-point deficits to beat Richmond and Harvard. Sam Tuckerman was the top kicker in the league. He averaged 8.5 points per game, booted 43 extra points and had 14 field goals, five more than any other player. In the 105-year history of the Yale Bowl, Yale played on artificial turf for the first time. The turf was donated by twin brothers Rob and Chris Michalik who played on the '89 Ivy League championship team.

Sept. 21: The Elis enjoyed the new rug with a 23–10 victory over Holy Cross. Zane Dudek, Caden Herring and QB Kurt Rawlings tallied TDs for the Bulldogs. Herring's TD came on a 24-yard toss from Rawlings. Tuckerman added a 28-yard field goal. Sophomore Elliott McElwain made Yale's longest run, a 54-yard sprint late in the game. Spencer Matthaei (4 tackles and a sack) and Kyle Ellis (5 tackles and 2 pass breakups) starred defensively for the Bulldogs.

Sept. 28: Yale defeated Cornell 27–16. The Bulldogs picked off four Big Red passes, two by Rodney Thomas II, the Ivy League defensive player of the week, who had 52 return yards and a touchdown.

Oct. 12: Following their win against Fordham the week before to start the season 3-0, Dartmouth blew away Yale 42–10 before a homecoming crowd of 6,796 in Hanover. Dartmouth entered the game leading the nation allowing just 8.0 points per game and continued its defensive approach which led to an early 21–0 first quarter lead that the Bulldogs could not overcome.

The Big Green scored on the first drive of the game and followed it with two first quarter picks off Rawlings which led to touchdowns.

Dartmouth senior QB Jared Gerbino ran for 59 yards and threw for 224 more. He also scored on a 12-yard TD run. Big Green receiver Drew Estrada finished with 203 receiving yards on five receptions. On the second play of the game Estrada went 75 yards for a score and added another early in the second half with a 61-yard touchdown catch.

First year Yale quarterback Nolan Grooms got his first snaps at a quarterback in the fourth quarter and went 4-for-4 for 39 yards and a touchdown pass to Darrion Carrington.

Oct. 19: Yale trailing by 20 points in the third quarter (27–7) erased a 27–14 deficit in the final 90 seconds at Richmond to complete an improbable comeback victory, 28–27. Rawlings threw for all four touchdowns and the Bulldogs came up with Sam Tuckerman's key onside kick.

Trailing by two touchdowns, Rawlings orchestrated the first score with a 15-yard TD pass to captain JP Shohfi with 1:23 left to play. Shohfi then came up with the needed onside kick recovery.

Rawlings completed the miracle comeback finding wide receiver Reed Klubnik with just nine second left to tie the game. Tuckerman drilled home the extra point to win the thriller.

Overall the Bel Air, Md. native passed for 249 yards (25-for 42). Two scores went to Klubnik while Shohfi and senior wideout Jaylan Sandifer each grabbed one. Spiders QB Joe Mancuso threw three touchdown passes and rushed for 117 yards on 13 carries. Richmond was coming off of its biggest win of the season, besting then-No. 18 Maine.

Oct. 26: In one of the wildest games seen in the Bowl, Yale downed Penn, 46–41. A total of 13 touchdowns were scored without a single field goal. The victory was fueled by Rawlings, who threw for a career high 388 yards (23 of 31) including a pair of touchdowns to go with 67 rushing yards and two more scores. For the day, he racked up 445 yards of total offense. In the process, Rawlings became Yale's all-time leader in career touchdown passes with 42 and 6,681 yards of total offense. All but five of his passing attempts went in the direction of Shohfi or Klubnik as the two book-end senior receivers combined for 20 catches and 349 yards. Two key plays in the game were Rawlings' 33-yard TD toss to Klubnik with two seconds remaining in the first half to give Yale a 20–13 lead at the break and sophomore safety Kyle Ellis' interception in the fourth quarter.

Penn rallied to take a 27–26 lead with 47 seconds left in the third quarter before Rawlings executed a scoring drive on the next possession.

Junior Zane Dudek rushed for 97 yards and three touchdowns. The line play of seniors Sterling Strother, Dieter Eiselen, Steve Cepalia, junior Cameron Warfield and sophomore Nick Gargiulo led to some impressive offensive numbers as the Yale offense collected 551 yards.

Penn QB Nick Robinson passed for 395 yards and three touchdowns with Ryan Cragun finishing with 208 yards on 13 receptions. Karekin Brooks, the leading rusher in the Ivy League ran for 72 yards including a two-yard TD late in the second quarter. Abe Willows (63 rushing yards) scored two TDs including his 20-yard scoring reception with 59 seconds left to play to pull the Quakers within a possible winning score. Penn attempted an onside kick that was recovered by Klubnik.

Nov. 2: The Rawlings-Shohfi connection continued its assault as Yale powered its way past visiting Columbia, 45–10. Shohfi, who opened the scoring early in the first quarter with a 17-yard TD grab, had 10 receptions, several in acrobatic fashion for a career high 189 yards. The TD was set up by Melvin Rouse's fumble recovery on Columbia's second offensive play. Rouse also had seven tackles on the day.

A key play in the game occurred in the first quarter when Yale's John Dean picked off a deflected pass when it appeared the Lions, trailing 7–3, would take the lead. The Bulldogs then navigated an 85-yard scoring drive capped by Rawlings' 5-yard run to make it 14–3 following a Sam Tuckerman extra point.

The Bulldogs scored again with 1:59 left in the first half on Darrion Carrington's 23-yard TD grab before adding a 38-yard Tuckerman FG on the first drive of the third quarter.

Rawlings racked up 390 yards in the air and ran for 33 yards. Dudek added a 45-yard TD run and Alan Lamar scored on a 5-yard TD reception from freshman QB Nolan Grooms.

Yale finished with a season high four sacks. Rodney Thomas II and Brandon Benn both had eight tackles. Starting cornerback Malcolm Dixon was ejected after being called for a targeting penalty. He was ineligible to play in the first half of the Brown game the following week. Yale coach Tony Reno believed that the targeting rule was misinterpreted by the officials.

Yale introduced its new video scoreboard thanks to the generosity of Sandy Cutler '73.

Nov. 9: In an offensive shootout on a cold Saturday afternoon at Brown Stadium, Yale pulled away late as Rawlings tossed a career high five touchdown passes, four to senior captain JP Shohfi, in the Elis 59–35 win. It was the most points the Elis had scored in 16 years. Shohfi had touchdown grabs of 23, 15, 11 and 9 yards. He pulled down 10 balls and went over 160 yards receiving for the third-straight game. It should be noted that the wunderkind Yale receiver holds the national high school season record for receiving yards when in 2015 playing for San Marino High School in California, he had 122 catches for 2,464yards and 29 TDs.

The game was a tale of two halves.

Yale totaled 627 yards of total offense, the first time the Bulldogs hit 600 total yards since 2014. The Yale defense also forced four turnovers on the afternoon.

The Bulldogs scored the first 17 points of the game, but Brown rallied as the Bears trailed 24–21 at the half and took the lead, 28–27, four minutes into the second half. Yale dominated from that point on however, outscoring Brown 32–7.

On the ground, Zane Dudek went for 216 yards, crossing the 2,000-yard rushing mark in his career, becoming just the 12th Bulldog to do so.

On defense, senior defensive tackle Spencer Matthaei led the charge with two sacks, three tackles for loss and a forced fumble. It was one of three forced fumbles in the game by the Bulldogs. Both senior Micah Awodiran freshman Brandon Benn were in on 10 tackles while Awodiran had 1.5 sacks and Benn had a forced fumble.

Nov. 16: Yale's offensive machine powered by the dynamic trifecta of Rawlings-Klubnik and Shohfi continued to roll as the Bulldogs dismantled the Princeton Tigers 51–14 in New Jersey. It was the first time since 1894 that Yale scored at least 50 points in back-to-back games. And the 37-point margin of victory tied for the largest number in the 142 meetings when ironically, Yale abused the Tigers by the same 51–14 score in 1931. The win allowed Yale to move into a first place tie with Dartmouth in the Ivy League after Cornell upset the previously undefeated Big Green, 20–17 in Hanover.

Statistically, it was an historic day in the annals of Yale football. Rawlings, the talented senior QB, set a Yale single-game record and tied the Ivy League record tossing six TD passes. Three fell into the hands of Klubnik who became Yale's leader in career receiving yards (2,396) passing Ralph Plumb '05. Shohfi, had eight catches for 141 yards and two scores. His remarkable 29-yard TD reception with nine seconds remaining in the first half despite double coverage led to a 30–7 lead at intermission and likely took the bite out of the Tiger.

Rawlings, who threw for 338 yards, became the tenth QB in Ivy League history with at least 7,000 career passing yards. For the fifth time this season he was selected the Ivy League Offensive Player of the Week. Patrick Conte caught an 18-yard TD pass, Alan Lamar crossed the goal line on a 1-yard run and Sam Tuckerman had 43-yard FG to round out the scoring.

Yale's defense was stellar as well holding Princeton's Collin Eaddy to 80 rushing yards, including a 15-yard TD run. This was a far cry from his 266 yards and three touchdowns in the 2018 contest. Kyle Ellis had a diving interception and Jaelin Alburg recovered a muffed Tigers' punt that led to Yale scores. Overall the Tigers were held to just 277 yards of total offense. During the season, the defense was bolstered by senior defensive linemen Spencer Matthaei and Charles Callender, senior linebacker Ryan Burke, senior defensive back Malcolm Dixon, and junior defensive backs Rodney Thomas II and Melvin Rouse II.

Nov. 23: Since 1875, a total of 136 Yale-Harvard games have been played but few, if any, can match The Game played on this date that was won by Yale 50–43 in two overtimes. It might or might not have been the greatest game played between the two rivals. But it certainly was the longest, with the noon start lasting 4 hours and 36 minutes because of a halftime climate change protest that held up the game for 40 minutes causing the game to finish in near darkness.

It may be forever known as "The Game in the Gloaming," a title coined by Tom Kokoska, a former Yale standout receiver who starred in Yale's win over Navy in '81.

The Elis down by 17 points early in the fourth quarter made a furious comeback to win the titillating contest earning a share of the Ivy League title with Dartmouth.

It was the third time in the last four years that the Bulldogs vaporized their ancient rivals and the first time since 1981 that Yale won the Ivy championship in two of the last three years. The Yale win put a damper on one of the greatest individual running performances in this series when Harvard freshman Aidan Borguet, rushed for 269 yards, including four touchdowns of 47, 59, 60 and 67 yards.

In the first offensive play of the game, Kurt Rawlings, Yale's magnificent QB, connected with Jaylen Sandifer for a 51-yard reception. The Elis got the ball to the Harvard four-yard line before Rawlings was sacked for a 16-yard loss. Sam Tuckerman's 34-yard FG put the Elis on top 3–0. Harvard answered on their first play of the game when Harvard QB Jake Smith fired a 60-yard pass to James Batch. The drive ended with a 27-yard FG by Jake McIntyre. The Crimson took a 9–3 lead after Rawlings was picked-off by Isaiah Wingfield which led to B.J. Watson's 27-yard TD run in the second quarter. McIntyre then missed the extra point that was partially blocked.

A Rawlings fumble then set up a 47-yard touchdown run by Borguet with 1:43 remaining in the first half. Harvard missed a razzle-dazzle two-point conversion attempt and went into halftime with a 15–3 lead.

Borguet, poison to the Elis the entire day, scooted for a 59-yard TD on the opening drive of the second half to give the Cantabs a 22–3 lead. Yale got back in the game when Jaelin Alburg recovered a Gavin Sharkey fumble on a knuckleball punt which led to Zane Dudek's four-yard TD run to make the score 22–10 after Tuckerman converted the extra point.

Wide receiver Reed Klubnik (14) is Yale's all-time leader in receiving yards with 2,627.

In 2019 wide receiver JP Shohfi (88) led the team in receiving yards (1,012) and TD receptions (10).

Tuckerman's 32-yard FG brought the Elis to within 22–13. But thanks to a pancake block by Harvard center Jackson Ward, Borguet went on an electrifying 60-yard run to give Harvard a 29–13 lead at the 6:52 mark of the third quarter. History will tell you, however, that it is not a good omen to have a 29–13 lead in a Yale-Harvard game reflecting back to the 1968 historic 29–29 tie game after the Elis led 29–13 with 42 seconds remaining. But on this sunny, brisk football day in New Haven, the script was reversed.

Yale answered back as Rawlings capped a scoring drive on a 5-yard TD run with 2:08 left in the third frame. But the try for two points failed and Harvard maintained a 29–19 lead. Borguet again spoiled Yale's momentum when early in the fourth quarter he broke for a 67-yard TD escaping the grasp of Yale linebacker Ryan Burke in the backfield. This gave the Crimson an apparent insurmountable 17- point lead, 36–19. It appeared the Johnnies had slayed the dragon while the Harvard band again played "Ten Thousand Men of Harvard." But the undaunted Bulldogs returned fire.

Tuckerman booted a 35-yard FG with 8:51 remaining to make it a two-possession game, 36–22. Rawlings subsequently engineered a 96-yard drive culminating with a 28-yard toss to freshman Mason Tipton followed by a 10-yard scoring pass to Tipton with 1:28 to play to make the score 36–29 after a Tuckerman PAT.

Tuckerman then executed an onside kick that was recovered by Klubnik. Harvard's victory dream transitioned into a nightmare. The Bulldogs marched to the Harvard seven before Rawlings fumbled with 22 seconds on the clock after a jarring hit. But Lady Luck was on Yale's side as the ball was recovered by Yale tackle Cameron Warfield. After a timeout, Rawlings hit captain JP Shohfi with a 7-yard TD toss to make the score 36–35. The Bowl crackled with excitement and the Yale band answered with "Bulldog," the school's fight song written by Cole Porter during his pre–World War I undergrad days at Yale. Tuckerman, a first team All-Ivy selection, then tied it with 18 seconds left in the game with the extra point. This sent the game into overtime and the crowd into a frenzy as daylight was rapidly bleeding toward dusk.

By this time, a large portion of the 44,989 fans who attended the game, had exited apparently thinking the Crimson had the game in hand.

On the first overtime play at 4:22 p.m., Harvard's Jake Smith connected with Cody Chrest for the 25-yard TD pass. The extra point made it 43–36 in favor of the Crimson. The drama continued as Yale answered with back-to-back completions to Shohfi and Caden Herring to send the game into a second pulsating overtime tied, 43–43. Shohfi set up another score with one of his patented circus catches before Dudek, who ran for 754 yards for the season, scored from four yards. This led to a 50–43 Yale advantage after Tuckerman's clutch PAT. The senior first team All-Ivy kicker played a major role in the win accounting for 14 points via three FGs and five extra points.

Harvard needed seven points to send the game into a third overtime but were stalled on a fourth down running play as Yale senior linebacker Ryan Burke thwarted Harvard's efforts when he tackled Watson about 1½ yards short of the first down. The roar from the approximate 10,000–15,000 that remained sounded like 70,000. Harvard's final ripple of hope had died. The game for the ages finally ended in near darkness at 4:39 p.m.

Final score: Yale 50 Harvard 43.

For Rawlings, who carried a California beach boy look with long blonde hair, the win included a free haircut in the locker room. The dynamic Yale QB promised several of his teammates that they could cut his golden locks if Yale beat Harvard. They wasted no time going to work on their beloved QB.

As for the crestfallen Harvards and their fans, it was a long trek back to Cambridge. For Yale fans, it was Nirvana as many partied into the night in the adjacent parking lots.

History was made in multiple ways. Yale's 19-point deficit (22–3) was the largest that either team came back from resulting in a win in the Y-H series. The combined 93 points was the most points registered in a Y-H game. Rawlings, after a sluggish start, engineered Yale's comeback victory. The unanimous All-Ivy first team selection put up a career high 417 passing yards. He shredded the Harvard defense accounting for 479 yards of total offense and 4 touchdowns. Shohfi caught 10 passes for 103 yards and Klubnik had 9 grabs for 141 yards. The two first team All-Ivy selections are only the second set of Ivy League teammates to have at least 1,000 receiving yards in the same season. The last time it happened was in 1983 when Derek Graham and Kevin Guthrie of Princeton accomplished the feat.

The game was marred by a halftime climate change protest involving students from both Yale and Harvard that lasted 40 minutes. Around 2 p.m. a group of about 50 students filtered onto the field entering from the southeast and northeast corner stands in the Bowl. The number of protestors that reportedly included alums and faculty members swelled to several hundred and refused to leave the mid-field. The protestors—Yale Endowment Justice Coalition and Divest Harvard—demanded that both universities clear their combined $71 billion endowments of investments in corporations tied to oil, gas and coal. They also protested the school's holdings in Puerto Rico debt, seen as exploitation of a poor besieged nation.

The protestors chanted, "Hey Hey! Ho Ho! Fossil fuels have got to go!"

The unprecedented Bowl protest was bizarre as the teams attempted to warm-up to resume the second half. But the protestors stood steadfast which led to the teams returning to their locker rooms around 2:15. Connecticut Governor Ned Lamont, both a Harvard and Yale alum, left his seat on the Yale side of the 50-yard line to join the protest. Lamont, who likely shared many of the objectives of the protesters, suggested that they talk off the field. Several student organizers followed him for a discussion of the compelling issues while the protesters dissipated.

The players reappeared on the field at 2:34 p.m. At 2:38 the field was finally cleared and play resumed at 2:48. The long delay, however, resulted in the game finishing in the dusk in lightless Yale Bowl. Ultimately 50 people who stayed on the field were arrested- 48 were issued summonses for disorderly conduct and two were criminally charged. Among those arrested was Sam Waterston, TV star of *Law and Order*, who was led off the field in handcuffs. The Academy Award–nominated actor is a Yale alum, class of '62.

During the delay Yale coach Tony Reno instituted his "lightning plan" that served this unexpected occasion well. Reno explained that if a game is ever halted because of lightning, his team is prepared to return to the locker room, have some food and get hydrated. Also, an area is cleared for stretching.

Entering the 2020 season, Yale and Harvard have met 136 times. Yale leads the series 68–60–8. Home field has not been a particular advantage for either team. Yale stands 32–29–3 in New Haven (24–27–1 in the Bowl) while on the road the Blue is 29–29–5 (26–26–3 at Harvard Stadium) and 7–2–0 at neutral sites. Yale has scored 1,912 points in the series to Harvard's 1,867. Since 1914 an estimated 2,958,647 fans have attended Y-H games in the Bowl. Overall over 6 million have attended Yale-Harvard games.

Harvard coach Tim Murphy has 18 wins, the most of any coach in the Y-H series.

In 2019, the *New York Post* came out with "The 20 Best Experiences College Football Has to Offer" and the Yale-Harvard game ranked No. 5 behind Clemson (Howard's Rock), Army-Navy, Notre Dame (TD Jesus) and Wisconsin's "Jump Around."

Nov. 24: Linebacker John Dean was elected captain of the 2020 Yale football team. Entering his senior year he has played in 28 games and has registered 88 tackles, four sacks and two picks.

Dec. 6: Superior Court Judge Philip Scarpellino sentenced the climate change protesters to five hours of community service without any criminal history or fine.

Dec. 9: Yale QB Curt Rawlings won the Bushnell Cup as the Ivy League's Offensive Player of the Year. Rawlings led the Ivy in passing yards (3,002), TD passes (27), passing yards per game (300.2) and efficiency (163.5). He tied the Ivy League record with five Offensive Player of the Week awards. He also ran for 314 yards. He is the second player in Ivy league history to have five straight games with at least 300 passing yards. His 60 career touchdown passes ranks third in Ivy history and he is fourth with 7,638 passing yards. His career passing rating of 149.69 is second best in league history.

Appendix: All-Time First Team All-Ivy League Selections

1956–2019

1956
Paul Lopata '57e, E
Denny McGill '57e, HB
Al Ward '57, HB

1957
Mike Cavallon '58, E
Curt Coker '58, FB
Jack Embersits '58, G
Dick Winterbauer '58, QB

1959
Harry Olivar '60, T
Mike Pyle '61, C

1960
Ben Balme '61, G
Bob Blanchard '61, FB
Mike Pyle '61, T
Tom Singleton '61, QB
Hardy Will '61, C

1961
Matt Black '62, C

1962
Perry Wickstrom '64, T

1963
Abbott Lawrence '65, T

1964
Chuck Benoit '65, G
Jim Howard '66, DB
Robert Kenney '67, E
Chuck Mercein '65, FB
Dave Strong '65, T

1965
Chris Beutler '66, S
Dave Laidley '66, DG
Greg Weiss '66, G

1966
Bob Greenlee '67, DT
Bill Hilgendorf '67, LB
Tom Schmidt '68, DG
Rod Watson '68, DE

1967
Don Barrows '68, FB
Dan Begel '68, K
Brian Dowling '69, QB
Kyle Gee '69, OT
Glenn Greenberg '68, DT
Calvin Hill '69, RB
Rick McCarthy '68, OG
Fred Morris '69, C
Tom Schmidt '68, MG
Paul Tully '68, OT

Appendix

1968
Mike Bouscaren '69, LB
Brian Dowling '69, QB
Ed Franklin '69, DB
Kyle Gee '69, OT
Calvin Hill '69, RB
Pat Madden '69, DB
Del Marting '69, E
Fred Morris '69, C
Bruce Weinstein '69, E
Dick Williams '69, MG

1969
John Biancamano '70, MG
Andy Coe '70, LB
Jim Gallagher '71, DE
Rich Maher '72, E
Tom Neville '71, DT
Bill Primps '71, HB
Bart Whiteman '70, OG

1970
Jim Gallagher '71, DE
Dick Jauron '73, FB
Matt Jordan '72, OT
Rich Lolotai '72, MG
Ron Kell '71, LB
Rich Maher '72, E
Tom Neville '71, DT

1971
Dick Jauron '73, FB
Matt Jordan '72, OT
Bob Leyen '73, OG
Rich Maher '72, E

1972
Dick Jauron '73, HB
Bob Leyen '73, OT
Mike Noetzel '73, DB
Bob Perschel '73, LB

1973
Elvin Charity '75, DB
Rick Fehling '74, DE
Rudy Green '75, HB
Carl Lewis '74, DB
Al Moras '75, OT
Gary Wilhelm '74, LB

1974
Brian Ameche '75, DE
John Cahill '76, MB
Elvin Charity '75, DB
Greg Dubinetz '75, OG
Bob Fernandez '75, TE
Rich Feryok '75, DT
Rudy Green '75, HB
Mark McAndrews '76, DB
Al Moras '75, OT
Charlie Palmer '76, OT
John Smoot '76, LB
Andy Walker '75, C

1975
John Cahill '76, MB
Gary Fencik '76, SE
Don Gesicki '76, HB
Scott Keller '76, DE
Charlie Palmer '76, OT
John Smoot '76, LB
Mike Southworth '77, P
Victor Staffieri '77, OG

1976
Pete Bonacum '77, DE
Steve Carfora '78, OG
Jim McDonnell '78, OT
Kurt Nondorf '79, DB
John Pagliaro '78, HB
Victor Staffieri '77, OG

1977
Steve Carfora '78, OG
Bill Crowley '79, LB
Paul Denza '78, DT
Jim McDonnell '78, OT
John Pagliaro '78, RB

Appendix

Bob Rizzo '78, QB
John Spagnola '79, TE
Clint Streit '79, DE

1978
Bill Crowley '79, LB
Arnie Pinkston '80, DB
Bob Skoronski '79, DT
John Spagnola '79, TE
Clint Streit '79, DE

1979
Dave Conrad '80, DT
Jim Dwyer '80, DE
Ken Hill '80, RB
Bob Regan '81, OT
Tim Tumpane '80, LB

1980
Kevin Czinger '81, MG
Rich Diana '82, RB
Fred Leone '82, DE
Bob Regan '81, OT
Dennis Tulsiak '82, DT

1981
Rich Diana '82, RB
Curt Grieve '82, WR
Tony Jones '82, P/K
Fred Leone '82, DE
Serge Mihaly '82, DT
Jeff Rohrer '82, LB

1982
Paul Andrie '84, RB

1983
Tom Giella '84, DT

1984
Hank Eaton '85, P
John Zanieski '85, MG

1985
Kevin Moriarty '86, WR
Steve Skwara '86, OT

1987
Dean Athanasia '88, TE
Jeff Rudolph '89, OG
Kelly Ryan '88, QB
Mike Stewart '87, TB

1988
Art Kalman '89, OT
Jeff Rudolph '89, OG

1989
Chris Gaughan '91, LB
Rich Huff '90, DB
Darin Kehler '91, QB
Glover Lawrence '90, DT
Ed Perks '92, K
Jon Reese '90, LB

1990
John Furjanic '91, DB

1991
Kevin Allen '92, OT
Nick Crawford '92, QB
Chris Kouri '92, RB
Erik Lee '93, DT
David Russell '92, OG

1992
Erik Lee '93, DL
Bart Newman '93, OG

1993
Jim Langford '94, TE

1994
Carl Ricci '95, LB

1996
Rob Masella '97, DB
Jack Hill '97, C

1998
Rashad Bartholomew '01, TB
Mike Murawczyk '01, K
Marek Rubin '99, OT

Appendix

1999
Jeff Hockenbrock '00, DE
Jim Keppel '02, FB
Than Merrill '01, S
Mike Murawczyk '01, K
Peter Sarantos '00, DE
Todd Tomich '01, CB

2000
Eric Johnson '01, WR
Peter Maloney '01, DT
Peter Mazza '01, LB
Than Merrill '01, DB
Matt Proto '01, OL
Todd Tomich '01, DB

2002
Robert Carr '05, TB
David Farrell '03, C
Jason Lange '03, DT

2003
Rory Hennessey '05, OT
Jake Kohl '04, OT
Nate Lawrie '04, TE

2004
Rory Hennessey '05, OT

2005
Ed McCarthy '07, OT
Ashley Wright '07, WR

2006
Bobby Abare '09, LB
Brandt Hollander '08, NT
Ed McCarthy '07, OT
Mike McLeod '09, RB
Jeff Monaco '08, OG

2007
Bobby Abare '09, LB
Brandt Hollander '08, NT
Langston Johnson '08, TE
Mike McLeod '09, RB
Jeff Monaco '08, OG

2008
Bobby Abare '09, LB
Darius Dale '09, OT
Kyle Hawari '09, DT
Mike McLeod '09, RB

2009
Tom Mante '10, P
Adam Money '11, DB
Paul Rice '10, LB
John Sheffield '10, H-B

2010
Adam Money '11, DB
Tom McCarthy '10, DL
Jordan Haynes '12, LB

2012
Tyler Varga '15, RB

2013
Deon Randall '15, WR

2014
Ben Carbery '15, OT
Kyle Cazzetta '15, PK
Deon Randall '15, WR
Tyler Varga '15, TB
Grant Wallace '15, WR

2015
Luke Longinotti '16, C
Spencer Rymiszewski '18, DB
Copache Tyler '17, DT

2017
Jon Bezney '18, T
Zane Dudek '21, RB
Hayden Carlson '18, DB
Jaeden Graham '18, TE
John Herubin '18, DL

Appendix

Karl Marback '18, T
Matthew Oplinger '18, LB
Spencer Rymiszewski '18, DB

2018
Reed Klubnik '20, WR
Alan Lamar '20, RB

2019
Kurt Rawlings QB
Dieter Eislen OL
Reed Klubnik WR
JP Shohfi WR

Yale Football All-Time Records: Through the 2019 Season

(Courtesy Yale Athletic Department)

Single-Game Rushing Yards

1. Mike McLeod (2007 vs. Lehigh) 276
2. Mike McLeod (2007 vs. Holy Cross) 256
3. Tyler Varga (2013 vs. Colgate) 236
4. Robert Carr (2002 vs. Cornell) 235
5. Deshawn Salter (2015 vs. Lehigh) 233

Single-Game Best Passing Yards

1. Griffin O'Connor (2018 vs. Princeton) 465 (3TDs)
2. Alvin Cowan (2003 vs. Harvard) 438 (2 TDs)
3. Joe Walland (1999 vs. Harvard) 437 (3 TDs)
4. Griffin O'Connor (2018 vs. Brown) 436 (4 TDs)
5. Kelly Ryan (1986 vs. Army) 426 (0 TDs)

Single-Game Most Catches

1. Eric Johnson 21 (1999 vs. Harvard) 244 yards 1 TD
2. Ralph Plumb 18 (2004 vs. Brown) 258 yards 0 TD
3. Nate Lawrie 16 (2003 Colgate) 167 yards 0 TD
4. Ralph Plumb 15 (2003 vs. Harvard) 158 yards 0 TD
5. Deon Randall 14 (2014 vs. Lehigh) 172 yards 2 TDs

Single-Game Most Receiving Yards

1. Ralph Plumb (2004 vs. Brown) 258 yards (18 catches) 0 TD
2. Eric Johnson (1999 vs. Harvard) 244 yards (21 catches) 1 TD
3. Reed Klubnik (2018 vs. Princeton) 234 yards (8 catches) 1 TD
4. Eric Johnson (2000 vs. Penn) 202 yards (13 catches) 2 TDs
5. Ashley Wright (2005 vs. Cornell) 198 yards (7 catches) 3 TDs

Single-Game Best Total Offense

1. Alvin Cowan (2003 vs. Colgate) 466 yards (45 rush; 421 pass)
2. Griffin O'Connor (2018 vs.

Appendix

Princeton) 464 yards (-1 rush; 465 pass)
3. Griffin O'Connor (2018) vs. Brown) 452 yards (16 rush; 436 pass)
4. Alvin Cowan (2003 vs. Harvard) 450 yards (12 rush; 438 pass)
5. T.J. Hyland (2001 vs. Harvard) 444 yards (171 rush; 273 pass)

Single Season Records Through the 2019 Season

Top Five Rushing Yards
1. Mike McLeod (2007) 1619
2. Rich Diana (1981) 1442
3. Tyler Varga (2014) 1423
4. Mike McLeod (2006) 1364
5. Rashad Bartholomew (2000) 1232

Top Five Rushing TDs
1. Mike McLeod (2007) 23
2. Tyler Varga (2014) 22
3. Mike McLeod (2006) 19
4. John Pagliaro (1976) 16
5. Zane Dudek (2017) 15

Top Five Passing Yards
1. Morgan Roberts (2014) 3220
2. Kurt Rawlings (2019) 3002
3. Alvin Cowan (2003) 2994
4. Morgan Roberts (2015) 2613
5. Jeff Mroz (2005) 2484

Top Passing TDs
1. Kurt Rawlings (2019) 27
2. Morgan Roberts (2014) 22
   Jeff Mroz (2005) 22
   Alvin Cowan (2003) 22
3. Kurt Rawlings (2017) 19
   Peter Lee (2000) 19
   Brian Dowling (1968) 19

Top Five Total Offense Rush Pass Yards
1. Alvin Cowan (2003) 435 2994 3429
2. Morgan Roberts (2014) 197 3220 3417
3. Kurt Rawlings (2019) 314 3002 3316
4. Morgan Roberts (2015) 57 2613 2670
5. Joe Walland (1999) 364 2207 2571

Top Five Receiving Yards
1. Reed Klubnik ('18) 1143
2. Grant Wallace ('14) 1139
3. JP Shohfi ('19) 1012
4. Eric Johnson ('00) 1007
5. Reed Klubnik ('19) 1002

Top Five TD Receptions
1. Eric Johnson ('00) 14
2. Curt Grieve ('81) 12
3. Ed Woodsum ('52) 11
4. Ashley Wright ('05) 10
   JP Shohfi ('19) 10
5. Reed Klubnik ('19) 9
   Eric Johnson ('99) 9

Appendix

Top Five Punt Return Yardage
1. Charles Ewart ('36) 299 yards
2. Gio Christodoulo ('08) 286 yards
3. Todd Tomich ('99) 274 yards
4. Gio Christodoulo ('11) 229 yards
5. Gary Fencik ('74) 209 yards

Top Five Kickoff Return Yardage
1. Chris Smith ('10) 732 yards
2. Jamal Locke ('15) 636 yards
3. Jake Fuller ('99) 548 yards
4. Robert Clemons ('13) 521 yards
5. Tyler Varga ('12) 519 yards

Most Interceptions
1. Mark Wallrapp (1995) 7
   Clint Frank (1936) 7
   Rich Huff (1989) 7
2. Todd Tomich (1999) 6
   Vanderveer Kirk (1945) 6
   Frank DeNezzo (1946) 6
   Arnie Pinkston (1978) 6
   11 tied with 5

Most Sacks
1. Kevin Czinger ('80) 14
2. Matthew Oplinger ('17) 11.5
3. Jeff Hockenbrock ('99) 10.5
4. Peter Sarantos ('98) 10
5. Harry Flaster ('02) 9.5
   Tony Cappellino ('87) 9.5

Career Records Through the 2019 Season

Top Five Rushing (Total Yards)
1. Mike McLeod (2005–08) 4514
2. Robert Carr (2001–04) 3393
3. Rashad Bartholomew (1998–2000) 3015
4. Tyler Varga (2012–14) 2985
5. Dick Jauron (1970–72) 2947

Top Five Rushing TD
1. Mike Mcleod (2005–08) 54
2. John Pagliaro (1975–77) 34
3. Tyler Varga (2012–14) 31
4. Robert Carr (2001–04) 29
5. Dick Jauron (1970–72) 27

Longest Runs from Scrimmage
1. Kahlil Keys vs. Columbia (2013) 94 yards
2. Denny McGill vs. Dartmouth (1956) 93 yards
3. Chris Kouri at Princeton (1991) 90 yards
4. Dick Jauron vs. Columbia (1972) 87 yards
5. Deshawn Salter vs. Cornell (2017) 82 yards
6. Buddy Zachery vs. Army (1998) 82 yards

Top Five Longest Passing Plays
1. Eric Williams to Cameron Sandquist at Georgetown (2012) 98 yards
2. Don Gesicki to Gary Fencik at Princeton (1975) 97 yards
3. Joe Massey to Bob Milligan vs. UConn (1969) 93 yards
4. Steve Mills to Dave Iwan vs. Dartmouth (1993) 90 yards

Appendix

5. Kurt Rawlings to JP Shohfi vs. Brown (2017) 83 yards

Top Five Passing TDs
1. Kurt Rawlings (2016–19) 59
2. Alvin Cowan (2000–04) 41
3. Morgan Roberts (2013–15) 37
   Patrick Witt (2009–11) 37
   Jeff Mroz (2002–05) 37

Top Five Passing Yards
1. Kurt Rawlings (2016–19) 7638
2. Morgan Roberts (2013–15) 6182
3. Patrick Witt (2009–11) 6033
4. Alvin Cowan (2000–04) 6024
5. Joe Walland (1997–99) 4832

Top Five QB Completions
1. Kurt Rawlings (2016–19) 583
2. Patrick Witt (2009–11) 549
3. Morgan Roberts (2013–15) 530
4. Joe Walland (1997–99) 430
5. Alvin Cowan (2000–04) 428

Top Five Receiving Yards
1. Reed Klubnik (2016–19) 2627
2. JP Shohfi (2016–19) 2501
3. Ralph Plumb (2001–04) 2396
4. Deon Randall (2010–14) 2320
5. Eric Johnson (1997–000) 2144

Top TD Receptions
1. Eric Johnson (1997–00) 23
2. Reed Klubnik (2016–19) 21
3. JP Shohfi (2016–19) 20
   Curt Grieve (1979–81) 20
4. Deon Randall (2010–14) 17
5. Ralph Plumb (2001–04) 16

Top Five Total Offense
1. Kurt Rawlings (2016–19) rush (1104) pass (7638) Total 8742 yards
2. Morgan Roberts (2013–15) rush (312) pass (6182) Total 6494 yards
3. Alvin Cowan (2000–04) rush (543) pass (5481) Total 6024 yards
4. Patrick Witt (2009–11) rush (minus 205 yards) pass (6033) Total 5828 yards
5. Joe Walland (1997–99) rush (776) pass (4832) Total 5608 yards

Top Five Punt Return Yardage
1. Gio Christodoulou (2007–11) 834
2. Todd Tomich (1997–00) 788
3. Charles Ewart (1935–37) 724
4. Gary Fencik (1973–75) 443
5. Jason Alessi (2014–17) 416

Longest Kickoff Returns
1. Melvin Rouse II (2018) 100 yards at Holy Cross
   Ken Hill (1978) 100 yards vs. Cornell
3. Nick Kangas (1959) (handoff from Lou Muller) 98 yards at Princeton
4. Jim Ryan (1950) 97 yards vs. Fordham
5. David Knox (2002) 96 yards vs. Penn

Longest Field Goals
1. Tom Mante vs. Cornell (2009) 54 yards
   Otis Guernsey vs. Princeton (1915) 54 yards
2. Jim Braden at Harvard (1919) 53 yards
3. Charlie O'Hearn vs. Carnegie Tech (1922) 52 yards
   Ed Perks vs. Cornell (1990) 52 yards
   Bill Moore vs. Princeton (1982) 52 yards

Appendix

Top Five Kickoff Return Yardage
1. Chris Smith (2008–13) 1726
2. Robert Carr (2001–04) 1401
3. Jamal Locke (2014-present) 1208
4. Rob Masella (1993–96) 1143 225
5. Buddy Zachery (1986–88) 1034

Top Five Longest Punt Returns
1. Herb Hallas vs. Penn (1958) 94 yards
2. Gio Christodoulou vs. Harvard (2007) 87 yards
3. Jason Alessi vs. Lehigh (2016) 82 yards
4. Jason Alessi vs. Columbia (2015) 80 yards
5. Rich Diana vs. UConn (1980) 77 yards (no TD)

Top Five Solo Tackles
1. Jon Reese (1987–89) 257
2. Don Lund (1986–88) 245
3. Carl Ricci (1992–94) 234
4. Gary Wilhelm (1971–73) 173
5. Bob Pershel (1970–72) 157

Top Five Tackles (since 1970)
1. Jon Reese 395
2. Don Lund 386
3. Carl Ricci 374
4. Gary Wilhelm 344
5. Bob Perschel 326

Top Five Sack Leaders
1. Kevin Czinger (1978–80) 27.0
2. Jeff Hockenbrock (1996–99) 22.5
3. Mathew Oplinger (2014–17) 21.5
4. John Zanieski (1982–84) 21.0
5. Isaiah Wilson (1994–97) 19.5

Most Interceptions
1. Todd Tomich (1997–2000) 16
2. Vanderveer Kirk (1944–47) 12
3. Steven Santoro (2005–08) 11
   Arnie Pinkston (1977–79) 11
4. Rich Huff (1987–89) 10
   Mike Tjarksen (1983–85) 10
   Chip Kelly (1977–79) 10
   Elvin Charity (1972–74) 10
   Frank DeNezzo (1945–46) 10

Longest Interception Returns
1. Bob Blanchard vs. Colgate (1960) 99 yards
2. Nate Boxrucker vs. Princeton (1998) 83 yards
   Bill Conway vs. Dartmouth (1948) 83 yards
3. Benjamin Cutler vs. Maryland (1924) 80 yards
4. Adam Money vs. Brown (2009) 77 yards
   Tim Kotkiewicz vs. Dartmouth (1984) 77 yards (No TD)
   Jack Ford vs. Penn (1969) 77 yards

Ivy League Championships

1956 (outright)	1969	1979 (outright)	1999
1960 (outright)	1974	1980 (outright)	2006
1967 (outright)	1976	1981	2017 (outright)
1968	1977 (outright)	1989	2019

Bibliography

Bergin, Thomas G. *The Game: The Harvard-Yale Football Rivalry, 1875–1983.* New Haven: Yale University Press, 1984.
———. *Gridiron Glory: Yale Football 1952–72.* New Haven: Football Y Association, 1978.
Buck, Polly Stone. *We Minded the Store: Yale Life and Letters During WWII.* Hamden, CT: Self-published, 1972.
Cahn, Neil R., Ronald Feiman, and Christopher Vizas II, eds. *The Blue Football Book.* New Haven: Yale Banner, 1970.
Cohane, Tim. *The Yale Football Story.* New York: G.P. Putnam's Sons, 1951.
Cozza, Carm, with Rick Odermatt. *True Blue: The Carm Cozza Story.* New Haven: Yale University Press, 1999.
Elliott, Len. *One Hundred Years of Princeton Football.* Princeton Athletic News, 1969.
Goldstein, Richard. *Ivy League Autumns: An Illustrated History of College Football's Grand Old Rivalries.* New York: St. Martin's Press, 1996.
Jones, Wilbur D. *Football! Navy! War.* Jefferson, NC: McFarland, 2009.
Leavy, Jane. *The Big Fella.* New York: HarperCollins, 2018.
MacCambridge, Michael, ed. *ESPN College Football Encyclopedia: The Complete History of the Game.* New York: ESPN Books, 2005.
McCallum, John. *Ivy League Football since 1872.* Briarcliff Manor, NY: Stein and Day, 1977.
Rafferty, Kevin, ed. *Harvard Beats Yale 29–29.* New York: The Overlook Press, 2009.
Rubin, Sam. *Yale Football: Images of Sports.* Charleston, SC: Arcadia, 2006.
Summers, John D. *Yale Bowl and the Open Trolleys.* Pittsburgh: Dorrance, 1996.
Trudeau, Garry. *Bull Tales.* New Haven: Yale Daily News, 1969.
Wallace, William N. *Yale's Ironmen.* Lincoln: iUniverse, 2005.

Newspapers

Brooklyn Daily Eagle
Hartford Herald
New Haven Register
New York Herald
New York Post
New York Sun
New York Times
Washington Times

Index

Abare, Bobby 144–146, 149
Abare, Larry 144, 146, 149, 150
Aceto, Lou 94
Ackerman, Steve 85, 86
Acosta, John 39
Adams, Tyler 175
Adee, George 18
Ajala, Sam 155
Alburg, Jaelin 180, 181
Alcott, Clarence 26, 27
Aldrich, Malcolm P. 39, 40
Alessi, Jason 164, 168
Alexander, Miles 172
Allen, Dan 44
Alston, Spencer 174
Ameche, Brian 107
Amendola, Buddy 82, 95
Anderson, Kevin 165
Andrie, Paul 121
Andrus, Ham 28
Angell, James Rowland 40
Angelone, Rich 111, 112
Anthony, Susan B. 82
Arnold, William 4, 5
Athanasia, Dean 125
Aubin, Tom 126
Aulcino, David 144
Awodiran, Micah 179
Aylsworth, Rob 134
Ayres, Benjamin 21
Azelby, Joe 121

Babbidge, Homer 70
Bagnoli, Al 64, 158, 162
Baker, Eugene 6, 7, 38
Baker, Hobey 30
Baker, Pink 41
Balestracci, Dante 144
Balme, Ben 89, 96, 117
Balsam, Peter 149
Barabas, Al 56
Barber, Donn 32

Barksdale, Roger 72
Barnett, Ben 127
Barres, Herty 53
Barry, Nancy 153
Bartholemy, Alan 62–64
Bartholomew, Rashad 138, 140, 141
Bartl, Fred 93
Barton, Bob 172
Barzilauskas, Fritz 68
Barzilauskas, Tony 68
Bassett, Mike 91, 94
Bassette, Jeff
Batch, James 181
Bayne, Nervy 12
Beagle, Bill 80
Bech, Tiger 169
Beck, Charles 10
Beecher, Henry 12, 13
Bell, Tommy 82
Benanto, Joe 127
Bence, Dick 85
Benigno, Ron 142
Benn, Brandon 178, 179
Bergin, Thomas G. 51, 71
Bigby, Keiron 122
Biglow, Lucius Horatio "Ray" 26, 27
Birmingham, Frank 89
Bjorklund, Hank 104
Black, C.R., Jr. 35
Blackman, Bob 103, 129
Blagdon, Crawford 22
Blaik, Earl "Red" 58, 64, 74, 88, 162
Blair, Ted 42
Blake, Ben 138
Blake, Doug 104
Blake, Jack 120
Blake, Richard 133
Blanchard, B.S. 6
Blanchard, Bob 89, 90
Blevins, Jon 140
Bliss, Pop 17
Bloomer, Amelia 82

199

Index

Bobo, Mike 131
Bolger, Ray 56
Bolling, Raynal 36
Booe, Billy "Boola Boola" 70, 72, 75, 92
Booker, Charlie 166
Booth, Albie 48, 49- 55, 68, 88, 101
Booth, George 125
Borden, Jake 137, 140
Borguet, Aiden 180, 181
Boston, Chief 62
Botsford, Matt 83
Boulris, Chet 88, 89
Brackett, Sean 154
Braden, Jim 35, 38
Brait, Mike 106
Brewster, Kingman, Jr. 94
Brice, Fred 51
Brice, Kevin 128
Brickley, Charley 32, 37
Bright, Ray 78
Brinckerhoff, Samuel 19
Brink, Bobby 80, 83
Brooks, Karekin 178
Brooks, W.A. 20
Brown, Billy 141
Brown, Charley 67
Brown, Fr. Francis Gordon 22
Brown, H.G. 67
Brown, Larry 112
Brown, Walter 67
Browne, Mike 125
Browning, Jim 111
Brubaker Mark 128
Bryant, Eddie 64
Buell, Charley 39
Bull, Billy 13, 14
Bull, Webster M. 65
Bullard, H.B. 70
Bunnell, Philip W. 45
Burch, Robert B. 27
Burke, Ryan 174, 280, 182, 183
Burkitt, Bob 114
Burkus, Greg 117
Burr, Francis 25
Burr, Fred 62
Bursiek, Paul 90, 91
Bush, George H.W. 77, 164
Bush, Jon 77
Butler, Doug 121
Butterworth, Frank A.
Bydume, Pat 142
Byrnes, Rodney 144

Cagle, Christian "Red" 50
Cahill, John 107
Cain, Dean 122
Caldwell, Bruce 45-47

Caldwell, Charlie 81
Callahan, Eunice 39
Callahan, Kevin 127, 130
Callahan, Mary 38, 39
Callahan, Mike 38, 39
Callahan, Tim 38, 39
Callender, Charles 180
Callinan, Jim 114
Camp, Alice 14, 44
Camp, Walter 1, 6–9, 13, 15, 16, 17, 20, 25, 26, 38, 43, 44, 47, 166
Campbell, Bill 90
Carfora, Steve 111
Cargill, Mordecai 150–152
Carlson, Stephen 169
Carr, Robert 141, 142, 167
Carrington, Darrion 176, 178
Carruthers, Corwynne 137
Carter, Jimmy 164
Carter, Lord 99
Carter, Randy 108, 109
Casey, Eddie 38, 52
Cavallon, Mike 86
Cawthorne, Joseph 28
Cazzetta, Kyle 159
Celentano, William 75
Cepalia, Steve 177
Chadwick, George B. 23
Chamberlain, Burr 20, 21
Champi, Frank 100, 101
Champion, Cole 155, 161
Chandler, Spurgeon "Spud" 49
Chapple, Colton 154
Charity, Elvin 105
Charlesworth, John 46
Chauncey, Henry 46
Chauncey, Sam 46
Chism, Earl 169
Choquette, Paul 87
Chrest, Cody 183
Christodoulou, Gio 148, 153
Cimini, Meg 121
Cirie, Jack 93
Clarke, Brian 104, 106
Clemencau, Georges 41
Clemens, Walt 75
Clements, Vin 102
Clemons, Robert III 160–163
Cleveland, Frances 20
Cleveland, Grover 20
Cleveland, Richard 35
Clifford, Emmett 172
Clouse, Rich 117
Cochems, Eddie 26
Cochran, Bob 83
Coe, Andy 103
Coker, Gene 84, 85

200

Index

Cole, Bob 22
Collins, P.J. 141
Colwell, Dave 60
Conrad, Dave 114
Conran, Pat 113
Conroy, Robert J. 37
Constable, Pepper 57
Constantin, Gene 65
Conte, Patrick 172, 180
Conway, William E. 73
Cook, Charles 158
Cooney, Carroll 29
Corbin, William H. "Pa" 13, 69
Corelli, Connie 80
Corwin, Robert N. 12
Cowan, Alvin 141–144, 173
Cox, Duncan 47
Coxe, Alex 11
Coy, Sherman 22
Coy, Ted 27–30
Cozza, Carm 71, 95, 97- 99, 102- 110, 112–117, 119, 120, 122- 128, 130–135, 137, 163, 164, 171, 172, 174
Cragun, Ryan 178
Crawford, Nick 130, 131
Crickard, Jack 53
Crim, Gus 100
Crisler, Fritz 60
Crone, Eric 103, 104
Crosby, Bing 84
Cross, John W. 48
Crowle, Nick 171
Crowley, Bill 112
Crowley, Joe 53, 54
Cullen, Albie 88
Culver, John 81
Cummings, Pete 92
Cummock, Arthur 15
Cunningham, John 82
Curry, Jim 107
Curtain, Clare 55, 56
Curtin, Mike 122
Curtin, Peter 107
Curtin, Tommy 57
Curtis, Nathaniel 5
Cushing, H.W. 6
Cutler, Sandy 178
Cuyler, DeWitt 17
Cyr, Mike 122
Czinger, Kevin 111–115, 117

Dakos, Art 136
Daley, Fred J. 29
Dalley, Larry 69
Danko, Adam 149
Dashiell, Paul 25
Davis, Ernie 91

Davis, Glenn 67, 121
Davis, Justin 141, 159
Davis, Parke H. 7
Davis, Trocon 154
Dawson, Clifton 145
Dean, D.S. 15
Dean, John 178, 185
DeAngelis, Jim 56
Deland, Lorin 17
DeMars, Ted 105
Dent, Fred 64, 66
Derby, Dave 125
Dernbach, Elizabeth 153
Dershimer, Cyrus 4
de Saulles, Charles 20
DeWitt, John 24
Diana, Rich 114–118
Dickenson, Mel 41
Diehl, Bill 91
DiLieto, Biagio 123
Dillon, Eddie 27
Discepolo, Kevin 166
Dixon, Malcolm 170, 178, 180
Doherty, Pete 157
Donelli, Aldo "Buff" 90
Donohue, John 106
Doolittle, Jimmy 66
Dorsey, Martin 172
Dowling, Brian 94, 97–101, 174
Downey, John T. 102
Doyle, Tom 105, 106
Drahos, Nick 63
Drawl, Ross 156, 169
Driftmier, Lee 145
Drury, Eric 132
Dudek, Zane 167- 172, 176–179, 181, 183
Dudley, "Bullet Bll" 64
Dufek, Joe 118
Dunn, Dennis 112, 114
Durston, Alfred 21
Duryea, John 124
Dwyer, Jim 113
Dwyer, Martin 68
Dyches, Brandon 145

Eaddy, Collin 169, 174, 180
Eaton, Franklin M. 9
Eddy, Maxon H. 47
Ederer, John 78
Edison, Thomas 24
Edmonds, Chase 165
Edwards, Brian 144
Egloff, Randy 93, 94
Egurbide, Jose 124
Eichenlaub, Ray 32
Eiselen, Dieter 177
Ellis, Kyle 176, 177, 180

Index

Ellis, S.G. 21
Embersits, John 86
Engle, Rip 73
Epstein, Theo 133
Ernst, Steve 121
Estrada, Drew 176
Evashevski, Forest 62

Faherty, Alex 145
Fakava, Heikoti 125
Farwell, Arthur 10
Fehling, Rich 105
Feiereisen, Todd 145
Felton, Sam 31
Fencik, Gary 106–108
Ferguson, Jack 64
Ferraro, Ralph 121
Ferry, Charles 32
Feryok, Rich 106, 107
Fiedler, Jay 131, 132, 162
Field, John 30
Finney, Frank 86, 87
Fischer, Andrew 160
Fish, Hamilton III 27
Fisher, Bob 38, 39, 66
Fishwick, Dwight 46
Fitzgerald, Art 69, 71
Fitzpatrick, Ryan 142, 144
Flanders, Bob 152
Flanders, Henry 11
Flinn, Rex 25
Flippin, Royce 81, 83
Flutie, Doug 121
Foch, Marshal Ferdinand 40
Foley, Frank 61, 62
Forbes, Bob 25
Ford, Gerald R. 61, 64
Ford, Jack 102
Forney, Jordan 150
Forte, Don 64
Fortunato, Joe 79
Frank, Clint 1, 17, 57–61, 66, 103, 121, 129, 132
Freeman, Bruce 100
Freeman, Matt 87
French, Art 48
Friedman, Stanleigh 24
Friesele, W.H. 53
Fuchs, Jim 76
Fuller, Jake 138, 140
Furman, Henry 154, 155
Furse, Tex 71, 73, 74
Fusilli, Nick 68

Galiette, Dick 137, 145
Gallagher, Frank 65
Gallagher, Jim 117
Galland, Alex 167, 168, 170, 174
Galvez, Rocky 147
Gamble, Kenny 124
Gardner, Henry "Hessie" 57
Gardner, Kevin 109
Gargiulo, Nick 177
Garrett, Jason 125, 127
Garrett, Jim 129
Garrett, Judd 127, 129
Gasparella, James 143
Gaston, John 39
Gates, Artemus L. 36
Gates, Jack 37
Gatto, Rich 104
Gatto, Vic 100
Gedeon, Alex 153
Gehrke, Erwin 44
Gerbino, Jared 173, 176
Gesicki, Don 106, 108
Gher, Marlin "Buzzy" 67, 68
Giamatti, A. Bartlett 120
Gianelly, Tony 83
Giardi, Mike 132, 133
Giegengack, Bob 80
Giella, Tom 120
Gill, Charley O. 14
Gilliam, Spencer 172
Gilligan (Princeton) 45
Gillis, Frank 68
Gilmore, Tom 167
Glass, A.J. 165
Glass, Edgar "Ned" 23, 24
Godiva, Lady 82
Gogolak, Pete 93
Gonillo, Bill 125
Goodfriend, Dan 109
Goss, George 23, 24
Gosselin, William 137
Gould, Charles 22
Gouveia, Jim 131
Graham, Derek 118
Graham, Jaeden 1, 160, 167, 168
Grana, Bill 91, 93
Grange, Red 87
Grant, Wally 89, 92
Graves, Andrew B. 14
Graydon, Thomas 22
Green, Rudy 76, 106
Greene, Waldo W. 48
Grennough, Malcolm 44
Grieve, Curt 116–119, 133
Griffith, Charlie 85
Grochowski, Dan 156
Groninger, Jim 94
Grooms, Nolan 176, 178
Guarnaccia, Dave 48
Guernsey, Otis 35

202

Index

Gunn, George 4
Gustafson, Eric 51
Guthrie, Kevin 101

Halas, George 2
Hall, Greg 109
Hall, Louis 10
Hall, Norman 48
Hallas, Herb 86, 87, 133
Hallowell, Bob 18
Halstead, William 4
Halvorson, Ryan 166
Hamlin, Chan 23
Hammersley, Bill 47
Handlon, Matt 145
Handsome Dan I 14, 18
Handsome Dan II 56
Handsome Dan XII, "Bingo" 113, 114
Handsome Dan XVII, "Sherman" 164, 166
Handsome Dan XVIII, "Walter" 165, 166
Hansen, Westi 68
Harasymiak, Joe 173
Hardman, Lamartine 49
Hardwick, Tack 33
Harlow, Dick 58, 70, 73
Harmon, Tom 61, 62, 121
Harper, Jesse 33
Harris, Dale 162, 165
Harrison, Fred "Ted" 64
Harrison, Ted 63
Harshbarger, Scott 94
Hart, Brook 149
Hart, Pete 91
Hart, Ridge 24
Hartwell, Josh 19
Harvard, John 36, 54, 56
Haughton, Percy 28, 43, 141
Hayes, Norm 161
Haynes, Jordan 76, 151
Hempel, Connor 160
Heneghan, Jack 167
Henley, Chandler 143, 145
Hennen, Brian 127
Hennessey, Rory 144
Hennings, Tyrell 105, 106, 107
Herring, Caden 176, 183
Herubin, John 165
Hessberg, Al 57
Hetherington, Chris 112, 134
Hibben, John Grier 40
Hickman, Herman 31, 73, 74, 76–78, 123
Hickok, William Orville "Wild Bill" 17, 18
Higdon, Hank 91
Higginson, Henry Lee 20, 25
High, Dick 63
Hill, Calvin 93, 101, 117, 164, 174
Hill, Ken 112, 114, 172

Hill, Lonnie 143
Hillebrand, Arthur 21
Hines, Bo 161
Hinkey, Frank 16–18, 32, 34, 38
Hinojosa, Lyn 91
Hinz, Tony 126
Hirsch, Allan M. 22
Hockenbrock, Jeff 138
Hodges, Russ 79
Hogan, Jim 24
Holden, A.F. 12
Hollander, Brandt 147, 148
Hollingshead, Richard M. III 70
Holly, Bob 118
Holmes, Bryan 161
Holmes, Tommy 50
Holt, Henry 24, 30
Holt, Milt "Pineapple" 107
Hoopes, Townsend "Tim" 64
Hoover, Herbert 61
Horn, Blake 166
Horsted, Jesper 169
Horween, Arnold 38, 39, 46, 52
Hosch, Scott 161, 163
Howard, Jim 93
Howe, Art 30
Howland, JJ 172, 173
Hu, Eion 134
Huff, Rich 127, 129
Huguley, Art 52
Humphreville, Dave 109
Humphrey, George 93, 94, 96, 133
Humphrey, Gilbert "Bud" 58, 61, 96
Humphrey, Louise Ireland 133
Humphrey, Watts 61, 133
Hunnicutt, Drew 167
Husing, Ted 52
Hutcherson, John 89, 90
Hyland, T.J. 141

Iacavazzi, Cosmo 94, 99
Ilacqua, Carmen 123
Iwan, Dave 133

Jackson, Levi 55, 70–72, 74–76, 103, 141
Jacunski, Harry 116
Jauron, Dick 1, 103–105, 111, 117
Jefferson, Thomas Coolidge 33
Jenkins, Troy 122, 126
Jiggetts, Dan 108
Johnson, Billy 22
Johnson, Eric 1, 138–140
Johnson, Wayne 66, 67
Jolson, Al 47
Jones, Howard H. 28, 29, 31, 41, 43
Jones, Thomas Albert "T.A.D." 29, 34, 36, 38–47

Index

Jones, Tony 115–117
Jordan, Lloyd 76
Jordan, Ralph E. 40
Joslin, Jim 86
Joss, John H. 45
Julien, Al "Doggie" 67
Juszczyk, Kyle 152

Kaake, Ed 90
Kachmar, Mark 152
Kai, Michael 144
Kaminsky, Bill 129
Kanoff, Chad 162, 163, 169
Kasprzak, Don 70
Katzman, Joseph 38
Kay, Derek 123
Kazmaier, Dick 77, 78, 121
Kehler, Darin 127- 131
Kelcher, Melvin B. 38
Kell, Ron 104
Keller, Charley 74
Keller, John 125
Keller, Scott 106
Kelley, Larry 1, 56–60, 121, 140
Kelly, Bill 100
Kelly, James C. 54
Kemp, Jack 113
Kemp, Jeff 113, 115
Kempe, Connor 150
Kempton,Fido 39
Kennard, Vic 28
Kennedy, Bobby 73, 84, 93
Kennedy, Joe 84
Kennedy, John F. 84, 89, 93, 94
Kennedy, Ted 84
Ketcham, Henry H. 31
Keys, Kahlil 155
Kidd, Brian 94
Kieran, John 47
Kilday, Tom 51
Kilpatrick, John Reed 30, 66
Kimball, Alan 145, 146
King, Bill 92
King, Phil 18
Kinney, Ralph 24
Kirk, Brent 106
Kirk, Vandy 69
Klebanoff, Harry 102–104
Kline, Bill 44
Klubnik, Reed 165, 166, 172, 173, 175, 177–179, 183–184
Knapp, Bill 65
Knowles, Carroll 33
Knowles, Tim 107
Knowlton, Hugh 66
Knox, David 142
Knox, William 26, 27

Kokoska, Tom 117, 180
Koslowski, Stan 69
Kotkiewicz, Tom
Kouri, Chris 131
Koze, Rich 123
Krystyniak, Bob 112
Kusserow, Lou 74
Kyasky, Bob 82

Lahr, Bert 56
Laidley, Dave 164
Lake, Everett J. 40
Lalich, George 100
Lamar, Alan 164–166, 172, 174, 178, 180
Lamar, Henry 12
Lamont, Ned 185
Lange, Jason 141
Langford, W.S. 44
Langner, Gus 72
Lapham, Henry G. 42
Larkin, Andrew 156
Lassiter, Bob 52, 55
Lathman, Matt 120
Lawrence, Abbott H. 94
Lawrence, Rick 107
Lawrie,Nate 142
Leary, John J. 82
Leavy, Jane 46
Leckonby, Bill 90, 91
Lee, Fran 63, 64
Lee, Peter 141
Lee, Rich 141
Leeds, H.C. 6
LeGore, Harry 33, 34
Leone, Fred 113, 115–117
Levatino, Joe 129
Levering, Walt 55
Lewis, Dexter 81, 84
Lewis, Grace "Amazing"
Libbey, C.E. 38
Lieb, Fred 36
Liechty, Dale 31, 76
Liguori, Jackson 152
Linehan Fred 51
Little, Lou 73
Little, Sebastion 161
Locke, Fergie 55
Lockman, Jim 132
Loeser, Fred 51
Loftus, Charley 68, 76, 80, 82, 106
Lohnes, John E. 77
Lombardi, Vince 110, 116
Looney, Chris 154
Lopata, Paul 83, 86
Lopez, Jimmy 80
LoProto, Ryan 140
Lorditch, Chris 150

204

Index

Loucks, Dean 84–86
Loucks, Vern 84, 86
Loud, George 48
Loughery, John 115
Lovejoy, Winslow M. 43, 44
Lovett, John 165, 174
Lowenstein, Carroll 77
Lowery, Nick 110
Loyd, Faye 82
Luft, Matt 148
Luman, Richard 42
Lund, Don 126, 127
Lund, Ken 124
Lynch, Mike 108
Lynch, Paul 87

MacArthur, Douglas II 52
Macauley, Tim 122
MacDonald, Torby 62
MacLeish, Archibald 32
Mahan, Eddie "Packy" 33, 34, 155
Maher, Rich 104
Mallory, Bill "Memphis Bill," 42, 65, 66
Mancuso, Joe 177
Manley, Phil 115
Manora, Darius 160, 162, 163
Mante, Tom 148, 149
Marckwald, A.H. 22
Marietti, Nick 143
Marinaro, Ed 93, 192, 104
Marquis de la Falaise de la Coudraye, Henri 45
Marschner, Ken 137
Marsh, Lee 91
Martin, Bert 65
Martin, Dick 81
Martin, Don 102–104
Marting, Del 55, 99
Marting, Walter 55
Martinson, Marty 122
Masella, Rob 134, 135
Mathews, Sam 143
Matthaei, Spencer 169, 176, 179–180
Matthews, William Clarence 25
Matuszak, Walt 63
Mayes, Brad 164
Mays, Zach 161
Mayweather, Mike 127
Mazurkiewicz, Tony 134
Mazza, Corey 144
Mazza, Peter 140
McAndrews, Peter 48
McBirney, Hugh J. 4
McBride, Malcolm L. 21, 22
McCall, "Wild Bill" 52
McCallum, Napoleon 117
McCanus, Ryan 158

McCarney, Gavin 154
McCarthy, Ed 92, 95
McCarthy, Tom 150
McCartney, Paul 164, 170
McClellan, Mike 136
McClung, Thomas Lee "Bum" 15, 16
McCormack, Vance 49
McCormick, Vance 17
McDonagh, Trevor 162
McElwain, Elliott 176
McEwen, John 48
McGill, Dennis 83–86, 98, 155
McHale, Will 153
McInally, Pat 107
McIntyre, Jake 170, 181
McKenna, Leo 80
McKenzie, Scott 109
McKinnon, Don 92
McLaughry, Tuss 45
McLeod, Mike 12, 53, 145–149, 160
McNamara, Robert 82
McNamee, Graham 51, 52
McNicol, Don 64
Mellish, Dan 134
Melville, Jake 164
Mercein, Chuck 93–95
Merriwell, Frank 19, 52, 81
Metcalf, Harold 24
Meyer, Cord 36
Meyer, Quentin "Monk" 65
Michaels, Al 117
Michalik, Chris 176
Michalik, Rob 176
Mihaly, Serge 113, 117
Miller, Elliot S. 3
Miller, James E. 37
Miller, Ogden 63
Milligan, Bob 102
Milstead, Century 22, 42
Minot, Wayland 29
Mitchell, Ledyard 24
Mitinger, Joe 78
Moesta, Marty 160, 165
Moffie, Hal 75
Molloy, Ed 78, 79
Moore, Bill 120, 122
Moore, Sam 26
Moore, Tre 165
Moran, Marty 86
Moriarty, Kevin 122
Morris, Carl 111
Morrison, Scott 107
Morrissy, Anne 82
Morrow, Mitch 136
Morse, Sammy 25
Morton, Bill 52
Morton, Strat 57, 65

205

Index

Moseley, Spencer D. 65, 66
Mothander, David 155
Mott, Tony 56
Mroz, Jeff 142, 144, 145, 157
Mullen, Kyle 171
Mulligan, Hugh A. 73
Munger, George 62
Murawczyk, Mike 137, 140
Murphy, Fred 18
Murphy, Tim 142, 153, 160, 163, 185
Murrell, Hertz 50

Nadherny, Ferd "The Bull" 71, 75, 76
Nebrich, Mike 155
Neidlinger, Newell 42
Nelson, Emerson"Spike 63–65
Nelson, Lindsey 87
Nelson, Rob 134
Nettleton, George H. 47, 48
Neville, Tom 101, 103, 117
Ng, Derek 172
Nicholson, John 61
Nitti, John 114
Nixon, Richard M. 64
Nizialek, Cam 162
Noble, Larry 44
Nottingham, Jim 120
Novosel, Dave 113
Nwokocha, Chuck 140
Nyhan, Dave 91

O'Brien, Bill 71, 139
O'Brien, Pat 112
O'Connor, C.W. 24
O'Connor, Griffin 173–175
Odell, Howard 65–68, 70–73
O'Donnell. Hank 72
O'Hearn, Charles 40, 41
Olcott, Herman 22
Oliaro, Scott 130
Olivar, Jordan 78–81, 83, 84, 86–92, 123
Olson, Bill 74
Oluokun, Foyesade 1, 156, 161, 165, 168–170
Opara, Chism 140
Oplinger, Matt 158, 169
Ortmayer, Andrew 37
Osterman, Al 33, 134, 135
Osterweis, Rollin G. 113, 114
Owen, George 40, 41
Owseichik, Mike 84
Owsley, J.E. 25

Paci, Frank
Paglaiaro, John 109, 110
Palazzo, Nick 142
Palin, Beau 155
Panico, Philippe 150, 151

Parcells, Bob 78, 79
Parker, Dan 26
Parker, Robert 129
Parkin, Leland 41
Parseghian, Ara 117
Pataki, George 101
Paterno, Joe 74, 92
Patterson, Mark 142
Patton, Gilbert 19
Peabody, Endicott "Chub" 64, 65 93
Penna, Tim 141
Perks, Ed 128, 130
Perry, James 136
Perry, Ted 104
Perschel, Bob 105
Peters, Frank G.
Petruska, Bob 75
Pfaffman, Karl 41
Pharr, Fred 38
Phillips, John 80
Phillips, Stone 108
Pickett, Bob 65
Pilkerton, Jay 147
Pinkham, Lydia 82
Pinkston, Arnie 113
Pitts, Art 80
Pizzotti, Chris 148
Platt, William V. 61
Plumb, Ralph 142, 144, 179
Poe, Arthur 20, 21
Pollard, Fritz 34
Pond, Raymond "Ducky" 43, 44, 55–57, 59, 61–63, 66, 77
Pont, John 93–95, 123
Poole, Bobby 81
Porter, Cole 183
Porter, Skip 113
Powell, Mike 138
Powers, John 150
Prchlik, John 68
Price, Keith 132, 134
Primps, Bill 103
Proxmire, William 59
Pruett, Hub 81
Pumpelly, Harold "Pump" 31
Purrington, Roly 104, 105
Pyle, Mike 1, 89, 117

Quackenbush,Bradford H. 77
Quarrier, Sidney 46
Quill, Jim 25
Quinn, John 123

Rafferty, Charles D. 23
Rafferty, Kevin 65
Ragone, Billy 151
Rahne, Ricky 140

Index

Raines, Bobby 74–76
Randall, Deon 76, 144, 155, 156, 158–161
Rapp, Brian 92
Rapp, George 109
Ravenel, Charley 88- 90
Rawlings, Kurt 165–170, 172, 173, 176–184, 186
Ray, Carl 57
Reagan, Ron (son) 109
Reagan, Ronald (father) 109
Reams, Keith 141
Regan, Bob 115
Reid, Bill 21, 25
Reid, John 63
Remington, Frederick 16
Renaud, Bob 115
Reno, Larry 80, 81
Reno, Tony 153–155, 161, 163, 166, 171, 176, 178, 185
Repsher, Larry 88
Restic, Joe 104, 131–133
Rhodes, David 133
Rhodes, William C. 15, 17, 18
Ribicoff, Abe 84
Ricci, Carl 134
Rice, Grantland 41, 42
Rice, Paul 149
Rice, Travis 169
Rich, Chandler 156
Richards, Eugene L. 11
Richeson, Lyle 42
Rickey, Branch 59
Ristine, Albert 22
Rizzo, Bob 109, 110
Roberts, Archie 93
Roberts, Morgan 156, 158, 161–163
Robinson, Bradbury 26
Robinson, Nick 178
Roche, Charley 69
Rockne, Knute 2, 33, 43
Rockwell, Foster 24
Rodgers, James O. 20, 21
Rogan, John 113, 115–118, 170
Rogan, Kevin 106
Rohrer, Jeff 113, 115, 119
Roman, J. Hunter 161
Roney, Lew 100
Roome, Howard 27
Roosevelt, Theodore 21, 25, 28
Root, Reggie 72
Root, Reginald D. 55
Roper, Bill 41, 44
Roscoe, Jerry 56, 57
Rose, Neil 141, 142
Ross, Brendan 153
Rossides, Gene 74
Rostomily, Bob 113

Roth, Tyler 160
Rouse, Melvin II 166, 172, 178, 180
Rowley, kyle 141
Runyon, Damon 41
Russell, Derek 154, 155
Ruth, Babe 43, 55
Ruth, Claire 55
Rutishauser, Don 110
Ruwe, Pat 119, 171, 174
Ryan, Frank 120
Ryan, Jim 77, 78
Ryan, Kelly 122, 124, 125
Rymiszewski, Spencer 158, 162, 166

Saah, Maurice 129, 130
St. John, Burke 114
Salter, Deshawn 167
Sandifer, Jaylan 177, 180
Santiago, Robert 123
Santoro, Steve 147
Santos, Rob 132
Sarantos, Peter 138
Saunders, John 132
Savage, Russ 111
Scales, Treavor 154
Scarpellino, Philip 185
Schaff David Schley 3
Schmoke, Kurt 101
Schneider, Jack 26
Scholl, Rob 138
Schonbrun, Zach 153
Schuler, Bill 68
Schulze, Jay 141
Schwartz, Dave 110, 111
Schwieger, Nick 150, 151
Scott, Stewart 46
Scott, Todd 135
Scussel, Ray "Scooter" 67
Seamans, W.S. 6
Searle, Dan 138
Sedgwick, Harold 124
Self, Clarence 75
Senay, Ed 77
Seneca, Isaac, Jr. 19
Seymour, Hovey 64, 65
Shafnisky, Nick 164
Shampkin, Aaron 170
Sharkey, Gavin 181
Sharpe, Albert 21, 38
Shears, Pete 80
Sheehan, Connor 160
Sheehan, Joseph M. 92
Shelton-Mosley, Justice 163
Sheriden, Richard 52
Sherman, Tommy 3
Sheronas, Dave 132
Shevlin, Tom 24, 25, 30

Index

Shields, Wally 109
Shimer, Connie 90
Shohfi, JP 170, 173, 175–179, 182–184
Shoop, Bob 125
Short, Sarah 153
Shugart, Thorne 81
Shula, Dave 113
Shula, Don 113
Siedlecki, Jack 135–138, 140–142, 144, 145, 147, 149, 153, 168
Simourian, John 86
Simpson, Jessica 138
Singleton, Tom 88- 90
Siragusa, Michael 161
Skelton, John 149
Skol, Kevin 129, 132
Skoronski, Bob 109
Skrovan, Steve 174
Slager, Kyle 143
Smilow, Joel E. 126, 151
Smith, Chris 151
Smith, David 167
Smith, Don 142
Smith, Greg 141
Smith, Homer 79
Smith, Jake 170, 181, 183
Smith, Red 11, 82, 84
Smith, Vernon "Catfish" 49
Smoot, John 107, 108
Smullen, Rori 132
Smythe, George 42
Snavely, Carl 63
Snickenberger, Walt 104
Snyder, Ned 77
Sorbara, George 124
Sortal, Paul 105
Southmayd, William 94
Southworth, Mike 109
Spagnola, John 110, 112
Spalding, Jesse 31
Spears, Bob 77, 84
Spivack, Paul 122
Spreyer, Charley 63
Stack, William J. 62
Staffieri, Vic 108
Stagg, Amos Alonzo 26, 52, 55, 72
Stahura, Walt 84
Standish, Burt L., 19
Stanley, Chris 150
Stanton, Paul 155
Stein, Jon 115, 117
Steinberg, Rob 121
Stevens, Marvin "Mal" 42, 47–49, 51–55, 68
Stewart, Mike 125
Stewart, Tom 175
Stillman, George S. 22
Stillman, Joseph 37
Stillman, Phil 18
Stopa, Craig 123
Stover, Dink 81
Streit, Clint 109
Strother, Sterling 177
Stubby, "The Military Dog" 37
Stuhldreher, Harry 75
Sturhan, Cobbles 46
Sullivan, Andrew 144
Sullivan, Dennis 104
Sullivan, Mike 110–113
Swan, Joseph R. 23
Swanson, Gloria 45
Swayne, Noah H., Jr. 32

Taft, Charley 35
Taft, William Howard 35
Takamura, Jon 150
Talbott, Nelson S. "Bud" 32, 33
Tarasovic, Phil 80, 83, 84
Tataranowicz, Vic 70
Taylor, Bill 91, 93
Taylor, Cyrus R. 65
Taylor, Ed 64
Taylor, Tommy 49
Terrell, Jeff 146
Terry, Wyllys 11, 159
Thomas, Alex 150–152
Thomas, Ken
Thomas, Rodney II 176, 178, 180
Thomas, Tanner 165
Thompson, Beverly V. 33
Thompson, Everard 32
Thompson, Oliver 6, 7
Thompson, Roosevelt 165
Thorne, Sam "Brinck" 18
Ticknor, Ben 52
Tipton, Mason 183
Tisdale, Stu 76
Todd, Kay, Jr. 65
Tomich, Todd 140
Tompkins, Ray 9, 10, 38
Torgerson, Alek 162, 165
Tower, A.C. 6
Treat, Herb 41
Tripp, Roswell 25
Troost, John 143
Tsitsos, Alki 107
Tuckerman, Sam 176–178, 180–183
Tulsiak, Dennis 113
Tumpane, Tim 113
Twining, Arthur 32

Valle, Rudy 38
Valpey, Art 75, 76
Van de Graaff, Adrian S. 11

Index

van Eeghen, Mark 105
Van Tassel, Irwin 26
Van Wincklen F.M. 22
Varga, Tyler 53, 153- 158, 160
Vaughn, Marty 106
Veeder, Paul 26, 27
Veldman, Peter 142
Verduzco, Bob 126
Vincent, Francis T. "Fay" 51
Viviano, Joe III 166

Wade, Geoff 172
Wadsworth, Jerry 46
Wagner, Robert 84
Walker, Blake 67
Walker, Keith 127
Walker, Leon 39
Walker, Paul 67–69
Wallace, Bill 56, 75
Wallace, Grant 154, 156, 158, 160
Walland, Joe 137–140
Wallington, Travis 117
Wallrap, Mark 129, 134
Walsh, Christy 43
Wandle, Frank 58
Warburton, Don 87
Ward, Al 83–85, 98
Ward, Jackson 182
Warden, David 77
Warfield, Cameron
Warner, Chris 130
Warner, Glenn "Pop" 16, 43
Waterston, Sam 185
Watkinson, George 159
Watson, B.J. 181, 183
Watson, Justin 165
Watson, Robert W. 8, 9
Wayne, John 45
Webster, Bill 46, 47
Weeks, John W. 43
Weiner, Stan 65
Welsh, George 119
Wendell, Jack 25
Wersching, Ray 26
Westmoreland, William 82

White, Byron "Whizzer" 59
White, Frank 83
White, Henry S. 11
White, Jack 57
Whitehead, Mather K. 57
Whiteman, Bart 62
Whiteman, Hal 62
Whiting, Macauley 67
Whitney, Caspar 15
Widman, Kelly 144
Wilbur, John S. 54
Wilhelm, Gary 105
Williams, Dalyn 158, 161, 162
Williams, Eric 108
Williams, Dr. Henry 26, 30
Williams, Ricky 144
Williams, Steven 148
Williams, Tom 149–151, 153
Williams-Lopez, Christopher 163, 168
Williamson, Ivy 72
Willows, Abe 178
Wilson, Al 58
Wilson, Harry 108
Wilson, Alex D. 33, 37
Winkler, Rich 87, 88
Winterbauer, Dick 83, 85, 86
Winters, Collier 150, 152
Winters, John 48
Witt, Patrick 149–153
Wolcott, Roger 21
Wolfe, Isaac 48
Wolfe, Ken 89, 90
Wood, Barry 51, 52, 54
Wood, Gary 92
Woodsum, Ed 78, 79

Yeager, Charlie 79, 84
Yohe, Tom 124
York, Theodore 31
Young, Ryan 173
Yovicson, John 87

Zachery, Buddy 124, 127, 128
Zanieski, John 122

www.ingramcontent.com/pod-product-compliance
Ingram Content Group UK Ltd.
Pitfield, Milton Keynes, MK11 3LW, UK
UKHW042001140426
5217IPUK00015B/925